STUDIES IN AMERICAN POPULAR
HISTORY AND CULTURE

Edited by
Jerome Nadelhaft
University of Maine

A ROUTLEDGE SERIES

Studies in American Popular History and Culture

Jerome Nadelhaft, *General Editor*

Hollywood and the Rise of Physical Culture
Heather Addison

Homelessness in American Literature
Romanticism, Realism, and Testimony
John Allen

No Way of Knowing
Crime, Urban Legends, and the Internet
Pamela Donovan

The Making of the Primitive Baptists
A Cultural and Intellectual History of the Antimission Movement, 1800–1840
James R. Mathis

Women and Comedy in Solo Performance
Phyllis Diller, Lily Tomlin, and Roseanne
Suzanne Lavin

The Literature of Immigration and Racial Formation
Becoming White, Becoming Other, Becoming American in the Late Progressive Era
Linda Joyce Brown

Popular Culture and the Enduring Myth of Chicago, 1871–1968
Lisa Krissoff Boehm

America's Fight over Water
The Environmental and Political Effects of Large-Scale Water Systems
Kevin Wehr

Daughters of Eve
Pregnant Brides and Unwed Mothers in Seventeenth-Century Massachusetts
Else L. Hambleton

Narrative, Political Unconscious, and Racial Violence in Wilmington, North Carolina
Leslie H. Hossfeld

Validating Bachelorhood
Audience, Patriarchy, and Charles Brockden Brown's Editorship of the Monthly Magazine and American Review
Scott Slawinski

Children and the Criminal Law in Connecticut, 1635–1855
Changing Perceptions of Childhood
Nancy Hathaway Steenburg

Books and Libraries in American Society during World War II
Weapons in the War of Ideas
Patti Clayton Becker

Mistresses of the Transient Hearth
American Army Officers' Wives and Material Culture, 1840–1880
Robin Dell Campbell

The Farm Press, Reform, and Rural Change, 1895–1920
John J. Fry

State of 'The Union'
Marriage and Free Love in the Late 1800s
Sandra Ellen Schroer

"My Pen and My Soul Have Ever Gone Together"
Thomas Paine and the American Revolution
Vikki J. Vickers

"My Pen and My Soul Have Ever Gone Together"
Thomas Paine and the American Revolution

Vikki J. Vickers

Routledge
New York & London

Published in 2006 by
Routledge
Taylor & Francis Group
270 Madison Avenue
New York, NY 10016

Published in Great Britain by
Routledge
Taylor & Francis Group
2 Park Square
Milton Park, Abingdon
Oxon OX14 4RN

© 2006 by Taylor & Francis Group, LLC
Routledge is an imprint of Taylor & Francis Group

Transferred to Digital Printing 2008

International Standard Book Number-10: 0-415-97652-9 (Hardcover)
International Standard Book Number-10: 0-415-99645-7 (Softcover)
International Standard Book Number-13: 978-0-415-97652-7 (Hardcover)
International Standard Book Number-13: 978-0-415-99645-7 (Softcover)

Library of Congress Card Number 2005020482

No part of this book may be reprinted, reproduced, transmitted, or utilized in any form by any electronic, mechanical, or other means, now known or hereafter invented, including photocopying, microfilming, and recording, or in any information storage or retrieval system, without written permission from the publishers.

Trademark Notice: Product or corporate names may be trademarks or registered trademarks, and are used only for identification and explanation without intent to infringe.

Library of Congress Cataloging-in-Publication Data

Vickers, Vikki J.
  My pen and my soul have ever gone together : Thomas Paine and the American Revolution / by Vikki J. Vickers.-- 1st ed.
      p. cm. -- (Studies in american popular history and culture)
  Includes bibliographical references and index.
  ISBN 0-415-97652-9
  1. Paine, Thomas, 1737-1809. 2. Revolutionaries--United States--Biography. 3. Political scientists--United States--Biography. I. Title. II. Series: American popular history and culture (Routledge (Firm))

JC178.V5V53 2005
320.51'092--dc22   2005020482

Taylor & Francis Group
is the Academic Division of Informa plc.

Visit the Taylor & Francis Web site at
http://www.taylorandfrancis.com

and the Routledge Web site at
http://www.routledge-ny.com

Publisher's Note
The publisher has gone to great lengths to ensure the quality of this reprint but points out that some imperfections in the original may be apparent.

To Steve,

*Who forced his heart and nerve and sinew
To serve their turn long after they were gone*

Contents

Acknowledgments	ix
Introduction	1
Chapter One The Pennsylvania Magazine	13
Chapter Two The Devil's Advocate: Thomas Paine and the Making of *Common Sense*	35
Chapter Three Why Thomas Paine?	59
Chapter Four The Origins and Significance of Thomas Paine's Religious Beliefs	77
Chapter Five "One God and No More": The Strange Mission of Thomas Paine	105
Conclusion	127
Appendix *Common Sense:* An Historiographical Overview	133
Notes	143

Bibliography 173

Index 183

Acknowledgments

In the eight years it took to write this book I had the great fortune to be guided, advised, and supported by many wonderful people. I forbear to mention them all, but there are a few to whom I am especially indebted.

First and foremost I need to thank my parents, Robert and Claire. Their love and support has been immeasurable and invaluable. To John L. Bullion, who gave me free reign to explore this topic and never failed to remind me of its significance. A special thank you to Chad Ross who continues to teach me that sometimes the trees are as important as the forest. And to Hazel Burgess, my colleague Down Under, I would like to express my thanks for her article on Paine, and for sharing information she would probably have preferred to keep to herself.

Finally, I'd like to thank James E. Murray, Gerard Clarfield, Noble E. Cunningham, Jr., and Richard Hocks—teachers and professors who inspired me to study history and taught me the skills I would need to pursue it professionally.

Introduction

Thomas Paine was born in Thetford, England in the county of Norfolk, on January 29, 1737. He was the son of Joseph Pain and Frances Cocke Pain (Thomas added the "e" shortly before he came to America). Joseph Pain was a stay-maker by trade[1] The Pains were not a poor family, nor did Joseph's occupation qualify as one that would afford a luxurious lifestyle for his family. Rather the Pains were of the "middling sort," able to afford to send young Thomas to the local grammar school in Thetford until he was thirteen. At the age of thirteen Paine's father removed him from school to apprentice him into the family trade.

Uninterested in the path his father had chosen for him, Paine, as an adult, drifted from one occupation to another, financial success always eluding him. At the age of twenty he enlisted aboard an English privateer during the Seven Years' War. When he returned from his adventure he worked as a journeyman stay-maker in Kent, where he met and married his first wife, Mary Lambert. She died within a year of their nuptials (cause unknown) and Paine returned home to Thetford to study for a position as an exciseman.[2] He drifted between positions as an excise officer, English teacher, and stay-maker until he settled in Lewes in 1768. Here he continued as an exciseman, and upon his landlord Samuel Ollive's death, Paine married his daughter, Elizabeth. Paine then also became responsible for the tobacco and grocery store that Elizabeth inherited from her father. After the failure of his business and his dismissal from the excise in 1774, Paine decided to start over in America. While in London he became acquainted with Dr. Benjamin Franklin, and with letters of introduction from the renowned diplomat and scientist, he departed for America in late October of 1774.

Paine arrived in America on November 30, 1774 after a rough passage which left him weak and sick with what was probably typhoid. He came to America with the intention of starting his own school and settling down to a quiet life. Instead, he commenced his literary career by becoming an editor and contributor to *The Pennsylvania Magazine*. The battles of Lexington and Concord in April 1775 so moved Paine that he fully adopted the cause of American Independence from his native Britain, and set out to convince his fellow Americans to take up arms. Thus *Common Sense* (1776) was born, and likewise the political career and notoriety of Thomas Paine. He enlisted in the Continental Army (and was reputedly a much better writer than soldier) and served as aide de camp for Generals Nathanael Greene and George Washington. In addition, he was nominated by John Adams to the Continental Congress as a secretary to the Committee for Foreign Affairs. Paine's patriotism knew no bounds, and he insisted that all of the proceeds from his revolutionary writings (including *Common Sense* and *The American Crisis* papers) be donated to the war effort.

At the conclusion of the war, Paine pursued scientific interests; he had plans to build a single-arch iron bridge of his own design over the Schuylkill River in Pennsylvania. His bridge was officially endorsed by both the Royal Society in London and the Académie des Sciences in Paris, but soon Paine's attentions turned to another political cause: the French Revolution. The French had read and studied Paine's incendiary pamphlet *Common Sense*, and when the author arrived on their shores they rewarded him with a seat as a delegate in the National Convention, and an honorary French citizenship in honor of his dedication to the principles of liberty, equality, and fraternity.[3] In 1789 it appeared to Paine that his goal of freeing mankind from the shackles of political and religious tyranny would soon be realized on yet another continent. The Revolution in France being perhaps more important because of its proximity to England, a country Paine viewed as having the most despotic of all governments. Paine had long ceased to think of himself as an Englishman—it was the United States of America that Paine claimed as his country—a nation free of tyranny that he had helped to create. Paine was optimistic that the French would establish a republic much like America's and in much the same manner. He therefore was greatly incensed by Edmund Burke's early denunciation of the Revolution in his work, *Reflections on the Revolution in France* (1790). Paine countered with *The Rights of Man*, and gained the admiration of not only France, but America and the radical fringe in Great Britain. *The Rights of Man* so aroused the masses in England and Ireland that Britain outlawed the work and convicted Paine, in absentia, of seditious libel. The conviction carried a sentence of life in prison or execution, and Paine never again set foot on English soil.

Paine was eventually imprisoned, but not in England. His eagerness to establish a true republic in France ultimately led to his own incarceration.

Paine was appalled at the Convention's advocacy of the execution of Louis XVI and his queen, Marie Antoinette. To begin a republic by shedding innocent blood was anathema to him, and he spoke out on the Convention floor (with the aid of an interpreter) against such actions.[4] Unfortunately for Paine, Robespierre and the Jacobins did not share his sentiments and the leader of the new Republic ordered Paine's arrest and imprisonment in late December 1793. Paine had anticipated Robespierre's decision to incarcerate him and he rushed to complete what he believed would be his final work: *The Age of Reason*. Paine purposely waited until the latter part of his life to publish a work on his deistic beliefs, as he was aware of the potential controversy his views on religion might cause. He completed the first volume of the work literally minutes before officers of the Committee for Public Safety arrived at his apartment and arrested him. That night, he gave the manuscript to his good friend and confidante Joel Barlow in the hope that Barlow would find a publisher. Barlow was successful, and readers devoured the pamphlet on two continents, but Paine could not enjoy his accomplishment: he was in the Luxembourg prison awaiting possible execution.

Paine remained in prison for nearly a year, and by his own account he narrowly escaped death on two occasions. While incarcerated he developed a critical illness which incapacitated him for three months, and then he was nearly guillotined. James Monroe, who became the U.S. Minister to France in 1794, secured Paine's release from prison. Paine's disillusionment with the way the French Revolution had progressed and the bloodshed that occurred during the Reign of Terror made him long to return to his home in America.

When he left America for England in 1783, Paine had not intended to be away for very long; nonetheless nineteen years had passed since he had been in the United States and much had changed. Paine's homecoming on October 30, 1802, was marked not by celebrations, but by censure. The popularity of his deist tract *The Age of Reason* had caused considerable consternation for the clerical and scholastic communities in America. The election of Thomas Jefferson in 1800 (whose own deist beliefs had been the subject of much sensationalism and condemnation during the election campaign) provided the Federalist party with a much desired target at which to aim its wrath. Paine became the pawn in the political wrangling between the Federalist and Republican parties. The clergy and the Federalist press dealt several deadly blows to Paine's reputation from which it never recovered in his lifetime. Paine continued to write in defense of his beliefs and to champion humanitarian causes until 1806 when he suffered a disabling stroke. His physical health declined steadily thereafter and he died on his farm in New Rochelle, New York in 1809 at the age of 72.

Scholars have agreed upon these essential elements of Paine's life and career. It is in the details, however, where much discussion and scholarly debate has taken place. After the publication of *The Age of Reason,* Paine's reputation suffered terribly at the hands of partisan politics and clergymen in the throes of the beginning of the Second Great Awakening. In his own time the majority of his critics acknowledged that Paine was a deist—that as he stated clearly in his pamphlet he did believe in God—but they railed against his denunciation of Christianity and the Bible. Meanwhile all of his achievements during the Revolution were cast aside as partisan politicians undermined the man they once revered as one of their Founding Fathers because of his unorthodox views. The damage to Paine's stature would certainly have been restored over time, and he would have again resumed his place alongside his other revolutionary compatriots like George Washington and John Adams—had it not been for Theodore Roosevelt.

Despite Paine's repeated public assertions that he believed in a Supreme Being, the most lasting blow to Paine's reputation came one hundred years after his death. President Theodore Roosevelt said that Paine was a "filthy little atheist," and Americans believed him.[5] Seemingly with one stroke, all of the progress made by historians attempting to reclaim Paine's proper place in American history vanished, and scholars spent the next century trying desperately to undo what Roosevelt had done.

Sadly, because of Roosevelt's comment, scholars have spent so much time setting the record straight with regard to Paine's religious beliefs, or in attempting to remind America of Paine's contributions, that they have done little else. In fact, Paine scholarship following Roosevelt's statement evolved into a strange dichotomy: one set of scholars trying so zealously to prove Roosevelt wrong and redeem Paine's reputation that they appear to be almost worshipers rather than historians; the other set acknowledging that while Roosevelt was wrong about Paine's religion, the underlying feelings behind Roosevelt's words were correct—Paine does not belong in the same class as Jefferson or Franklin or Adams. The devotees of Paine tend, more often than not, to be biographers; the skeptics tend to be serious scholars and historians. An unbiased history of Paine still waits to be told.

Paine's first biographer was George Chalmers, who wrote under the pseudonym "Francis Oldys." Chalmers' biography was published in 1791, after the appearance of Paine's *Rights of Man.* The British government commissioned Chalmers' work to diffuse the radicalism in England that Paine incited with his attack on the parliamentary system. It was, therefore, a biography written to discredit and mock Thomas Paine—it was not a critical edition, nor were all the facts entirely correct. Given the circumstances surrounding the motives of the author it should be treated for what it is: a proprietary biography written with malice at the behest of the British government. Unfortunately, too many biographers (even modern ones) still refer to Chalmers' work as having some truths. How they decipher the truths from the falsehoods is beyond conception.

The next earliest biography of Paine was written the year that Paine died by a New York editor. James Cheetham, like Chalmers, was no friend of Paine—nor was his biography critical. It was Chalmers who wrote (rather absurdly) that Paine had an illicit affair and illegitimate child with the wife of his good friend, Nicholas de Bonneville. (Madame de Bonneville quickly sued Cheetham for libel and easily won the case.) Cheetham's biography is as superficial as Chalmers' and equally as forgettable. Paine's next several biographers, continuing well into the twentieth century, wrote what can best be described as hagiographies.[6]

The two most recent biographies of Paine, by Jack Fruchtman, Jr. (1994) and John Keane (1995), warrant closer examination.[7] Both are equally lengthy—each over four hundred pages of text—but both also suffer from the same lack of analysis and errors. The central problem, as one reviewer identified it, is that "both Keane and Fruchtman are serious scholars, but neither is a professional historian. . . ."[8] Both lack the appropriate historical knowledge and context to portray Paine and his activities accurately. As a result there are a number of glaring deficiencies which detract from what are otherwise well written books.[9]

While the biographers of Paine tend typically to be devotees, the opposite is true of the other class of Paine researchers: academicians. But there is also an interesting polarization present in these studies as well: some study Paine's politics, others his religion, still more his rhetoric, but rarely do these threads ever intersect in scholarship related to Paine.[10] Among the more sensational elements evident in studies of Paine's life and career is the question of Paine's alcoholism and possible sexual dysfunction. (These subjects are explored most often in biographical studies of Paine.) The latter is almost too ridiculous to confront, the former is too pervasive not to. Looking closely at the historical record, it seems evident that Paine developed a serious drinking problem during the 1790s. Neither his friends nor his enemies seemed to notice any intemperance in Paine before that time. Benjamin Rush was a friend of Paine during the Revolution, but as a devout Christian, he was incensed by Paine's deist tract, and refused to have any further contact with him. Still, in 1809 Rush wrote that during the Revolution Paine "spoke but little but was always inoffensive in his manner and conversation."[11] Paine's best friend, Clio Rickman observed that "during [Paine's] residence with me in and about the year 1792, and in the course of his life previous to that time, he was not in the habit of drinking to excess."[12] Finally, Joel Barlow, Paine's devoted friend in France, noted that when Paine's friends in America neglected him because of his activism in the French Revolution, "he gave himself very much to drink."[13]

Paine kept company with the elite of three nations, yet comments on his drinking only surface while in France in the 1790s, around the time of his imprisonment and alienation from the affections of former friends. It is a matter of speculation, but the most likely cause of Paine's new drinking habits was what would today be called a clinical depression. Paine in fact became very despondent about the excessive violence in France, the rise of factionalism in American politics, his criminal conviction in England, and his own personal denunciation as an atheist. In fact, the letters Paine wrote during his imprisonment contained very dark, and even suicidal thoughts. Paine was also in ill health from the time of his imprisonment until his death. He had never fully recovered from the nearly fatal fever that he contracted in prison, and he had an abscess (most likely a bedsore) that would not heal properly. Therefore it is also possible that Paine drank heavily as a pain remedy or as a restorative.

This is not meant to be an excuse for Paine's possible alcoholism, but rather to make a larger point which is that it is completely irrelevant whether Paine was an alcoholic or not. His drinking habits are only worthy of serious consideration if he thought, acted, and wrote one way while drinking and another while sober. This is simply not the case. There is a remarkable continuity in the thoughts and actions of Thomas Paine (as will be demonstrated). Alcoholism may not have won Paine many friends after 1793, but it certainly did not create enemies—political factionalism and his controversial writing did that. It is a waste of time for a serious scholar to allow any discussion of alcoholism to overshadow Paine's words or actions; its value is purely sensational and does not have a place among serious studies. It is worth mentioning as well that it is well known that Americans in the eighteenth and nineteenth centuries drank to excess on a regular basis. If W.J. Rorbaugh's argument is to be believed, Paine was not an exception but rather the rule needing only to be placed in the appropriate social and cultural context.[14]

As far as Paine's sexual impotence is concerned, there is simply no proof. The origins of discussions of Paine's sexual inadequacies arise from the mysterious circumstances surrounding Paine's separation from his second wife. Oldys and others claimed maliciously (again, without proof) that Paine could not perform sexually and therefore the marriage dissolved. Surprisingly, Rickman supported this conclusion insisting that "[Paine] did not cohabit with [his wife] from the moment they left the altar till the day of their separation, a space of three years . . . is an indubitable truth."[15] The difficulty in trusting Rickman is that he admitted asking Paine repeatedly to divulge the reason for the separation, and each time Paine told him that the reasons were his to know and no one else's. Paine never divulged to anyone, even his best friend, the reason for the failure of his marriage—should it then be believed that he revealed to Rickman that he was impotent? In any event, this ridiculous discussion among historians must come to a close—it has no bearing whatsoever on Paine's contribution to world history and it is degrading to scholarship to pursue it further.[16]

Among those who study Paine's politics, "the major point of controversy between scholars' concerns . . . the originality of his thought versus the originality of expression and communication."[17] The number of journal articles and book paragraphs devoted to wrestling with this question is too high to count, and the debate is still ongoing.[18] A similar bias is apparent in comparisons of Paine to other Founding Fathers. Inevitably in works on the Revolution or in studies of Paine, scholars seem to feel the need to rank Paine's contribution and assign him a place based on how he compares with his fellow patriots. Sean Wilentz characterized Paine as lacking "Madison's realism and originality as a political theorist or Hamilton's frightening genius as a financial visionary."[19] Wilentz instead argues that Paine's genius lies in his ability to translate the theories and ideas of his social betters and diffuse them to the masses.

The central problem with these arguments is the elitism that most writers try cleverly to hide, but that readers easily discover. It is quite clear from reading Paine scholarship (or rather reading between the lines of Paine scholarship) that the real reason why researchers are quick to dismiss the idea that Paine had original theories is because he was the uneducated, bankrupt son of a lower-middle class artisan from a remote English country town. It is also evident in reading the literature on Paine that scholars find it discomfiting to place Paine alongside a giant like Thomas Jefferson, let alone John Locke. These were well educated men who had read all the works and studied all the theories that Paine probably only knew about second-hand. Scholars have therefore cast Paine aside as a lesser figure; an imitator of his more educated brethren.

By choosing to spend their time in these pursuits, scholars commit the dual fallacy of studying Paine in miniature and not studying him in the appropriate broader context. If nothing else, the American Revolution proved that ordinary men could do extraordinary things. The Revolution, as most scholars will readily concede, was not conducted solely from the floor of the Continental Congress but from battlefields, farmhouses, shops, and wharves. The Revolution proved that eighteenth-century Americans excelled in making the impossible possible and Paine—a poor uneducated corset-maker—led the way.

Among the other strands of criticism related to Paine's politics is the constant observation that Paine was more of an idealist than a realist. Arnold King points out that "Paine was clearly in water over his head when he came to designing a scheme of government, and he knew it."[20] Likewise, Cecilia Kenyon notes that "among the Americans of his day he remained a prophet rather than an effective leader because he was incapable of bridging the gap between what was and what might be."[21] This is a curious line of inquiry because beginning with *Common Sense,* and throughout all of his works, Paine readily acknowledged this inadequacy. He admitted that "I only presume to offer hints, not plans."[22] Paine's significance lies not in his ability to create perfectly workable programs, but rather in the fact that he offered plans at a time when most had no plans at all. Moreover, Paine's effectiveness as a leader is not a matter of doubt; he led one continent to Revolution and another to republicanism.

Paine envisioned an America that had a strong federal government to preserve the strength of the Union. He envisioned nations (in particular Great Britain) that took responsibility for the welfare of its citizens. He imagined a nation, the United States, that would be a great power based on its commerce with all the world. But Paine did more than dream, he actively worked for these changes; he should be credited at least with being the one who vocally demanded radical changes when others were unwilling or afraid.

Scholars seemingly do not know what to do with Thomas Paine. For so long now the criteria for those who have qualified to be called Founding Fathers has been limited to a select group of (usually educated) white males—the Jeffersons, Madisons, and Adamses of the eighteenth-century world. Paine meets only one of these criteria and yet his contribution to the Revolution and the founding of the United States was no less than these men; his peers comfortably ranked him among the first order of patriots. How is it then, that Paine never has achieved the title of Founding Father among scholars? The answer is fairly simple: social historians have an aversion to the celebration of the accomplishments of "dead white European males" over the achievements of the common man. They typically prefer a narrative where the ordinary person makes history. But who was more ordinary than Thomas Paine?

Studies of Paine's religious beliefs have not been as exhaustive as studies of his politics. Perhaps this is because his political activities consumed most of his life and overshadowed his religious works, which did not take prominence until the last decade of his life. It is also probable that, due in part to statements like Roosevelt's, scholars who research Paine's religion had to expend most of their energy in refuting the claim that Paine was an atheist. Whatever the cause, studies of Paine's theology have evolved much like that of his politics: piecemeal.

Historians interested in Paine's deist theology tend to isolate single aspects as potential influences. Most studies focus on the importance of his father's Quaker beliefs. Others focus instead on Newtonian science as the root cause of Paine's adoption of deism.[23] Walter Woll argues that "there are good reasons to assume that the author was not so much influenced by his mother's Anglican views but by the Quakerism of his father."[24] These interpretations are problematic because they are too limiting. A full analysis of the origins of Paine's deism and a clear explication of those beliefs is critical because understanding his deism is the key to understanding Thomas Paine.

This lack of understanding is responsible for another problem with scholarship surrounding Paine's religion: errors. For a man who was acclaimed by his contemporaries for his rhetorical simplicity and clarity, Paine seems to have baffled most scholars when it comes to understanding his religious beliefs. They cannot agree on what exactly Paine's theology entailed. Why scholars have such difficulty with Paine's religious beliefs is worthy of separate study, but this work will attempt to make Paine's belief system as clear as possible, relying almost exclusively upon Paine's own words.

Another current common to research on Paine's religious beliefs is the continual disagreement among scholars about when exactly Paine became a deist. Paine himself is the source of the confusion because, as Wilentz points out, "his most important American pamphlet, *Common Sense,* was actually filled with Biblical references and quotations in support of his arguments."[25] This incongruity has proved to be strangely prohibitive: scholars have shied away from a thorough analysis of the evolution of Paine's deist beliefs. However, the evidence contained in this work will bear out Gregory Claeys' assertion that "his deism . . . was certainly settled by the time of the American Revolution."[26] Another incongruity discussed by historians of late, is the possibility that Paine may have been a Methodist preacher while in England. This too will be investigated thoroughly.

This jigsaw puzzle method of trying to put together the various pieces of Paine's religious life has led to considerable confusion among scholars about exactly how to interpret and analyze Paine and his beliefs. Aspects of his theology that are perfectly simple, by not being analyzed in the appropriate context, appear complex. Aspects that are complex, by the same token, are often analyzed too simplistically. Now is the time to put the pieces together and trace the evolution of Paine's beliefs from his birth until the publication of *The Age of Reason* in 1794 when he opened his mind to the world.

PURPOSE OF THE STUDY

It should not be surprising that those who study Thomas Paine agree on very little about their subject. Biographers cannot decide whether or not Paine was an heroic figure of pathos or a short-sided rabble-rouser. Scholars and academicians are unsure whether or not the radical pamphleteer was an intelligent, astute political analyst or simply a naturally gifted writer lucky enough to be in the right place at the right time. And yet there is universal agreement upon one aspect of Paine's life and works: all agree that Paine's political activities were heavily influenced and motivated by his religious beliefs. Even so, in the year 2005, after over two hundred years of research and scholarship no one has yet undertaken an in-depth study of the impact Paine's religious beliefs had on his life or his politics. This area of Paine studies has been neglected for too long.

With all the apparent dissonance in Paine studies, another note of harmony also resounds loudly among scholars: Paine's politics and religion must be studied simultaneously. There is almost a universal accord on this principle; Harry Hayden Clark, the first person to analyze with any significance the connection between Paine's religion and politics, argued in the 1930s that "[a modern skeptic] cannot ignore religion in the case of Paine, for it was the fountainhead of his concrete work, and without understanding his religion one can scarcely understand and interpret correctly his practical programs."[27] Forty years later Robert Smith concurred: "Paine's work can only be viewed within the context of his theology."[28] And yet, while scholars agree that this kind of interpretation is necessary, it has not yet been attempted. In 1977, even after Foner's brilliant work, Smith observed that "the full impact of Paine's religious principles on his political, social, and economic views has never been completely explored."[29] Here, in the succeeding chapters, it will be.

In his exceptional study of Paine and Philadelphia during the Revolution, Eric Foner noted, "Paine's ideas . . . [have never been] successfully located within the social context of his age."[30] Foner seems to understand, better than his colleagues, that studying select elements of Paine's life and works is not productive. Because of this approach, "Paine's ideas, indeed, have never been grasped in their full complexity . . . [and] no one has shown why, when, and how the various strands became integrated into [a] coherent ideology."[31] Foner, perhaps more than any other historian, has studied Paine in that proper context and placed him among his revolutionary peers in Pennsylvania. Unfortunately, as valuable as Foner's study is, it is not a biography of Paine; in many ways it is more significant as a microhistory of Revolutionary Philadelphia. But Foner did issue an important challenge to historians: the challenge of producing a complete study to explain how Paine's beliefs developed and their significance.

That is the purpose of this study—to investigate who Thomas Paine was, what he believed, how those beliefs motivated him to political action and how those actions helped to found the United States of America. It is the first intellectual biography of Paine; an attempt to explain how and when Paine's "coherent ideology" was formed. It is also a work that will demonstrate the importance of context when studying Thomas Paine. As Bernard Bailyn wrote, understanding a writer's "personal culture" is key to understanding the uniqueness of an author's ideas and their impact.[32] It should be noted, also, that Paine's context was not merely his role as founder of the United States, but rather the broader transatlantic world of the eighteenth century.

The time has now come for social historians to embrace Thomas Paine with enthusiasm; the symbol of, as Alfred Young so eloquently put it, "the kind of [revolutionary] leader for whom most historians have never found a place."[33] The definition of Founding Father must be widened to encompass Paine and others like him. (Of course social history should also not forget to include the Founding Mothers, but that is beyond the scope of this work.)[34] When social historians embrace a wider definition of the term "founder," Paine will once again be able to stand among his revolutionary peers as "a plain man speaking the common language of radicalism, speaking for and as one of the people simultaneously."[35]

SCOPE AND LIMITATIONS OF THE STUDY

The time-frame of this study is limited primarily to the years 1737–1783. However, because two of Paine's most significant works were written after 1783 this work will seemingly encompass more than Paine's American revolutionary career. These two works, *The Rights of Man* (1791/2) and *The Age of Reason* (1794/5), must be included because (1) they are critical to demonstrating continuity in Paine's thought, (2) because it is in *The Age of Reason* that Paine first declares his deist principles, and (3) both works contain significant (and rare) autobiographical evidence of the formation of his political and religious ideology. Finally, at all times this work will attempt to place Paine in his appropriate eighteenth-century transatlantic context.

One of the joys for Paine researchers is that nearly all of his extant works (publications and correspondence) have been published in various collected works. The most complete (although somewhat flawed editorially) is Philip Foner's two volumes.[36] One of the difficulties for Paine researchers is that the papers Paine kept, including the first two volumes of his autobiography, burned in a fire in St. Louis in the early part of the nineteenth-century. (The principal dilemma here is knowing that an autobiography actually existed—it positively tortures the researcher who craves answers to unanswerable questions.) These difficulties are complicated by the fact that there is no single repository for Paine's letters, works, etc. Various documents are scattered throughout the United States which makes it arduous—and expensive—to utilize unpublished documents. The largest U.S. collection is perhaps the Colonel Richard Gimbel Collection at the American Philosophical Society Library in Philadelphia. However, this collection is mostly secondary sources related to Paine; the original documents related to Paine have already been published. The other significant collection is in the Thetford Library in Thetford, (Norfolk County) England—Paine's birthplace. The obvious problem here, as the astute local librarian observed, is that East Anglia "isn't on the way to anywhere."[37] Like the Gimbel collection, it is primarily secondary sources. Perhaps in the near future Paine's materials can all be scanned and placed on-line for the convenience of scholars everywhere. Until that date, researchers limited by time, money, and Paine's own reticence (he was an exceedingly private man) will have to utilize all that is available to create as accurate a portrait of the subject as possible. By looking broadly at Paine's works both during and after the Revolution this study will attempt exactly that.

Chapter One
The Pennsylvania Magazine

CHARTING A NEW COURSE

Starting over was something that Thomas Paine had long been accustomed to. As a young man he left his trade as a corset-maker to sail the seas as a privateer, only to return to England and his former trade. As a young widower he again set aside his life as an artisan to pursue a career in the civil service. Finally, after his dismissal from the Excise and another brief stint as a corset-maker he found himself in a small town, newly married. He was recently reinstated as an excise officer, and served as a vestryman. Time and again Paine managed to reinvent a new life for himself, and though none of his occupations had led to prosperity, there had always been the possibility of a new chance for success. However, by the autumn of 1774, Paine had run out of opportunities in England and had to look elsewhere for his future.

Paine and his fellow excise officers in Lewes suffered under the constraints of an annual salary that barely kept them out of debt. His fellow officers decided to petition Parliament for a pay increase, and they asked Paine to be their advocate. After two long years traveling between his home in Lewes and his work on behalf of the officers of Excise in London, Paine reached an impasse. His marriage of convenience had crumbled and his wife sought a separation agreement. The grocery store Elizabeth Ollive Paine owned in Lewes (jointly operated by her and Thomas) was bankrupt, and Paine's two-year political campaign to get Parliament to hear the grievances of excise officers had failed outright. As if all this were not enough, Paine was summarily dismissed from the service.

At the age of thirty-seven, Paine had simply run out of options. Despite the length of time he lived there, and the friends he had acquired, there was really nothing left in Lewes for him to go back to. Given the cost of living in London, he could not remain there unless he found respectable

13

employment and quickly. Paine was a trained and experienced corsetmaker, but it was a form of employment he despised at the best of times and merely tolerated at the worst. Even if Paine had been considering returning to his trade, he would undoubtedly have concluded that this would not have been a viable option. Paine had simply been away from his craft for far too long. It had been nearly a decade since Paine was last in practice; modes of fashion had passed him by, he had no clientele, and the physical fitness required for such demanding work would have been difficult for him to reacquire at such an advanced age. It should also be noted that, even if he could manage to find a town that required his services, Paine would have been competing against far younger, more experienced, more capable craftsmen. Unfortunately for Paine he had not been trained for anything else. His career as a civil servant was over and his reputation as a troublemaker would have kept him from other areas of government service as well. He had been a privateer, but Britain was once again at peace. A career as an author might once have been considered by Paine, but given the dismal failure of his first serious effort, *Case of the Officers of Excise,* and his lack of any formal training, it is exceedingly doubtful that Paine gave the matter any further thought. Paine's best options in the Autumn of 1774 did not entail remaining in England.

Through his acquaintance with George Lewis Scott, a commissioner on the Board of Excise, Paine met Benjamin Franklin. Franklin was in England serving as a colonial agent for the colony of Massachusetts seeking a peaceful reconciliation agreement between the colonies and Great Britain. By 1774 the American situation had become very serious indeed. Britain's century-old policy of salutary neglect towards its North American colonies had led to unforeseen—and dire—consequences. The colonists had not only learned how to govern themselves, but they had also come to accept this as an absolute right guaranteed to all British subjects. Thus in 1764 when Parliament tried to reign in its lucrative but defiantly independent colonies, Americans resisted immediately and forcefully. Ten years of organized protests by Americans against parliamentary measures (and occasional isolated incidents of bloodshed) by 1774 had culminated in a full-scale rebellion. Some Americans, like Samuel Adams, agitated for a complete break from Great Britain; others like John Dickinson pleaded for a reconciliation. There were still others who were not sure at all what course of action was appropriate. The simple truth was that America was a land in turmoil; she could not turn back and yet there was not enough momentum, even from the radicals, to move her forward.

Benjamin Franklin was well acquainted with this awkward status of the colonies. He, perhaps more so than any other American, was in a better position to understand what it meant to have divided loyalties. Franklin was an American and proud of his heritage. But he was also an Anglophile, and had a strong reverence for all things British—as befitting a loyal colonial subject. Franklin loved America but he also loved England, which was why, in 1774, he was in London seeking a reconciliation. However, Franklin's loyalty to England had been sorely tested in the months just prior to meeting Thomas Paine.

In 1774, Benjamin Franklin was in the midst of a political scandal that he unwittingly caused. In 1772 Franklin disclosed (very indiscreetly) a packet of letters written between Massachusetts Royal Governor Thomas Hutchinson and his Lieutenant Governor Andrew Oliver. The letters, penned during the turmoil of the 1760s, revealed that the governors were alarmed by the resistance in the colonies and felt that more direct, decisive action from Parliament was required to subdue the colonists. Franklin, ever the champion of the "rights of Englishmen," had hoped that, in the right hands, the letters would demonstrate that Parliament was not to blame for the colonies' troubles, but rather the Crown's appointed local officials. Instead, when the letters went public (much to Franklin's dismay), the Massachusetts colonists revolted against what they perceived as a tyrannical threat from the Royal Governor. This caused considerable embarrassment for King and Parliament.

Long before the news reached England, but only days after the Boston Tea Party in December 1773, Franklin admitted publicly to being the source of the Hutchinson-Oliver letters. About a month later the story of the Tea Party reached London, and the British government—reeling from the embarrassment of open defiance by its colonists—sought an explanation and retribution. On January 29, 1774, Paine's thirty-seventh birthday, Franklin was summoned to appear before the Privy Council. There he was humiliated in front of not only the Council but spectators who had been invited for the purpose of taunting Franklin. He was chastised for inciting the treasonous conduct of his Massachusetts brethren by releasing the Hutchinson-Oliver letters. That day at the Privy Council hearing Franklin suffered an embarrassment he never forgot or forgave.

Franklin's views about England began to alter dramatically. He had come to view England as corrupt, and as a result "his idealization of America proceeded apace."[1] Despite his new outlook, Franklin was still determined to push for reconciliation. Months after the Privy Council incident, in August 1774, Paine met with Prime Minister William Pitt to forge a coalition of parliamentarians to negotiate a settlement.[2] As late as October 1774, when he met Thomas Paine, Franklin still believed that reconciliation was in the colonies' best interest. It was this Benjamin Franklin that

Thomas Paine became acquainted with in London: bitter, angry, and disillusioned but not the ardent patriot Franklin later became.

Because neither left records, it is only possible to speculate about what Franklin told Paine about America and his chances there, but it is fairly easy to conjecture. They met through a mutual acquaintance who was a scientist; both Franklin and Paine were (to a degree) scientists. Therefore it would seem logical that they had some discussion of scientific studies of the day. Franklin probably told Paine that Philadelphia was a haven for scientists because of institutions like the American Philosophical Society. Both Paine and Franklin were or had once been disgruntled civil servants in the pay of the British government; it is likely that they discussed the pride and perils associated with such work.

Paine would probably have been in awe of the famous Dr. Franklin but Franklin was also clearly impressed with Thomas Paine—he wrote him a recommendation letter which, in most American circles in 1774, was as good as gold. To whatever extent they discussed the situation in the colonies, it is improbable that Franklin mentioned the necessity for independence. Franklin himself had not yet reached that conclusion. Instead he probably presented Paine with a persuasive argument for the necessity of reconciliation. Franklin might have argued that reconciliation was a better alternative than war. He would most likely have told Paine that America (whatever ministerial difficulties she had with Britain) was a land of opportunity for industrious young men. Franklin would also probably have told Paine that with a personal recommendation from him, many prosperous doors would be readily opened to him. He likely added further that America needed talented and ambitious men like Thomas Paine.

It is unknown exactly what Paine knew of the American situation before he departed England. It is unlikely that he knew much about the American cause outside of what he learned from Franklin. The English papers and magazines that Paine read were biased and cast Americans as the villains, yet Paine did not come to America with any such prejudices. It is also possible that Paine did not follow the American colonial conflict at all. His own life had not been uneventful since the troubles started in 1765; it is entirely likely that Paine was far too consumed with his own personal difficulties to take notice of colonial resistance. England was the source of Paine's woes as an excise officer, corset maker, and political activist—not America. Ironically, because of his inability to seek redress from Parliament for his grievances, Paine had more in common with his future countrymen than even he probably knew.

Whatever Paine knew about the troubles in the colonies it did not keep him from determining that moving to America was his best option. He further decided that the occupation best suited to his tastes and talent was that of teacher. He had taught briefly in London for a year before he moved to Lewes in 1768, and now planned on journeying to America "to establish an academy" based upon the London design he was most familiar with.[3] Benjamin Rush, one of Paine's first new friends in America, concurred that Paine told him that "his object was to teach a School, or to give private lessons upon geography to young ladies and gentlemen."[4] It is clear that Paine had no intention of seeking a career in America as a writer. In October 1774 Thomas Paine booked passage to the colonies.

By late autumn 1774 the colonists' exasperation with parliamentary policies had reached a fevered pitch. The Coercive Acts, issued largely as a punishment following the Boston Tea Party, were being oppressively enforced in Boston. That city suffered terribly by the closure of its port and everywhere colonists rallied (illegally) to aid them. The First Continental Congress—itself an extralegal body—was under considerable pressure to act decisively on behalf of the colonies in their cause against Britain. In October, the month that Paine left England, Joseph Warren of Massachusetts presented the Congress with the Suffolk Resolves, demanding that the fledgling American government actively resist Britain's rule. The Continental Congress finally responded to mounting pressure on October 14th with its Declaration of Rights. The Declaration clearly stated that their rights of representation and local taxation were absolute, and Parliament had violated those rights. The Declaration stopped short of demanding an open break with Britain; rather the Congress acknowledged their allegiance to Britain but demanded that their rights be respected. Clearly the Congress was not ready to seek independence for America. Days later, on October 20th, the Continental Association was formed. Its sole purpose was to organize a national boycott of British and Irish goods as a means of resistance. Nonconsumption had already begun, but the Association boycott was scheduled to begin officially on December 1st. To say the least, by late 1774 the American situation had reached critical levels.

Philadelphia, Paine's destination, was as much a part of the turmoil as the beleaguered Boston. The City of Brotherly Love was comprised largely of artisans, servants (of varying status), and merchants. The artisans were considerably literate, self-educated, and increasingly politically active.[5] According to Eric Foner they "made up a large portion of the audiences at Philadelphia's popular lectures on scientific subjects."[6] Evidently, Paine would not have to worry about fitting in in Philadelphia—he had chosen a place that hosted a large community of kindred spirits.

Philadelphia was an important port city like Boston, but not as committed to resistance—at least not in the beginning. In 1774 Philadelphia became the seat of the Continental Congress and consequently the center of the action. However, Philadelphia had not always been a hub of radical activity. Largely due to Franklin's influence, the large artisan community continued to remain loyal to the powers of King and Parliament, and obeisant to the city's powerful mercantile elite. In fact, Philadelphia did not really become fully active in the resistance movement until after 1770.[7] As Eric Foner has noted, "By 1774 . . . the artisans had emerged as a self-conscious, aggressively anti-British element in Philadelphia politics."[8] In fact, because of the "politicization of the mass of Philadelphians," the city began to exhibit distinct leveling tendencies.[9] According to Foner, "[artisans] awakened to political consciousness and articulated a fiercely egalitarian ideology."[10] Slowly, these newly awakened political participants began to initiate a new political order in Philadelphia—one in which the average citizen had power and a voice in government. In 1774 the artisan community there organized a protest movement to lend support to the Continental Association boycott. They also organized Committees of Correspondence and mustered thirty organized militia companies. In fact, by 1775, Philadelphia was the epicenter of American radicalism.

In October 1774 Paine booked passage on the *London Packet,* captained by a man named Cooke. Unlike most new British immigrants to America, Paine did not indenture himself in exchange for his fare; he paid it in full from the £30 he received from his wife in their separation settlement. His passage to America was like his life in England: precarious. A few months after his arrival, Paine wrote to his benefactor Franklin that during the voyage "a putrid fever broke out among the servants . . . we buried five."[11] He further added that while he did not suffer from the same severity of affliction as the servants did, he "suffered dreadfully with the fever" and "had very little hopes that [I] would live to see America."[12] The fact that Paine was able to pay his own fare may very well have saved his life; had he been quartered with the servants the results might have been fatal.

When Paine's ship docked in Philadelphia harbor on November 30, he was too weak from his illness to disembark under his own power. When a doctor named John Kearsley met the ship, Paine told him that he had arrived in America on Benjamin Franklin's recommendation. Kearsley immediately sent for two men to bring Paine ashore by chaise. Paine was so ill that he "could not at that time turn in my bed without help."[13] Kearsley additionally provided lodging for Paine while he recuperated; he was "six weeks on shore" before he could finally present Franklin's recommendation letter to his son-in-law Richard Bache.[14]

After he presented himself to Bache in early January 1775, the doors of opportunity opened to the nearly thirty-eight-year old Paine. He wrote to Franklin that "I have been applied to by several gentlemen to instruct their sons, on very advantageous terms to myself."[15] His plan to become a teacher in America was coming to fruition, albeit as a private tutor. It seems also that these unknown gentlemen offered Paine ample compensation for his services. A fulfilling career awaited him and Paine had economic prosperity at his fingertips. However, even though opportunities as a tutor beckoned, Paine chose a different path. Robert Aitken, a Philadelphia printer and bookseller, approached Paine with an offer. He was "a man of reputation, and property" who asked for Paine's assistance in his newest venture: the creation of a new uniquely American magazine.[16] Paine wrote to Franklin that Aitken approached him because Aitken had "little or no turn that way himself."[17] In other words, Aitken did not know the first thing about founding a new magazine and hoped that Paine might. According to Paine, Aitken "had not above 600 subscribers when I first assisted him."[18]

Robert Aitken's earliest subscription difficulties may have been caused by the nature of his magazine. No less than sixteen magazines had been attempted in America—all failures.[19] Aitken determined to succeed where others had failed, but wanted his publication to be different from the others—it was to be "an 'American magazine' that would print original American essays and poetry."[20] Most of the other magazines published in America were distinctly British in content; Aitken hired Paine, the Englishmen, to help create a new voice for Americans. Because of Paine's familiarity with English magazines, Aitken thought he would be a perfect candidate for the job. It is also likely that Aitken was impressed by Franklin's support of Paine. It is important to remember that not only did Paine have no experience working on a magazine (let alone editing one) he had never published a word in his life. However, Paine did possess one quality that Aitken probably recognized: he was a scientifically-minded artisan who enjoyed magazines and knew the English format. Who better to put together an instructive, entertaining magazine to appeal to the large artisan community in Philadelphia but one of their very own? *The Pennsylvania Magazine* was a national publication, but Aitken knew Paine's most immediate audience and potential subscribers would be Philadelphians.

THE PENNSYLVANIA MAGAZINE

Paine's contributions to *The Pennsylvania Magazine* have posed an interesting challenging for historians: how to identify Paine's work from the efforts of other writers. The difficulty stems from the fact that Paine insisted on always using pseudonyms—even long after he became famous. There have traditionally been a number of essays and poems attributed to Paine. The majority of these were written by "Atlanticus," but some were also written by "Esop," and "The Old Bachelor." Unfortunately for scholars Paine never claimed that any of the works now attributed to him came from his pen. Moreover, Paine's recollections of his published works in correspondence and published material always begin with *Common Sense*. Yet we know through the recollection of Paine's peers and the careful research of historians that Paine may have contributed to the magazine.[21]

To date the most meticulous researcher and analyst of Paine's contributions has been Frank Smith.[22] Smith based his assessment partly on a 1797 advertisement for a new edition of Paine's collected works, and partly on a detailed literary analysis of Paine's writings. In the advertisement for the 1797 volumes, editor James Carey stated that Aitken wrote him a letter listing Paine's contributions.[23] Aitken listed only ten; among them "Introduction to *The Pennsylvania Magazine*," "To the Publisher on the Utility of Magazines," "New Anecdotes of Alexander the Great," and "The Farmer's Dog Porter."[24] Smith therefore further extrapolated that all articles written using those same pseudonyms should also be included bringing the total to fourteen. Another essay, "A Mathematical Question Proposed" written by "P.," Smith also assumed was Paine's own work. Smith also included another dozen or so essays based on a comparison of Paine's later works to those contributed to the magazine.

Smith's assertions sparked considerable debate among historians, most concurring with Smith. This is unfortunate because Smith's conclusions rest on rather dubious evidence. Smith does not give any citation for the "advertisement" he claims he discovered, thus calling into question this very valuable source of authenticity. Secondly, his literary analysis rests on a comparison of Paine with Paine—neglecting a comparison of the dozens of other writers who contributed not only to *The Pennsylvania Magazine* but also to other contemporary publications. Finally, with regard to the essay signed "P.," had Smith been more thorough he might have discovered that *The Pennsylvania Packet* contained at least two essays written by someone known as "P." One essay, "*Trifles, light as air, Are to the jealous confirmations strong.*" was published in 1773 (before Paine arrived in America), but "Of Love of Country" was published in January 1775—within days of the publication of "A Mathematical Question Proposed."[25] Might this not be the same "P."? Or perhaps someone writing under the pseudonym "Pacificus" in the *Packet* November 1773 begging for unity among the colonists? Is it possible that by 1775, given the increase in tensions, this person became "Atlanticus"?[26]

Maybe the only thing scholars can be sure of is what Paine did not write for the magazine. For example, it was Smith who discovered that a work often attributed to Paine, "An Occasional Letter to the Female Sex," was not written by him at all. Published in August 1775 after Paine's tenure had ended, anthologies and collected works astonishingly continue to include this as an example of Paine's early writings as proof of an early inclination towards egalitarianism. Even as late as 2001, the Bedford Series included this essay to showcase Paine's earliest works in a newly published edition of *Common Sense*. The problem: Paine's authorship of the essay was disproven conclusively by Smith in 1930. Smith discovered that the essay "was lifted bodily from the Russell translation of M.A.L. Thomas's *Essai sur le Caractére, le Moeurs, et l'Esprit de Femmes dans les Différents Siécles*, which had come out in . . . Philadelphia in 1774."[27] It is unfortunate that so many scholars, editors, and publishers have ignored Smith's discovery.

The plain truth is that scholars will never know with any degree of certainty what Paine wrote. There simply is no concrete evidence to link him conclusively to any of these essays. To be sure, many of those written by "Atlanticus" and others do closely resemble Paine's style. But to say definitively that Paine wrote this essay or that poem would not be good scholarship. Worst of all, it has been a waste of time on the part of historians to quibble over such matters. Consequently, the debate still continues over how much or how little Paine's early American writings resemble his later output like *Common Sense*. Scholars, in an attempt to explore the evolution of Paine's political thought, have turned often to these magazine contributions in hopes of finding a Paine diamond in the rough. Historians continue to agree with Eric Foner that these early works "provided an inkling—but only that—of the fully developed political outlook . . . which Paine would soon express in *Common Sense*."[28]

Given the fact that there is no conclusive proof of what Paine did or did not write for the magazine this continued wrangling has been unnecessarily counterproductive. In doing so scholars have too narrowly focused their microscope on this year of Paine's life at the loss of a broader analysis and the larger significance of his time at the magazine. It should be recalled that as editor of the magazine, Paine was in charge of choosing the articles, essays, and other works to be included for publication. *The Pennsylvania Magazine* was Paine's first canvas; how he chose to paint it is what should occupy the attention of scholars now.

Although Paine was the contributing editor, Aitken was still the publisher and owner—he therefore gave Paine explicit guidelines which he was bound to follow. Aitken established the parameters of his new venture in his proposal for the magazine, published (before Paine's arrival in America) in *The Pennsylvania Packet* on November 21st, 1774. In the proposal Aitken announced that the magazine would be organized in such a manner that "a proportion of nearly the same number of pages in each Magazine will be set apart for original American productions."[29] As for the actual subject matter, Aitken solicited works on "the whole circle of science, including politics and religion as objects of philosophical disquisition," but not opinion pieces.[30] He insisted that his choice of submissions would be aimed at "excluding controversy in both [politics and religion]."[31] Aitken assured his potential readers that he would take care that "Lest this should offend any, all the political controversy proper for this periodical publication, will fall under the article of news."[32] In an additional notice published in the *Packet* alongside his proposal, Aitken affirmed that he had already found willing contributors for his new venture. However, Aitken assured potential subscribers that these anonymous contributors agreed to submit essays only if Aitken "continues to make his Magazine the decent repository of useful and ornamental *Science,* excluding from it every indelicate; every party production."[33] It is obvious that Aitken intended, whatever the atmosphere in the colonies, to avoid engaging in or creating any contemporary political debate. The magazine was to remain strictly nonpartisan. In other words, an informed discussion of Locke's *Second Treatise* would be welcome, but discourse about the lawfulness of the Coercive Acts would not. The publisher then instructed his future readers that he would attempt to follow the example of his publishing peers abroad by studying the English and Scottish magazines when making his selections.[34] The magazine subscriptions cost a reasonable one shilling per month plus one additional shilling for a yearly supplement. Aitken assured his future subscribers that (barring difficulties procuring printing paper) he intended to publish on the first Wednesday of every month starting in February 1775.[35]

In January 1775 (one month earlier than its anticipated debut) the first issue of *The Pennsylvania Magazine* rolled off the presses. Paine was not the editor of the inaugural issue; he may not even have been a contributor. When he sent a copy of the February issue to Benjamin Franklin in March, Paine wrote, "This is only the second number, the first I was not concerned in."[36] In the "Publisher's Preface" of the first issue Aitken reiterated his earlier promise to subscribers to offer a variety of subject matter. The magazine was, after all, a "miscellaneous work;" the true merits of which resided in its ability to "furnish entertainment to the different tastes and capacities of its numerous readers."[37] Aitken also noted the limitations of attempting a magazine in America. He reminded his readers that European magazines were replete with "Discoveries of the curious remains of antiquity"—something his audience would have to learn to live without because of America's youth.[38] However, Aitken acknowledged that the biggest challenge confronting his new venture was the growing rift between America and Britain. He admitted that procuring talented writers would be difficult because "Those, whose leisure and abilities might lead them to a successful application to the Muses, now turn their attention to the rude preparations for war."[39] Moreover, Aitken regretted that "Every heart and hand seem to be engaged in the interesting struggle for *American Liberty.*"[40] He ended his preface with a simple prayer: "that this once happy country may again enjoy the unviolated blessings of the *British Constitution.*"[41]

True to its promise, the content of the January issue was a motley mix of miscellanea. The Table of Contents included

- Meteorological Diary
- Utility of this work evinced
- Comparison of the Passions of Pride and Vanity
- Character of M. de Voltaire
- Account of the N. American Beaver
- History of Amelia Gray
- Mathematical Question Proposed
- Description of a New Electrical Machine
- The Learned Lady's Soliloquy[42]

There was also an essay on how to cure fevers, literary news items from Britain, and a news section (both foreign and domestic) entitled "Monthly Intelligence."[43] The content of the January issue was nonpartisan and did not touch on any significant political or religious issues of the day. Even the news section was nothing more than reports from abroad (from various countries) and general domestic news. The magazine clearly began with the format intended by Aitken and demanded by promised contributors. However, the unknown author of "Utility of this work evinced," most probably Thomas Paine, declared "There is nothing which obtains so general an influence over the manners and morals of a people as the Press; from *that,* as from a fountain, the streams of vice or virtue are poured forth over a country."[44] Apparently for this anonymous author, the magazine was meant to be more than mere entertainment—it was to be a vehicle to influence the minds of its readers. Aitken may have plainly established the parameters of the magazine but it did not take his editor long to violate them. After Paine assumed stewardship in February, the tone of the magazine changed significantly. As Larkin observed, "Paine's involvement compromised Aitken's intentions from the outset because Paine brought what proved to be a decidedly political voice to the magazine."[45]

The contents of Paine's February issue were markedly different from January. There was considerable variety of subject matter and genre, yet a noticeable theme developed also. The Table of Contents for February included

- Useful and Entertaining Hints
- Description of a New Threshing Instrument
- Internal Riches of the Colonies
- Anecdotes of Alexander the Great
- Interesting Queries on Bloodletting
- Substitutes for Tea
- Select Passages from the Newest British Publications
- Prologue, Critic and the Snow-Drop[46]

"Useful and Entertaining Hints," written by "Atlanticus" was a short essay detailing the abundant natural resources (particularly mineral ore) in America and urging Americans to tap into those resources. It is an unabashedly patriotic work proclaiming America's greatness: "*The degree of improvement which America has already arrived at is unparalleled and astonishing,* but 'tis miniature to what she will one day boast of."[47] The author reiterates, "The world does not at this day exhibit a parallel, neither can history produce its equal."[48] In the mind of this author, America was the promised land and Americans were God's chosen people.[49] "Atlanticus" repeated this argument again in "Internal Riches of the Colonies." "Anecdotes of Alexander the Great," by "Esop," was a stinging denunciation of ruthless conquerors, and "Substitutes for Tea" directly addressed (against Aitken's promises) controversial political and social issues of the day. Whether the evidence is overt or subtextual, clearly there was a new bias in favor of the American situation discernible in the magazine after Paine took the helm in February.

By March even the variety of genres had changed. Paine had chosen fewer scientific articles—the principal purpose of the magazine—and instead chose more poetry and occasional pieces like "The Monk and the Jew." The denunciation of conquerors continued in March, but this time the subject was an English conqueror: Robert Lord Clive. In "Life and Death of Lord Clive," "Atlanticus" recounted the horrific nature of Clive's conquest of India and his honorable (indeed celebrated) return home to England. In the essay, Clive is evil personified: "Fear and terror march like pioneers before his camp, murder and rapine accompany it, famine and wretchedness follow in the rear."[50] The English people do not fare much better; those who welcomed Clive back to England enthusiastically

"Atlanticus" vilifies by declaring, "'Tis the peculiar temper of the English to applaud before they think."[51] Even after the truth was uncovered and "the torrent stops," the English were still beyond redemption because their anger rushed back again with the same violence."[52] Thus "Atlanticus" presented an image of a ruthless English conqueror and an English nation that was gullible and inconstant. In a mere two months Paine's magazine went from patriotically praising America to openly denigrating the English.

By April, however, the American situation changed dramatically. On April 19, 1775, the Revolutionary War began in Massachusetts following the armed conflicts at Lexington and Concord. It was not the first time American blood had been spilled by British troops, nor was it even the first time for Massachusetts—the Boston Massacre of 1770 was still an open wound. However, the skirmishes at Lexington and Concord were another matter entirely; this was not a conflict initiated by an angry American mob that escalated with tragic results. Lexington and Concord involved the concerted movement of British troops with the specific purpose of subduing resistance by seizing ringleaders Samuel Adams and John Hancock, and American munitions—using force if necessary. The fighting began on the 19th of April, but it took a few days for word to reach all of the colonies; Philadelphia received the news on the 24th. Usually *The Pennsylvania Magazine* was available to subscribers around the 10th of each month, but the April issue included extensive news coverage—six full pages—devoted to the battles of Lexington and Concord. (Paine had apparently fallen almost two weeks behind in his editorial obligations.) However, the extensive coverage of the battles was in itself significant: the news included only the American accounts of the story.

There also appeared in the May issue a curious essay entitled "Cupid and Hymen" written by "Esop." The story was simple: in an idyllic country village Cupid meets a poor shepherd who is saddened by the fact that his love, Ruralinda, is going to marry Gothic, the wealthy and aged Lord of the Manor. The marriage was arranged by Ruralinda's parents; Ruralinda would be wealthy and Gothic would have the pleasure of a young, beautiful wife. Cupid was furious because the marriage was not authorized by him and he suspected that Hymen, his assistant, had usurped his authority and sanctioned the union. Cupid chastised Hymen vehemently while Hymen proclaimed his right to act independently of Cupid. The God of Marriages won by placing Gothic and Ruralinda in a walking trance as they proceeded to the altar. Cupid allowed both parties to see their first seven years of marriage; it was not a pretty sight. At the end of the seven years Ruralinda was so miserable—because she had chosen money over love—that she wished her husband dead. Gothic, likewise, was tormented because his young wife continually sought companionship with younger men. Cupid's plan worked; Ruralinda and Gothic realized their mistake, Hymen was ordered never to return again without summons, and the shepherd married his true love.

This simple essay has been largely overlooked by scholars. Most seem to analyze it too simplistically, arguing that it is merely the story of an unhappy union symbolizing the unhappy union between Britain and America. However, a closer look reveals that there is considerably more in the essay. Reading more carefully, it is arguably a short history of America's struggle against British authority. Cupid, which represents America, is the source of all legitimate authority and has control over all local matters (like Ruralinda's marriage). As long as Cupid is in charge, true marriages are created and lasting happiness is assured. When Hymen, Cupid's helper (but not equal) intervenes and usurps that local authority misery is the result. Cupid is forced to remind Hymen, "I am your master. Indulgent Jove gave you to me as a clerk, not as a rival, much less a superior. 'Tis my province to form the union, and yours to witness it."[53] In other words, America and Britain were business partners, but Britain had no rights to interfere in local colonial affairs. Britain's only role was that of "witness" or signatory—a kind of rubber stamp writ large for America's commercial affairs. Cupid and Hymen, like America and Britain, could have worked well together, but Hymen "treacherously assumed to set up for [himself]."[54] Britain's attempts to enforce direct taxation, for example, had sparked the resistance movement in 1765 because the colonists felt taxes were a matter for local government and therefore not the purview of Parliament. Thus "Esop" unveils very cleverly one of the causes for America's grievance against her mother country.

Another reason why colonists resisted British authority was the growing perception that Britain cared little for (let alone understood) the American people and instead cared only for the wealth that its colonies generated. This led colonists to further associate Britain with moral bankruptcy, cunning, and corruption; consequently, America became virtuous and wholesome. Cupid's only master is Love; Hymen's new master is Wealth. In "Esop's" tale Hymen lashes out at Cupid's assertions of independence by revealing, "Plutus [God of Riches] and I are greater than Cupid."[55] As for Cupid's assumptions of moral superiority and power, Hymen counters with "you are not of such importance in the world as your vanity thinks."[56] Parliament similarly asserted its power in 1766 when it proclaimed boldly in the Declaratory Act that it had the right to "bind the colonies in all cases whatsoever." Cupid's reply to Hymen—"You have not a grace but what is borrowed from me"—was perhaps yet another assertion of American purity in contrast to the ruthlessness of Britain.[57]

Finally, as with any good fable, there is a moral at the end of the story. The "seven years of wretched matrimony" Cupid vividly displays to Gothic and Ruralinda mirrors the seven years of resistance by America following the passage of the Townshend duties.[58] In those mythical seven years the couple, yoked together for superficial reasons, made one another miserable. Ruralinda sought only material gain, Gothic sought only a youthful, beautifully adorned trophy. Their marriage was not based on mutual trust, affection, honesty, or love. In short, nothing bound them together except their individual selfishness. Britain neglected its management of the colonies to reap the rewards of nearly unchecked enterprise, only to discover that her colonies no longer needed her. Consequently, America took great advantage of life in the British Empire, free from direct Parliamentary control, but nonetheless benefiting from the trade. America unhappily realized that in her quest for prosperity, she forgot who was in charge, choosing instead to believe that a modicum of independence was not only proper but an inviolable right. Thus, like Ruralinda and Gothic, each party gained exactly what they sought but were made terribly unhappy in the bargain. The solution for Ruralinda and Gothic was simple: separation. Each person should be free to seek his or her own happiness. For America, in 1775, that solution—while not yet publicly debated—also became a more viable option than it ever had been before. "Esop" may not have directly demanded independence, but he certainly suggested that it was the key to America's future happiness.

By summer the magazine was anything but nonpartisan. Allegorical tales like "Cupid and Hymen" in April gave way to more explicit essays like "On the Fall of Empires" in May.[59] That month news from the committees of correspondence featured prominently in the "Monthly Intelligence" section as well as lists of men who were missing, killed, or wounded in Massachusetts. Interestingly, none of the lists included the names of British casualties—only Americans. In June the magazine contained two articles describing in detail the method and necessity of making saltpeter (potassium nitrate), a compound that, when added to sulfur and charcoal, produces gunpowder.[60] In this instance, Paine had not strayed far from the scientific origins of the magazine, but instead of miscellaneous descriptions of new machines or wildlife, he tried to help the American war effort by promoting the manufacture of saltpeter. Moreover, the June issue also included an elegy to those Americans killed at Lexington and Concord, more lists of men who were killed or wounded, and an allegorical essay ("The Dream Interpreted") detailing America's eventual triumph over Great Britain.[61]

In "The Dream Interpreted," author "Bucks County" relates the story of a man who falls asleep in a country wood and has a horrific nightmare. In the dream, he is awakened by a storm, "a confusion of distant thunders," which becomes "a general discharge of the whole artillery of heaven."[62] The dreamer seeks refuge in a cave where he observes that the lightning "exhibited the landscape of a world on fire," and "floods of water, resembled another deluge."[63] When the storm ends, and the narrator emerges from his shelter, he expects to find "a world in ruins, which nothing but a new creation could have restored."[64] Instead, he discovers that the earth is "lovely and inviting, and has all the promising appearance of exceeding its former glory."[65] The lesson here, of course, was that war with Britain would be devastating and dangerous, but that it was necessary to purge America of evil in order to begin anew. (The biblical parallel here to the great flood is unmistakable.) Once cleansed, America's future would be assured and the narrator understood that "what I dreaded as an evil, became a blessing."[66] This was precisely the kind of political content that Aitken promised the magazine would not contain, yet Paine continued to ignore his employer's wishes. The July issue included "On the Continental Fast," and a poem entitled "Liberty Tree."[67] "A Lover of Peace" dispensed with the usual cryptic allegories in "Thoughts on a Defensive War." By July Paine was bold enough to allow his author to declare "we live not in a world of angels. The reign of Satan is not ended; neither are we to expect to be defended by miracles."[68] The essay was explicitly a call to arms; America needed to defend herself at any cost.

There were only two news items in the "Monthly Intelligence" section of the magazine in July: George III's opening address to Parliament in May and the Continental Congress' declaration of the "CAUSES and NECESSITY of their taking up ARMS." In his speech the King warned the colonists that "if the *sword must be drawn,* your faithful Commons will do every thing in their power to maintain and support the supremacy of *this* legislature."[69] George III further added his regrets to Parliament that "the unhappy disturbances in some of my colonies have obliged me to propose to you an augmentation of my army," no doubt intending to strike fear in the rebellious Americans.[70] Paine followed up the king's address with a bold assertion by the Continental Congress of their intention to continue their defensive war. Congress insisted that "we have not raised armies with ambitious designs of separating from Great Britain," rather that they were fighting to defend their rights as Englishmen.[71] It was not a call for independence, but it is significant that Paine accompanied this declaration with the story of a man dreaming of a glorious rebirth for America, and a poem celebrating the "Liberty Tree." Under Paine's editorial tenure, the magazine had clearly become the voice of the patriot cause.

In a letter to Henry Laurens, dated 1779, Paine told his friend that he edited *The Pennsylvania Magazine* for six months.[72] Assuming Paine meant six full months, he may also have been responsible for the August issue's contents. The August issue contained "References to the Plan of Gen. Gage's Lines," complete with a fold-out map detailing Britain's occupation of Boston. There was also yet another essay describing the proper method of making saltpeter. Paine's attempts at aiding the American war effort were now fully transparent. Paine's tenure at the magazine came to a rather abrupt (and apparently bitter) end sometime between July and August 1775. Paine later wrote that he and Aitken had never been able to reach a salary agreement. Paine had worked on the magazine for six months without a contract, and despite attempts to come to terms with Aitken they parted ways during negotiations.[73] It is unknown whether or not Paine ever received any compensation at all for his work as editor. This turn of events was unfortunate, because Paine had been successful. When he wrote to Benjamin Franklin in March of 1775 he happily reported that "We have now upwards of 1500 [subscribers] and daily increasing."[74] Thus after working at the magazine for only two months—only one of which was he the acting editor—Paine had more than doubled the number of subscribers. Apparently Aitken's gamble had paid off, although he was probably not happy with the political turn the magazine had taken.

In September, the month that Aitken resumed editorial control, "Method of Making Mortar Impenetrable to Moisture" appeared.[75] However, the issue also included a curious essay entitled "Arabella's *Complaint of the* CONGRESS." In the article a decidedly unpatriotic woman complains about the deprivation she is forced to endure. She asks, "are we forever to be disbarred the use of *India* Teas! are we to have no more new fashions; no more fine things from *England?* we may as well all be dead and buried at once."[76] Perhaps Aitken was trying to restore some political balance to the magazine, but by October the publication had returned to its original scientific/ miscellaneous format. There was less news, no political content, and many lighter essays and poems. The following months also continued this same format. There were, in fact, no political essays, articles, or poems in October or November at all.[77] The magazine was no longer Paine's soapbox: it now resonated with the voice of nonpartisanship.

TOWARDS A REINTERPRETATION

The most comprehensive study to date of Paine's tenure at the *Pennsylvania Magazine* (1775) is Edward Larkin's 1998 article "Inventing an American Public: Thomas Paine, *The Pennsylvania Magazine,* and American Revolutionary Discourse."[78] The fact that this is really the only significant work on Paine's brief editing career is surprising. According to Larkin this scholarly void "is perhaps the most overlooked aspect of [Paine's] emergence as a major figure in revolutionary American politics."[79] This deficiency is all the more startling, Larkin declares, because "it is difficult to imagine Paine writing *Common Sense* without the experience of editing *The Pennsylvania Magazine.*"[80] Larkin's assertion is correct—Paine's work at the magazine did have a significant impact on his political development—although not necessarily for the reasons that Larkin claims.

Larkin uses a rhetorical analysis of Paine's contributions to *The Pennsylvania Magazine* to bolster his thesis. First, Larkin argues that while at the magazine Paine had to invent a new political language to reach nontraditional readers and activists. According to Larkin, Paine developed a new form of discourse "that would represent them as legitimate participants in the public sphere."[81] Larkin further claims that Paine deemed this necessary because he "had been one of the first to understand that in order for the revolution to take place in the minds of the people . . . it first had to be made available to them."[82] Next, Larkin argues that Paine, by inventing this new political language, invented a new public "which he could then claim to represent in his writings."[83] This new public "would then provide him with a legitimating constituency," which was "radically different from the public that was typically included in eighteenth-century political debates."[84] In order to develop this new discourse and this new "public," Larkin asserts that Paine gave the magazine a decidedly political voice, albeit rarely explicitly so. Rather than confront political issues of the day directly, Larkin avows that Paine as writer and editor chose selections which addressed political matters and other issues by displacing them onto other benign subjects. Finally, Larkin claims that because Paine created a new audience the magazine was clearly an important stepping stone to Paine's universally appealing polemic *Common Sense*.[85]

The assertion Larkin makes that Paine invented a new language and a new public is problematic.[86] Larkin attempts to argue that as editor of *The Pennsylvania Magazine* Paine "attempted to make politics and political action available to a broader segment of the population than was previously thought desirable or imagined possible."[87] Unfortunately Larkin, who is not an historian, fails to take into account the fact that by the time Paine became editor that "broader segment of the population" was not only fully attuned to Philadelphia politics but they were in charge of it. Paine did not have to draw Philadelphians into the political sphere—he only had to capitalize upon the prevailing political power shift in the city. Philadelphia's radical politics aside, all across America by 1775 the "public" that Paine supposedly created already contained artisans, farmers, mechanics, and other traditional outsiders of the political landscape. The Sons of Liberty, the nonimportation movement, and committees of correspondence across the colonies had drawn in increasing numbers of Americans (male and female) who were not only engrossed with the growing conflict between Britain and her colonies but who also played a role in it. Thus the national "public" that Larkin claims Paine "invented" already existed; Paine had only to nourish their already voracious appetites for information.

Larkin's postulate that during Paine's editorship the magazine was rarely explicitly political is also worthy of examination. The principal flaw in this argument is that Larkin fails to look at the magazine as a whole. In doing so, Larkin fails to take into account the fact that a magazine is the sum of all of its parts; the entire magazine must be examined to draw any such conclusions about its essential character. Furthermore, there are more ways than articles or occasional pieces to engage in political debate. A comparison study of Paine's editorship versus that of Aitken reveals that clearly Paine brought a radical political voice to *The Pennsylvania Magazine*—whether or not one of those voices was his own is irrelevant.

THE IMPACT OF THE MAGAZINE ON PAINE'S POLITICAL EVOLUTION

As Larkin and others have asserted, Paine's tenure at the magazine was pivotal to his development as a political figure. The mere fact that Paine chose to work on the magazine at all is worthy of interest. He had been offered several lucrative teaching positions which he rejected in favor of Aitken's offer. An offer which, apparently, did not include any definitive term of service or salary. In choosing uncertainty over security, Paine had not only looked the gift horse in the mouth, but also turned away from his planned teaching career. This decision has been largely overlooked by historians but it is important because Paine's decision to edit *The Pennsylvania Magazine* proved to be an important step in his evolution as a professional writer—albeit not for the reasons commonly assumed by scholars.

The fact that Paine chose to work at the magazine without pay instead of private tutoring with a guaranteed salary, indicates—at the very least—that his economic situation was of little interest to him. It further indicates that he was not afraid of risky ventures; nor was he afraid of being a literary pioneer. Perhaps more importantly, this decision exposes an important character trait of Paine: ambitiousness. A glimmer of this was visible during his long campaign for the officers of excise, even though it was not initiated by Paine. Becoming the editor of a potentially popular magazine, however, would have been a feather in Paine's personal cap. It would have made him famous in his own right and given him a reputation and position in America that he could have truly called his own. This might very well account for the fact that money was not (at least in the short-term) of primary importance to him; the opportunity to make his own way in the world may have been of more interest.

It is also important to note that as a contributing editor of the magazine his stock-in-trade was information. In order to succeed in publishing Paine would have to be an effective salesman, not just a mere copy editor. He would have to persuade Americans that they needed to read his publication, and he would have to find ways to keep them interested. Always of concern was the necessity of maintaining a readership and selling subscriptions to keep the venture (and his livelihood) afloat. To do so would mean that Paine would have to have a keen understanding of what Americans might be interested in, or, perhaps more significantly, Paine would have to find ways to arouse their interest in his product. In other words, Paine's words or his selection of others' words had to be persuasive. He had to know (or learn) how to woo his readers with ideas. This ultimately became the hallmark of his political writings and the principal source of his success as a polemicist.

As a teacher or tutor Paine would also have been a purveyor of information—but on a much smaller scale. As a tutor he could only change one mind at a time; as a teacher perhaps dozens. But as a Philadelphia-based magazine editor Paine could reach the minds of thousands. Put simply, in choosing the magazine over teaching, Paine's occupation made him responsible for reaching out to the multitude of Americans. Paine's ability to engage a wider audience than previously targeted by political discourse is another important and distinctive characteristic of Paine's political writings. Clearly in choosing *The Pennsylvania Magazine,* Paine took an important step in his evolution as a famous writer and revolutionary.

Paine's development of a new, broader world view can also be traced to his work at the magazine. During his time at the helm of the new publication Paine had ceased to think like an Englishman; he adopted the cause of America as his own and used his position to further that cause. Paine, to use the common vernacular, had begun to see "the big picture." His concerns now were no longer those of an individual, but of an entire continent. In a matter of months he went from groveling to Parliament on behalf of poorly-paid civil servants to portraying the English as ruthless conquerors. He urged Americans to make gunpowder to kill his former countrymen, while his magazine promised Americans a new Eden following the brutal—but necessary—conflict. A dramatic change in Paine's outlook had occurred in 1775, but the full force of his new beliefs had yet to be unleashed.

Finally, and perhaps most auspiciously, the magazine had one other significant role in Paine's political development: it introduced him to the radical faction in Philadelphia. Because of his work at *The Pennsylvania Magazine*, Paine became an insider in Philadelphia politics. He became close friends with the radical patriots there, including such men as Timothy Matlack, David Rittenhouse, and even Boston's own Samuel Adams. Politics does make strange bedfellows, and Paine could count among his new friends the most ardent and most active of America's rebels. His continued association with these men throughout 1775 partially accounts for Paine's new American bias. One influence in particular, however, deserves a separate mention: Dr. Benjamin Rush. Rush was an Edinburgh-trained physician of considerable reputation and notoriety. He was also one of the leaders of Philadelphia's radical political faction. It was Benjamin Rush, whom Paine met while working at the magazine, who urged Paine to write a daring new pamphlet arguing the necessity of American Independence. That pamphlet was *Common Sense*.

Chapter Two
The Devil's Advocate: Thomas Paine and the Making of *Common Sense*

Thomas Paine was one among thousands of British immigrants who arrived in America in the years just prior to Independence. Like Paine, these travelers left Britain seeking new opportunities and a better life in America. Setting aside his plans to start his own school, Paine quickly found work as a newspaper editor on *The Pennsylvania Magazine*. It was while working at the magazine that Paine became familiar with colonial politics. When word reached Philadelphia in 1775 that the British had fired upon colonists in Massachusetts, Paine was stunned. Perhaps because he was a recent émigré—seeking a life of peace and prosperity—the news of the Massachusetts battles struck Paine with unusual force. Years later he vividly recalled, "Scarcely had I put my foot into the country but it was set on fire about my ears."[1] Paine confessed that, until he found out about Lexington and Concord, "I had no thoughts of independence or arms. The world could not then have persuaded me that I should be either a soldier or an author."[2] However, immediately after he learned of the bloodshed in Massachusetts Paine eagerly cast his lot with the Patriots.

Paine's ardent commitment to Independence notwithstanding, he was obligated to Robert Aitken in the spring of 1775. Their contract negotiations were ongoing, but Paine was still editor of *The Pennsylvania Magazine* and he continued to perform his usual duties. Although he was bound to the magazine it did not stop Paine from expressing his new radical political beliefs. Rather, the magazine became a convenient outlet for his patriotism. By April 1775 Paine had been editor of the magazine for four months but he had only edited two issues (February and March) when he received the accounts of Lexington and Concord. In the April issue six full pages were dedicated to the pivotal events in Massachusetts; easily three

35

times the length of previous months' news items. As Paine was responsible for the content of the magazine, the impact of Lexington and Concord began to color his personal political outlook and likewise that of his publication. The periodical's previously more cryptic pro-America essays like February's "Useful and Entertaining Hints" gave way to more explicit items in June like "Account on the Manufactory of Salt-Petre." Under Paine's stewardship in 1775, the magazine became a decidedly political, even Patriotic, organ through which Paine could lend his support for the American cause. Still, the magazine was only an indirect outlet for Paine's views; a safe and anonymous way for its editor to express his political opinions. The magazine provided the earliest outlet for Paine's new radicalism, but it was only temporary; by August he had lost his job and his political voice. Benjamin Rush provided Paine with the perfect opportunity to continue his activism.

The exact date that Rush met Paine for the first time is unknown, but it must have been sometime after April 24th and before August 1775. This is a simple deduction, based on the fact that Paine was a patriot when he met Rush, and he was still editor of *The Pennsylvania Magazine*. According to Rush, "in one of my visits to Mr. Aitken's bookstore I met with Mr. Paine, and was introduced to him by Mr. Aitken."[3] Rush remembered being fascinated with Paine from the first moment of their acquaintance. He wrote years later that his conversation with Paine "became at once interesting."[4] Rush then immediately asked Paine to visit him at his home and Paine accepted the invitation a few days later. "Our subjects of conversation were political," Rush recalled.[5] He further stated that "I perceived with pleasure that he had realized the independance [sic] of the American colonies upon Great Britain."[6] Rush was convinced that Paine had reached the conclusion that independence was necessary "to bring war to a speedy and successful issue."[7]

Rush then informed Paine that he had started writing an address to the colonists broaching the subject of independence, but had thought better of it. "I hesitated as to the time," Rush recalled, "and I shuddered at the prospect of the consequence of its not being well received."[8] The good doctor was apparently worried that Americans were not ready to consider a plea for separation, a desire that was shared only by the radical fringe in America. Rush was content to move quietly in radical circles, but he knew all too well that "a great majority of the citizens [of Philadelphia] . . . were hostile to a separation."[9] Rush was also worried about his own reputation and safety if his identity as author became public or if his work was not well received. Rush feared, "my profession and connections, which tied me to Philadelphia . . . forbad me to come forward as a pioneer in that important controversy."[10] Paine's situation, Rush noted, was quite different. Paine had no familial ties in America; no reputation to uphold or protect. He was virtually unknown in Philadelphia, to say nothing of the rest of the American colonies. If Paine risked writing a publication calling for independence and it was not well received, he could simply vanish—Rush could not. Even if people found out the work was authored by "Thomas Paine," Americans would only be able to wonder about the identity of the mysterious author. If Rush had been discovered, his freedom (like that of Samuel Adams or John Hancock) would have been compromised. In other words, Paine was expendable.

It was on these terms that Rush couched his proposal to Paine. "I mentioned the subject to Mr. Paine," Rush recalled, "and asked him what he thought of writing a pamphlet upon it."[11] He further encouraged Paine by adding, "I suggested to him that he had nothing to fear from the popular odium to which such a publication might expose him, for he could live anywhere."[12] According to Rush, Paine "readily assented to the proposal."[13] John Adams, also writing years later, corroborated Rush's account in his autobiography, adding that Rush "furnished [Paine] with the Arguments which had been urged in Congress an hundred times."[14] Upon completion of the pamphlet Paine asked Rush to supply the title for his work. The Scotland-trained physician appropriately dubbed the pamphlet *Common Sense*.[15]

Paine eagerly agreed to Rush's proposition in order to aid the war effort. Paine decided to take up his pen because "I saw an opportunity in which I thought I could do some good."[16] In fact it was Paine's intention to accept no profits from the sale of *Common Sense*; rather it was his plan to use any profits to buy mittens for the troops going to Quebec.[17] He was completely in favor of America's separation from Great Britain, and wanted to do whatever was in his power to persuade the colonists to choose that course. If he believed Benjamin Rush (and there is no reason to think that he did not) then he may have found some comfort in the fact that his anonymity afforded him some protection. Finally, Paine really had almost nothing to lose by writing the pamphlet while he had everything to gain: American Independence and peace in his adopted land.

Some historians have taken issue with Rush's recollections, claiming that Rush tried to steal Paine's thunder by claiming that *Common Sense* was from first to last his idea.[18] This is unfortunate because Rush never takes credit for the pamphlet itself, only the proposal to Paine. The actual work, which Rush readily acknowledged, was all Thomas Paine. Neither did Rush, nor any of the other men who read draft copies have any say in the actual wording of the pamphlet. Therefore all of the credit for the actual success of the pamphlet belonged to Thomas Paine alone—a fact that Rush also acknowledged.[19] Regardless of the impetus, Paine accepted Rush's challenge and began writing the work that made him the world's preeminent pamphleteer.

By the time Paine sat down to write *Common Sense* in 1775 Americans were at a crossroads. One path led to reconciliation and a possible end to the growing bloodshed. The other led to revolution and independence from the Mother Country. Reconciliation was a matter of public debate; independence was not. While there yet remained the slightest possibility of ending the bloodshed and remaining a part of the illustrious British Empire, the Continental Congress would not consider a complete separation. Even after the casualties continued to mount following the bloody battle at Bunker Hill, as late as July 1775 the Continental Congress submitted the Olive Branch petition to King George III attempting to solicit a reconciliation.[20] The war notwithstanding, America's leaders were simply not prepared to take such drastic measures as seeking full independence. Even the radical faction in Congress had not yet reached the conclusion that a complete separation was desirable.[21] Americans fought on, but Revolution was not what they were fighting for.

Paine's charge, then, was to convince Americans—all Americans—that reconciliation was not merely unthinkable but onerous. Paine had to find a way to make Americans believe that not only could they survive without Britain, but that they could actually prosper from the separation. He wanted to convince Americans that there was only one option—complete and absolute independence. In other words, what Paine needed was to create a conversion experience for the masses. Just as Lexington and Concord had converted Paine to the doctrine of Independence, now he sought to convert the American colonists. In order to accomplish this Paine launched the literary equivalent of a two-pronged attack. He used prevailing Enlightenment natural law political theory to appeal to Americans' reason, and inflammatory anti-British rhetoric to appeal to their emotions. At times, the lines between Paine's dual argument blurred. Like a New Light minister preaching to his wayward congregation, Paine presented the cause of American Independence as nothing less than a moral imperative. In *Common Sense,* Paine portrayed Revolution as the way of righteousness and reconciliation as the route to eternal damnation. The American struggle was a battle between good and evil, and Paine exhorted the American people and the Continental Congress to act boldly. For America to retain her virtue and remain God's chosen people she would first have to cut her ties with the Great Satan, Great Britain. Thus at times Paine's rational, political arguments were infused with emotion and righteous indignation as he forced his fellow countrymen to choose between paradise and purgatory.

THE DEVIL'S ADVOCATE

Paine's opening argument in *Common Sense* might just as easily have been written by John Locke. The educated leaders of the colonial rebellion were well acquainted with the seventeenth-century philosopher's natural law theory, and it was predominantly this crowd that Paine addressed with his summation of "the Origin and Design of Government."[22] Nearly a century before the Stamp Act Crisis that produced that famous phrase, John Locke introduced his theory on the origins of government. In his second *Treatise of Government,* Locke asserted that mankind was born free in a State of Nature, placed there by God. Moreover, this state of nature "has a Law of Nature to govern it . . . And Reason, which is that Law, teaches all Mankind."[23] All mankind were subject to the law because according to Locke, all men were created equal, "being all the Workmanship of one Omnipotent, and infinitely wise Maker."[24] Thus all men were created equal, but subordinate to the deity that created them and placed them upon the earth. In this state of nature, men acquired property by employing their labor to put resources into production. This, however, led to competition, and because of mankind's failure to remain strictly altruistic, Locke argued, conflict ensued. "Were the impulses of consciences clear, uniform and irresistibly obeyed," Paine insists, "man would need no other law-giver."[25] To resolve these conflicts, men voluntarily sacrificed absolute freedom to establish a government that Locke declared, "has no other end but the preservation of Property."[26] Government became a necessary evil, and therefore in Paine's evaluation, "the badge of lost innocence."[27] Natural law theory was at the very core of the colonists' assertion that "taxation without representation is tyranny."

Paine was also well aware that the simplicity of natural law theory was very attractive to colonial rebel leaders; it dictated that governments easily established were just as easily (in theory) disestablished. According to Locke's theory, since government was formed voluntarily by the people, its power was therefore derived from the people. When government ceased to protect the people or abused its power, Locke argued, the people had the absolute right to alter or abolish that government and establish a new one. Government of the people and by the people, according to Paine, "is our natural right."[28] Paine too was drawn to the simplicity of natural law philosophy, as he was drawn to simplicity in all matters of philosophy and principle. In *Common Sense* Paine declared, "I draw my idea of the form of government from a principle in nature which no art can overturn, viz. that the more simple anything is, the less liable it is to be disordered, and the easier repaired when disordered."[29] Similarly, in his attack on the British government, Paine argued that "absolute governments . . . have this advantage with them, they are simple; if the people suffer, they know the head from which their suffering springs; know likewise the remedy."[30] However, Paine reminded his readers in *Common Sense* that England's constitutional monarchy was anything but simple. "The Constitution of England is so exceedingly complex," Paine wrote, "that the nation may suffer for years together without being able to discover in which part the fault lies."[31] For Paine, the British system with its unwritten Constitution that nevertheless bound the Parliament and King by its invisible laws, was so incomprehensible that it was oppressive. Under such a system, the British people obeyed the laws out of habit, not understanding. "The prejudice of Englishmen, in favor of their own government," Paine lamented, "arises as much or more from national pride than reason."[32] Because of the complexity of the British system, the people revered rather than questioned their government, which gave king, lords, and commons inordinate power over their everyday lives. If the American colonists were ever to return to a simpler, more natural and just government, they would first have to free themselves from this kind of "obstinate prejudice."[33]

Another, somewhat lesser component of Paine's natural justifications for revolution, included an appeal to the laws of nature and scientific reasoning. Stating a simple geographical fact, Paine pointed out to his readers that "the distance at which the Almighty hath placed England and America is a strong and natural proof that the authority of the one over the other, was never the design of heaven."[34] Moreover, "In no instance hath nature made the satellite larger than its primary planet."[35] In Paine's estimation, "there is something absurd, in supposing a Continent to be perpetually governed by an island."[36] Indeed, the very idea of America remaining subject to the will of Great Britain was "repugnant to reason, to the universal order of things."[37] "Reconciliation," Paine declared, "is *now* a fallacious dream. Nature hath deserted the connection."[38] According to *Common Sense,* because innocent blood had been spilt, the law of nature now demanded justice. Paine insisted that "There are injuries which nature cannot forgive."[39] He therefore instructed his readers that reconciliation was no longer an option. He reminded Americans of the words of John Milton: "never can true reconcilement grow where wounds of deadly hate have pierced so deep."[40]

What is intriguing about this particular phrase from Milton is who uttered it: Satan. In Milton's work *Paradise Lost,* Satan made this remark to his fellow fallen angels to demonstrate his contempt for God. Lucifer made it clear to his brethren in Hell that, even with eternal salvation and God's love hanging in the balance, he was too wounded by God's actions to seek forgiveness or reconciliation. Satan may have been relegated to the depths of Hell, but his fall from grace had secured his independence from the King of Heaven. With this one quotation Paine summed up the bulk of his rational arguments, and in choosing Satan's words and actions as illustration for his argument he became—quite literally—the Devil's Advocate. In his role as Devil's Advocate Paine forced Americans and the Continental Congress to examine closely what they envisioned as a worst-case scenario: separation from Britain. Through his examination America realized, like Satan in Milton's fable, that Independence was actually the best of all possible solutions.

Taking each of the arguments against independence separately, Paine showed Americans how misguided and illogical their apprehensions were. He began by taking issue with the widespread belief that America could not survive economically without England. Paine reminded his readers that America's primary economic strength lay in its production of foodstuffs, and would therefore "always have a market while eating is the custom of Europe."[41] No longer bound by parliamentary law to use British ports only, an independent America would be welcomed by the rest of the trading world, "because it is the interest of all Europe to have America a free port."[42] Furthermore, Paine reminded his readers of the fact that westward expansion would be unchecked without parliamentary regulation, and such expansion would lead to even greater domestic economic power. In Paine's estimation, "no nation under heaven hath such an advantage as this."[43] Finally, *Common Sense* laid to rest any worries about foreign invaders taking advantage of a new nation no longer protected by the powerful British navy. Europe's dependence upon America's commerce would secure protection of her ports, and America's "barrenness of gold and silver" would keep potential invaders away.[44]

Foes of independence argued vociferously that the colonies' safety and security depended upon the protection of Great Britain. Moreover they argued that Americans were obliged to the Mother Country for her protection of her children across the water; a debt that required nothing short of total submission. Paine countered such rhetoric by reminding Americans that Britain's military involvement in the colonies had nothing to do with familial loyalty or affection. "Her motive was *interest* not *attachment*," Paine insisted.[45] To Paine this mistaken affection on the part of Britain had led to the far more dangerous proposition that together England and America "might bid defiance to the world," costing Americans their lives out of a sense of service and devotion to King and Country.[46] He lamented that in refusing to acknowledge that Britain's interest in America was purely economic, the colonists had "made large sacrifices to superstition."[47] With independence and the equivalent wealth of King Solomon's mines within their grasp, Paine pondered, "what have we to do with setting the world at defiance?"[48] Let Englishmen fight English wars: "our plan is commerce."[49] Still, the question remained of how an independent America could defend her borders. Without the British navy to protect them, detractors painted a portrait of a nation that was not only ungrateful, but helpless and vulnerable. Paine again argued the opposite: "No country on the globe is so happily situated, or so internally capable of raising a fleet as America. Tar, timber, iron and cordage are her natural produce. We need go abroad for nothing."[50] Furthermore, *Common Sense* reminded Americans that not only did they have the resources to build their own navy, but they also had the advantage of a trained army. The recent French and Indian War had given many Americans real military experience, and Paine urged the colonists to act while that experience was still fresh and could be taught to the next generation.[51]

There was still yet another, more compelling reason why an independent America would be a safer America. "Any submission to, or dependence on, Great Britain," Paine warned, "tends directly to involve this continent in European wars and quarrels."[52] American commerce and safety could be assured, but only if those directing her foreign policy heeded the following caveat: "Europe is too thickly planted with kingdoms to be long at peace, and whenever a war breaks out between England and any foreign power, the trade of America goes to ruin, *because of her connection with Britain.*"[53] Disengaging themselves from Britain meant not only a safe present, but more significantly, a peaceful and prosperous future. "France and Spain never were, nor perhaps ever will be, our enemies as *Americans,*" Paine asserted, "but as our being *subjects of Great Britain.*"[54] The key to securing this future resided in the colonists viewing themselves as one united people, rather than as separate entities. To this end, in *Common Sense* Paine always referred to the colonists as "Americans" suggesting unity, a common struggle, and a shared destiny. A nation that regarded itself as one unified people could not be divided or conquered. Paine reminded Americans that in their recent struggles against Parliament, in the very formation of a Continental Congress, they had acted as one nation. The troubles they had endured had created bonds that transcended colonial borders. "The friendship which is formed in misfortune, are of all others the most lasting and unalterable . . . we are young, and we have been distressed; but our concord hath withstood our troubles," he wrote.[55] He therefore challenged the assumption of Parliament and colonial loyalists that "the colonies have no relation to each other but through the parent country."[56] Paine argued that with independence and unity America could attain both strength and safety.

As subjects of Great Britain, the colonists had been accustomed to regarding England as the Mother Country, and themselves as her obedient children. Familial language and the concomitant paternalism that pervaded political discourse and policy for much of the colonies' history had never been challenged in any significant fashion. In *Common Sense* Paine unleashed the first volley and directly attacked the customary loyalty to Crown and Country. If England was truly America's parent, Paine chastened, "then the more shame upon her conduct. Even brutes do not devour their young, nor savages make war upon their families."[57] Paine asked his readers to recall the privation of Boston, whose citizens suffered miserably under the oppressive Coercive Acts: "the seat of wretchedness will teach us wisdom, and instruct us for ever to renounce a power in whom we can have no trust."[58] Finally, for those whose loyalty to Mother England remained steadfast, he countered with a much simpler yet more compelling argument: "Europe, and not England, is the parent country of America. This new world hath been the asylum . . . from *every part* of Europe."[59] How could England truly claim to be the parent of German, Finnish, Swedish, French, Irish, and Scottish Americans? The American colonies had become their own parent country to immigrants from around the globe; immigrants not fettered by England's matronly apron strings. Paine thus urged Americans to disregard forever more "the violated unmeaning names of parent and child."[60]

As Devil's Advocate, Paine confronted what was perhaps the greatest and most pervasive obstacle to serious consideration of Independence: fear. Much of the arguments against the colonies striking out on their own centered around a fear not only of the unknown, but worse still, the known dangers involved in such an undertaking. In *Common Sense* Paine deftly countered any economic concerns Americans harbored by reminding them of their role as the world's breadbasket. Paine also laid to rest any fears related to America's ability to defend itself against hostile nations by demonstrating that just as American lumber and labor had built the British navy, they could certainly build their own. However there was another, more obvious fear, that kept most colonists from contemplating independence: the knowledge that they would have to defeat the greatest military force in the world to achieve it.

Just as he had done with the other arguments against independence, Paine attempted to show Americans that however elusive victory against such a strong power seemed, in fact the opposite was true. Paine tried to reassure his audience by declaring, "we have contracted a false notion respecting the navy of England, and have talked as if we should have the whole of it to encounter at once."[61] Paine knew all too well that Britain would not be able to send its entire naval fleet to stop the American rebellion. England had considerable political and economic interests elsewhere; in concentrating her fleet in North America, she would shift the balance of power on the Continent to her European foes who would be able to take advantage of her vulnerability. Therefore whatever complement of ships Britain sent, America would be able to defeat them with her own navy, easily built from an abundance of resources and an experienced shipbuilding infrastructure. As for the British army—whom the Americans were already at war with—*Common Sense* urged Americans to take heart: "Our iron is superior to that of other countries . . . Cannon we can cast at pleasure. Saltpeter and gunpowder we are every day producing."[62] Not only did America have the weaponry, but far more importantly they had the manpower. Perhaps the greatest weapon in America's arsenal, Paine argued, was its sheer numbers. "Our present numbers are sufficient to repel the force of all the world," he wrote. Even though Paine believed a war of attrition would result in victory for the colonists, he also moved to reassure them that they need not fight alone. Paine urged his fellow Americans to consider the possibility of an alliance with England's European foes not only as a sound move diplomatically, but also militarily. He enticed his readers to accept the fact that "nothing can settle our affairs so expeditiously as an open and determined DECLARATION FOR INDEPENDENCE" because "under our present denominations of British subjects, we can neither be received nor heard abroad."[63] In other words, America did not require the help of a foreign power, but the aid of one (and hopefully several) would clearly shift the balance of military power in America's favor. *Common Sense* showed that with all of these military advantages (some already employed, others only imagined) there was simply no way that America could lose a war with Britain—thus laying the colonists' fears to rest.

Americans' fears about war with Britain were grounded in firsthand knowledge of the capabilities of England's fighting forces—colonists had recently fought with them against the French, and were currently fighting against them in Massachusetts. Paine therefore knew that the best way to calm such fears was to remind Americans of their own strength and power. This strategy was useless, however, against the colonists' other reason for trepidation: fear of the unknown. Supposing the colonists did defeat Britain and win their independence: then what? The uncertainty of how America would govern itself and maintain order as an independent nation loosed from the constraints of King and Parliament weighed heavily upon the minds of many. "If there is any true cause of fear respecting independence," Paine sympathized, "it is because no plan is yet laid down. Men do not see their way out."[64] Paine then offered his own "hints" for a plan of government, suggesting that the colonists use his ideas as "the means of giving rise to something better."[65] Paine's plan called for annual assemblies with a President and a Continental Congress that would be the ruling body of the colonies.[66] He further suggested that there should be an absolute minimum of thirty delegates per colony to the Continental Congress, and that congressional legislation should require a three-fifths majority for passage.[67] Finally, Paine advised America to create a "Continental Charter."[68] This charter (to be modeled after England's Magna Carta) would clearly delineate "the number and manner of choosing members of Congress, Members of Assembly . . . and drawing the line of business and jurisdiction between them."[69] In other words, the United Colonies (as he termed them) should have a written Constitution—a far more logical system than that of Great Britain.

Paine's arguments to quell the fears of colonists also included using their fear to argue for independence. In his role as the Devil's Advocate Paine argued that reconciliation and its consequences was by far the outcome to fear the most. Paine insisted that unless the issues between Parliament and the colonies were truly resolved to the satisfaction of both parties, reconciliation would only be a temporary solution. "There is ten times more to dread from a patched up connection," Paine wrote, "than from independence."[70] Eventually, the same problems that led to colonial rebellion would "be followed by a revolt some where or other, the consequences of which may be far more fatal than all the malice of Britain."[71] Those who had tasted liberty, and been close to a life of freedom; those who had suffered at the hands of British oppression or bloodshed would eventually act out if that liberty was taken from them by reconciliation. Civil war would be the inevitable result, and Paine warned that "nothing but independence . . . can keep the peace of the continent."[72] Americans needed to choose between complete submission or complete independence for their own safety's sake.

"TIME TO MURDER AND CREATE"[73]

As compelling as Paine's rational arguments for independence were in *Common Sense*, they often paled in comparison to the force of his emotional appeal. There are times when it seems that Paine's own anger at the British government overpowers his reason, resulting in a frenzy of insults and blood-chilling rage that nearly consume his arguments. Closer inspection reveals, however, that there was in fact method to Paine's madness. As Devil's Advocate, Paine had successfully demonstrated that independence was a logical and necessary goal for America. Paine realized, however, that "long standing prejudices" would not be overcome simply by natural law arguments and logic.[74] Paine was aware that as long as the colonists were "under the influence of some leading partiality," they were not capable of being guided by their reason.[75] Thus, in order to convert Americans to the doctrine of independence, he would have to appeal to both their hearts and their minds. The strong emotional ties that bound the colonists to Mother England would have to be destroyed lest they interfered with their ability to see the truth. To make a convincing case for separation, Paine reminded Americans of the "wounds of deadly hate" inflicted upon them by an unfeeling Parliament and king. He needed Americans to feel anti-British; to turn away from their Mother Country and cut their lingering emotional ties. In so doing, he could halt any further discussion of reconciliation and present Americans with a soothing alternative: independence. Destroying the colonists' emotional ties to Britain was therefore a key component of Paine's argument for independence in *Common Sense;* one that included stirring up the colonists' basest emotions and appealing to the authority of Scripture.

Arousing the anger of the colonists was a simple task for Paine in *Common Sense;* he had only to remind Americans of how they already felt about the war and the resulting bloodshed. The Continental Congress had always maintained that it was a defensive war; that Britain had fired first upon unassuming colonists in Concord, Massachusetts. The inflammatory language Paine used drew upon the colonists' assumptions that they were victims of British aggression. He called the British soldiers "murderers," and asked his readers "tell me whether you can hereafter love, honor, and faithfully serve the power that hath carried the sword into your land?"[76] Not only were the Redcoats murderers, but their actions had made the colonists murderers as well. The colonists had fought with Britain against France, and now Britain fought against America in the name of loyalty; two generations of Americans had been trained to kill in the name of Mother England. Paine pleaded with his readers, "for God's sake let us come to a final separation, and not leave the next generation to be cutting throats under the violated unmeaning names of parent and child."[77] *Common Sense* insisted that there was no hope for reconciliation after such brutality because there could be no forgiveness. "There are injuries which nature cannot forgive," wrote Paine, "she would cease to be nature if she did."[78] The only way to rid America of violence and bloodshed, protecting the next generation from such a fate, was to secure her independence.

Safety from British aggression was one thing; safety from the Almighty was quite another. By far the most significant portion of Paine's argument, "Of Monarchy and Hereditary Succession," played upon the colonists' darkest most unspeakable fear: the wrath of God. In this section of *Common Sense* (and indeed throughout the pamphlet) Paine argued that not only was monarchy contrary to natural law, but that it was in fact contrary to God's law, and was therefore evil. A continent of Americans who were loyal to the King, moreover, were not only blasphemers but condemned to suffer God's punishment unless they mended their ways—and quickly. They only way to make things right with the Creator, Paine argued, was for America to seek independence from Britain and establish a true system of government, according with God's laws. *Common Sense* was, in the words of Winthrop Jordan, a "political eucharist."[79] This term, more than any other, accurately describes the character of the work as both political and religious. In the pamphlet, Paine proposed a sort of communion (or reconciliation) with God through political action: the disestablishment of the monarchy. Paine in fact used Scripture and religious imagery to persuade Americans to become independent—for their own souls' sake.

Common Sense opened with a warning for the people of America: "the palaces of kings are built upon the ruins of the bowers of paradise."[80] This was clearly a reference to the doctrine of original sin and the fall of man. In this statement, Paine argued that monarchies developed after man's expulsion from Eden, and were therefore not the original design of heaven. "Mankind being originally equals in the order of creation," Paine averred, "equality could only be destroyed by some subsequent circumstance."[81] Using the Old Testament as historical evidence, Paine sought to illustrate that "the exalting one man so greatly above the rest cannot be justified on the equal rights of nature, so neither can it be defended on the authority of scripture."[82] Monarchy was thus an "unnatural" institution contrary to God's plan.[83] The "sinfulness of the origin" of such a system, according to Paine, could be traced directly to the ancient Hebrews.[84] It was the consequences of this "sin of the Jews," however, that Paine sought to warn the colonists about.[85]

According to Paine's reading of the Bible (specifically the Book of Samuel), heathens invented kingship, and the ancient Hebrews adopted the practice from them.[86] The Jewish people, "under a national delusion," requested a king to lead them—thus altering the "Republic" they were currently governed by.[87] For 3,000 years the Hebrews had no king because they "held it sinful to acknowledge any being under the title but the Lord of Hosts."[88] Then, after Gideon helped them defeat their foes in a mighty battle, the Hebrews cried out for him to become their king. Gideon replied, in Paine's estimation, in the only manner a God-fearing man should: "Gideon in the piety of his soul replied, *I will not rule over you, neither shall my son rule over you*. THE LORD SHALL RULE OVER YOU."[89] Paine explained to the colonists that "Gideon doth not decline the honor, but denieth their right to give it."⁹⁰ Unfortunately the Jewish people did not heed Gideon's refusal, nor the prophet Samuel's, but instead pleaded with Samuel to give them a king. Samuel sought guidance from God who lamented, "*they have not rejected thee, but they have rejected me,* THAT I SHOULD NOT REIGN OVER THEM."⁹¹

God told Samuel exactly what a king would give to the children of Israel: misery. The Almighty prophesied that a king would make soldiers of sons and force daughters to be his servants. The king would seize the peoples' farms and vineyards and give them to his servants and officers as patronage, and force the Jews to work for them.⁹² God said to Samuel, "*and ye shall cry out in that day because of your king which ye shall have chosen,* AND THE LORD WILL NOT HEAR YOU IN THAT DAY."⁹³ According to Paine, God then bade Samuel to tell all of this to the Israelites in an attempt to change their minds and make them see reason. Samuel obeyed, but the people continued to demand a king. The king they selected behaved just as God prophesied, demonstrating that "oppression . . . bribery, corruption, and favouritism, are the standing vices of kings."⁹⁴ Indeed the people did cry out for relief from God, praying to Samuel, "*Pray for thy servants unto the Lord thy God that we die not, for* WE HAVE ADDED UNTO OUR SINS THIS EVIL, TO ASK A KING."⁹⁵ God ignored their cries, and permitted their suffering as a punishment for their sins. For Paine, this was clear evidence—and a warning to be heeded—"that the almighty hath here entered his protest against monarchical government" which "so impiously invades the prerogative of heaven."⁹⁶

Because of his later professed devotion to deism, the origins of Paine's biblical argument in *Common Sense* has been the subject of much debate among scholars. In his autobiography, John Adams recalled a conversation he had with Paine shortly after he published *Common Sense:* "I told [Paine] further that his Reasoning from the Old Testament was ridiculous, and I could hardly think him sincere. At this time he laughed, and said he had taken his Ideas in that part from Milton. . . ."⁹⁷ Surprisingly, this possible connection between Paine and Milton has been virtually ignored by historians and Paine scholars alike. In fact, in 1984 Aldridge was the first to identify the quotation in *Common Sense*—that Paine attributes to Milton—as being a line from *Paradise Lost.*⁹⁸ For 200 years, scholars have ignored the presence of Milton in Paine's writing; to date only Aldridge has shown an interest, but even he dismissed the potential connection with little more than a few sentences.⁹⁹ This is unfortunate, because a closer analysis of Milton's work reveals a striking similarity to Paine's argument.

In 1658 Charles II was the object of Milton's scorn, and in his *Defence* he devoted one entire chapter to the origin of monarchy as an evil, blasphemous institution.[100] His evidence was taken largely from the Old Testament, based primarily on scriptures from Deuteronomy and the book of Samuel.[101] For further proof of his theory, Milton listed a number of chapters and verses (all from I Samuel) to aid his argument.[102] "All of these passages," Milton stated, "are proof that a king had been given to the Israelites as a result of God's anger."[103] Paine himself used one of these citations (I Samuel verse 7) verbatim in *Common Sense* also as proof of the Jews' betrayal of God.[104] Milton averred that the only way to right the wrong committed by the establishment of and obedience to a king was to depose him. "Whenever a people have created a king without some visible sign from God," Milton asserts, "they can by the same right of theirs cast the king out."[105] Furthermore, Milton reasoned, "to depose a tyrant is clearly a more divine action than to set him up."[106] Paine's argument (discussed previously) is more than an echo of Milton's; it is practically a carbon copy.[107]

The ancient Hebrews had committed an unpardonable sin in adopting monarchy, but for Paine, there was a far more troubling aspect to their blasphemous institution: it was hereditary. Paine described this component of monarchy as nothing less than "evil," and "an insult and imposition upon posterity."[108] Paine declared, "in their choice not only of a king but of a family of kings for ever, hath no parallel in or out of scripture but the doctrine of original sin, which supposed the free will of all men lost in Adam; and from such comparison, and it will admit of no other, hereditary succession can derive no glory."[109] "It unalterably follows," Paine reasoned, "that original sin and hereditary succession are parallels."[110] The fall of man guaranteed that the depravity of mankind was eternal; no mortal could hope to escape it. The same was not true, unfortunately, of the principle of virtue. Virtue was not hereditary, which therefore meant that in the case of hereditary monarchies, there was no way to guarantee that one just, honorable ruler would always be replaced by another. Such an "unnatural compact" created the possibility that "the next succession" would place people "under the government of a rogue or a fool."[111] As Paine pointed out to his readers, the theory of hereditary monarchy was predicated upon a fallacious assumption: "This is supposing the present race of kings in the world to have had an honorable origin."[112] The author of *Common Sense* illustrated that at least in the case of England, nothing could have been further from the truth. According to Paine, the fact "that William the Conqueror was an usurper is a fact not to be contradicted."[113] "The plain truth is," Paine asserted, "the antiquity of English monarchy will not bear looking into."[114]

In fact the history of the monarchy in England provided Paine with all the proof he needed of the evil of not only hereditary succession but of the institution itself. Hereditary succession often allowed minor children to inherit the throne (Henry VI's disastrous reign is a notable example), causing them to be vulnerable to courtly deception and corruption. Still worse, the institution itself did not provide any stability, and often created exactly the opposite: chaos and bloodshed. According to Paine, "Thirty kings and two minors have reigned in [England] since the conquest, in which time there has been (including the revolution) no less than eight civil wars and nineteen rebellions."[115] Not only was hereditary succession a sin but it also violated the laws of nature. The proof of which, Paine argued, was the endless succession of so many foolish, simpering monarchs. "Nature disapproves it," he wrote, "otherwise she would not so frequently turn it into ridicule, by giving mankind an *ass for a lion.*"[116]

Paine's humor and sarcasm notwithstanding, his fear for America's future under such a blasphemous regime was no laughing matter. Paine's historical account of the origin of monarchy, its evil nature, and the depravity of hereditary succession was meant to be more than a warning to Americans—it was meant to be a mirror. Paine hoped that the punishment inflicted upon the Hebrews—by an oppressive, self-aggrandizing king who turned his own people into murderers—would resonate with colonists in 1776. The colonists' loyalty to George III had been rewarded with oppressive taxation, the denial of a political voice in Parliament, bloodshed, and (at least in the case of Boston) starvation. Paine bemoaned the fact that monarchy "'tis a form of government which the word of God bears testimony against, and blood will attend it."[117] God's punishment was everywhere visible, according to Paine, and the only way to escape the Almighty's wrath was to form a government according to God's laws. "Ye that oppose independence now," Paine cautioned, "ye know not what ye do."[118] Any man who would choose George III and eternal damnation over equality and the rewards of heaven "would have joined Lucifer in his revolt."[119] By making this argument Paine forever altered the character of the debate. Revolution was no longer a matter of the "rights of Englishmen;" it was a struggle between good and evil, and Paine begged the colonists to choose wisely. To help the colonists make a more informed choice between loyalty to the king and independence, Paine stripped away the trappings of monarchy to expose the man, George Hanover, and all of his faults. In doing so, Paine thrust the burden of America's woes upon the king's shoulders, making him the object of their disaffection and his removal the source of their future happiness.

Paine began his assault on the character of George III by tracing his succession as King of England back to William the Conqueror, a "French bastard" and "a very paltry rascally original."[120] Paine employed this kind of brash language to demote the king from a revered sovereign to contemptible man. This time it was George the man that Paine attacked, not his office, in order to change the way the American people viewed him. By portraying him as a man, Paine made him fallible with all the sin that flesh is heir to. As an amiable, trusting man, George III was at the mercy of his evil ministers and diabolical Parliament, but as an incompetent and ruthless king directing events, George III himself could be blamed for the colonists' woes. Thus Paine denounced George III as "the royal brute of Great Britain," "an apostate from the order of manhood," and the "sullen-tempered Pharaoh of England."[121] In sharp contrast to the monarch the colonists toasted all the while decrying Parliamentary abuses, Paine's king "hath wickedly broken through every moral and human obligation, trampled nature and conscience beneath his feet."[122] "The naked and untutored Indian, is less savage than the king of Britain," who, according to Paine, was content to wage war upon his own colonists because of his monomania.[123]

The language that Paine used to describe George III was very interesting indeed. At a time when most writers characterized those who supported the crown as "unmanly" or effeminate, Paine turned the tables on his contemporaries. Apparently the king suffered from too much testosterone (a brute, a Pharaoh, a "ruffian," a savage) rather than too little.[124] In other words, King George was a tyrant. As a tyrant, the king became a ruler who dictated orders and bullied his lessers to achieve his own ends. George III was no longer the victim or the innocent bystander—Paine made him the grand maniacal architect of systematic colonial oppression. The only possible solution to the colonists' difficulties with England, therefore, was to rid themselves of their sovereign. Replacing George III with a government based on equality and reason assured Americans not only of freedom from British tyranny but freedom from God's vengeful grasp.

With his emotional rhetoric and his religious arguments Paine had successfully destroyed any lingering ties between the colonists and their mother country. As Winthrop Jordan has argued, Paine "killed" the King and any remaining affection between him and his people.[125] Doing so might have proven to be a danger in itself: what would the colonists' substitute for the loss of their identity as British subjects? For Paine the answer was simple: a sense of themselves as Americans. Paine had destroyed the colonists' emotional ties to Britain, but he created something entirely new to replace it: American nationalism. To do so Paine chose his words very carefully in *Common Sense,* always referring to America—in a way other pamphleteers had not—as one nation, not separate colonies. Unity was Paine's ultimate purpose in employing this rhetorical device (how else could the colonies defeat such an accomplished foe?) but the sense of nationalism he created was every bit as important to securing independence.

Paine avoided drawing attention to American loyalists as individuals, rather he focused his ire on George III—the object of their loyalty. Paine rarely ever referred to "the colonies," instead he repeatedly referred to "America" or "Americans." Similarly, Paine makes continued reference to the American continent, implying not only a broader vision of America beyond mere individual colonial possessions, but also an America that was geographically an enormous unified whole. American Independence was not "the affair of a city, a county, a province, or a kingdom, but of a continent," Paine proclaimed.[126] He demonstrated to the colonists that "a Continent" could not be governed by an island, and it was "this continent" of America that he warned against entangling alliances.[127] America was one nation, and the colonists were all equal citizens with a shared destiny: they were God's chosen people. It was their destiny to free themselves from their "sullen-tempered Pharaoh" George III to establish the New Israel in America.[128] History had proven, according to Paine, that this was indeed God's plan: "The Reformation was preceded by the discovery of America: As if the Almighty graciously meant to open a sanctuary to the persecuted in future years."[129] Implicit in the characterization of the colonists as God's chosen people, was the tacit assumption that Americans were superior to the British. "We have it in our power to begin the world over again," Paine entreated.[130] This language suggested that the colonists had a uniqueness that England could not lay claim to. They were Americans, blessed by the Almighty, possessing the strength and ability to make the world over again in their image. Independence was not only within the colonists' grasp, it was their divine right.

Paine's message was accompanied by an urgency that was meant to move Americans to boldly seek their Independence and frighten them with the consequences of inaction. America was at war with Great Britain, and whether or not she knew what she was fighting for was a moot point. "The Rubicon is passed," Paine declared.[131] There was no turning back; America would have to move forward to independence "or the whole continent will partake of the misfortune."[132] The time to act was now while America was young and able to develop sound principles based on reason and virtue, rather than centuries of British despotism. "Youth is the seed-time of good habits as well in nations as in individuals," Paine observed. The winter of 1776 was in fact "the seed time of continental union, faith and honor," and "worth an age if rightly employed."[133] "'Tis not the concern of a day, a year, or an age," Paine asserted; "posterity are virtually involved in the contest."[134] Not only America, but the fate of the entire world was at stake: "Many circumstances have, and will arise, which are not local, but universal, and through which the principles of all lovers of mankind are affected, and in the event of which their affections are interested."[135] Paine informed his readers that the world was waiting for the United States to accept its role as the guardian of freedom, and urged them to "prepare in time an asylum for mankind."[136] The time for pondering independence ended when American blood was shed. For Paine there remained only one course of action for the colonists that could quell the violence, forgive their sins, and fulfill their destiny: "'TIS TIME TO PART."[137]

LEARNING FROM HIS MISTAKES: A NEW LOOK AT THE *CASE OF THE OFFICERS OF EXCISE*

As previously mentioned, Paine's first foray into politics, the *Case of the Officers of the Excise* (1772), had failed miserably. For nearly two years he had campaigned to win over Parliament with his rhetoric but to no avail. Within a year of Paine's failure and his dismissal from the Excise, Rush asked Paine to attempt another persuasive essay. Only this time, it was not the salaries of a few English tax collectors that were at stake; this time, it was the fate of an entire nation. Given the fact that Paine's only other attempt at persuasive rhetoric was a failure, it stands to reason that however committed Paine may have been to independence, he was not likely to rush into another major political work without rethinking *Case of the Officers of Excise*. If Paine was to move Americans to revolution, he would clearly have to form better, more persuasive arguments. It seems likely then, that Paine may have tried to avoid making the same mistakes twice. Thus, it is time to reevaluate *Case of the Officers of Excise* in relation to its possible influence on the creation of *Common Sense* and Paine's development as a writer.

Until now, the scant scholarship surrounding *Case of the Officers of Excise* has revolved around one central question: how much does the style and tone of *Case of the Officers of Excise* resemble Paine's later works like *Common Sense?* A similar line of inquiry is also present, as previously mentioned, in studies of Paine's alleged contributions to *The Pennsylvania Magazine*. By comparing his style and grammatical structure, the results of both investigations have been predictably similar as well: a glimmer of the future radical and master of polemical prose is visible, but only in fledgling form. There is nothing inherently incorrect in this conclusion regarding the *Case*, and it is a perfectly legitimate question for scholars to investigate. However, to study the evolution of a man's career, mark changes and note possible turning points, requires a more thorough approach. Thus, the question to ask now is why—since they were Paine's first political works of any length in 1776—is there such a tremendous difference between *Case* and *Common Sense?* Finding the answer to this question could shed new light on the creation of America's first best-seller.

The lengthy subtitle of the *Case of the Officers of Excise* partially divulges its argument: "With remarks ... on the Numerous Evils Arising to the Revenue from the Insufficiency of the Present Salary."[138] According to Paine's introduction, his purpose was to present the situation of the revenue officers to Parliament before an official petition reached the House of Commons. In other words, Paine's goal was essentially to raise enough sympathy and political support for the salary increase so that when the petition was presented to the House, the required support for passage would already be in place. Paine believed that "when petitioners in any case ground their hopes of relief on having their case fully and perfectly known and understood" they would be assured of success.[139] It was a proactive move on the part of Paine and his fellow officers, hopefully providing some assurance of the measure's passage. Unfortunately, that confidence was not reflected in the pamphlet's argument.

Arguably the most conspicuous difference between the *Case* and *Common Sense* is the dissimilarity between the language and tone of the two works. Because the *Case* was "Humbly Addressed to the Members of Both Houses of Parliament," the tone is markedly different from Paine's later political writing which was addressed most often to ordinary citizens.[140] The forcefulness and urgency of *Common Sense* is nowhere visible in the *Case*; rather Paine's style is obsequious and deliberate. He was apparently aware of the need to command the acquiescence of his august audience and thus he treaded lightly. Similarly, there is a great degree of timidity in his arguments. Rather than making forceful statements, he often posed rhetorical questions. For example, he attempted to rouse the sympathy of Parliament by asking them to ponder "*if the poverty of the officers of excise, if the temptations of arising from their poverty . . . if the security of the revenue itself,* are matters of any weight."[141] Moreover, there are a number of conditional "if" statements throughout the essay which again distinguishes its style from the forceful conviction of his language and argument in *Common Sense*.

Paine's thesis consisted of two largely circular arguments: first, that excise officers who are poorly paid take bribes (which results in less national revenue), and secondly that the poor pay of officers is immoral, which causes families to live in wretchedness and resort to unethical behavior (like taking bribes). Paine therefore decided to make an emotional appeal on behalf of his fellow officers, attempting to demonstrate that immorality inhibited the growth of the national treasury. He argued that "the poverty of the officers is the fairest bait for a designing trader," because savvy businessmen "introduce themselves to the officer under the common plea of the insufficiency of the salary."[142] Officers, because they were so poorly paid, became easy prey for merchants trying to avoid taxation through bribery. This, in turn, corrupted the character of the collectors whose condition was "truly wretched and pitiable," leaving them a choice only between penury and larceny.[143] "Poverty in defiance of principle," Paine informed Parliament, "begets a meanness that will stoop to almost anything."[144] Paine further argued that insufficient salaries were an especially difficult problem for officers who had families. According to Paine, "a single man may barely live" on an officers' £50 per year salary.[145] Men with families, therefore, were subject to "powerful temptations."[146] Paine had been an officer as both a single and married man and therefore knew from whence he spoke.

Paine addressed his final remarks to critics who contended that positions in the excise were voluntary, and that those who were unhappy with their employment should simply resign. Paine responded indignantly, "what a mockery of pity would it be to give such an answer to an honest, faithful old officer in the excise, who had spent the prime of his life in the service, and was become unfit for anything else."[147] Again, Paine wrote from personal experience. He himself had given up a skilled occupation for work as one of His Majesty's revenue officers, and by 1772 when he wrote the *Case*, he too was unfit for employment in his former craft. Paine then concluded his argument with remarks on the "Qualifications of Officers," in an effort to garner yet more sympathy by reiterating the demands placed on dedicated officers and the mutual moral obligation of Parliament. Revenue officers were expected to be—at all times—honest, diligent, sober, and skillful.[148] "The want of any of these qualifications is a capital offense in the excise," Paine reminded Parliament, and "a complaint of drunkenness, negligence or ignorance, is certain death by the laws of the board."[149] He further added that "everyone knows that the excise is a place of labor, not of ease; of hazard, not of certainty; and that down right poverty finishes the character."[150] Revenue officers then, because so much was demanded of them, had the right to expect the same from their government in return. A living wage was not only just, but the absolute obligation of the government the officers so faithfully served.

The fatal flaw in Paine's work was undeniably the argument itself: it was unbalanced. Paine wrote only of the excise officers' torment with no attention given to the plight of the treasury. Paine may very well have succeeded in demonstrating the pitiable suffering of His Majesty's servants, but he failed to demonstrate how that suffering endangered the British economy. Paine simply did not discuss the problem from the perspective of Parliament, and therefore did not convince that body that increasing salaries would be beneficial. Paine repeatedly referred to "the revenue" and the damage inflicted upon it by smuggling and bribery, but his references to the economy were vague, and he failed to give any concrete evidence or hard facts to support his assertions. Paine offered no quantitative analysis to illustrate how much money was purloined from the treasury or how that loss might have damaged the national economy. Nor did he demonstrate in any way how the economy itself would benefit from increasing the salaries of officers. Moreover, Paine did not indicate where the government was supposed to find the money to increase salaries. This is particularly relevant given the fact that in 1772 Britain was reeling from an enormously high national debt following sixty years of nearly continuous warfare. The Seven Years' War had been especially costly for the British government, which eventually led to a political crisis with its American colonies. Paine completely ignored these glaring facts when he made his case.

Another miscalculation by Paine was his portrayal of human nature. Paine posits the assumption that officers only accepted bribes as a necessary evil in order to pay their living expenses. "Involuntary poverty," he warned, "will teach men to believe that to starve is more criminal than to steal."[151] For Paine it was nothing less than a Darwinian struggle for survival; men yielded to sin and corruption only to number themselves among the fittest. Paine's altruistic view of human nature discounted entirely that class of men who would steal from the government regardless of their salary. This oversight contributed to Paine's failure to show Parliament how they could benefit from decreasing smuggling or increasing "the revenue." Perhaps Parliament understood all too well that bribery and smuggling were detrimental but given human nature, also unstoppable. Thus the government had no incentive to pay untrustworthy, easily replaceable officials more money when they would continue to take bribes and rob the treasury. Increasing the salaries of officers would not make them angels, and in doing so Britain stood to lose even more money through a larger budgetary allocation. Put simply, this was an essay that was too narrowly focused; Paine did not examine the problem thoroughly thus his argument fell on deaf ears. The *Case of the Officers of Excise* was written from Paine's heart, not his head. The sophisticated and complex nature of national economic policy was not his primary concern, and thus Paine failed to garner the attention of those for whom it was their sole concern. Paine's principal interest was the individual plight of his fellow officers and his own personal financial difficulties. He simply could not see the forest for the trees. One year later, with American Independence and his own life hanging in the balance, Paine did not make the same mistake twice.

Whether Paine did it consciously or not, all of the inherent problems with his argument in the *Case of the Officers of Excise* were duly corrected when he wrote *Common Sense*. In fact, *Common Sense* is an absolute contrast

The Devil's Advocate

to the *Case*. It was as if Paine recognized how poorly executed his first political work was and made every attempt to do exactly the opposite. To begin with, instead of addressing the Continental Congress (Parliament's extralegal counterpart) Paine took his cause directly to the American people. Paine again offered an emotional appeal, but this time it was not pity he solicited, but rage. Moreover, Paine coupled his emotional appeal with reason and political practicality for a more balanced argument. Statistical analysis and concrete evidence supported his push for independence so he successfully avoided the evidentiary difficulties of the *Case*.[152] Likewise, Paine now had a new world view—a "big picture"—from which to draw upon to avoid the pitfalls of tunnel vision. Finally, unlike with the *Case*, Paine presented the question of independence from all sides, making every attempt to leave no question unanswered and no lingering doubts as to the merits of his cause. Interestingly, for *Common Sense*, Paine insisted on peer review for input. He published the work anonymously (this time to avoid possible execution instead of termination), unlike the *Case* which he signed his name to and took great pride in its authorship. Paine recognized that the stakes were high and when Americans needed direction the most he made every effort to be utterly convincing. Paine left Americans with no acceptable alternative to a complete separation from Britain, and portrayed Revolution as the road to America's eternal glory. The question that remains now is how Thomas Paine—an absolute nobody from nowhere—became the man who brought this message of political salvation to colonial America's multitude of unbelievers.

Chapter Three
Why Thomas Paine?

In 1973, as the 200th anniversary of *Common Sense* loomed, Bernard Bailyn dared to wonder, "What is one to make of this extraordinary document after 200 years? What questions . . . should one ask of it?"[1] Bailyn chose to focus his study on the "uncommon," or extraordinary elements of *Common Sense*.[2] That same year noted historian Winthrop Jordan also published an essay about *Common Sense* entitled "Familial Politics: Thomas Paine and the Killing of the King, 1776."[3] Whereas Bailyn chose to focus more on the unique rhetorical aspects of *Common Sense*, Jordan opted to inquire into "the subliminal sources of political influence" and pondered whether or not such an "arcane" study of a symbolic homicide should even be undertaken.[4] This has been the nature of Paine scholarship over the course of the past 200 years: a hodgepodge of theories and assessments ranging from the mundane to the truly esoteric and everything in between. Over the course of the past two centuries, rhetoricians, literary critics, political scientists, historians, and religious scholars have all taken an interest in Paine's explosive pamphlet.

Nearly 200 years of scholarship exists on Thomas Paine and yet there remains no answer to the most important question often posed by historians: "why Thomas Paine?" How was it that this man—a poor, unknown Englishman—wrote *Common Sense* transforming the nature of political debate on two continents? It is puzzling that after so long a time and after so much research that this is still a mystery. However, a close survey of the historiography of Paine's life and career reveals the reason for this gulf in Paine studies: improper or nonexistent contextualization. Scholars of rhetoric, history, political science, and religion, have studied Paine within their separate spheres, rather than communicating across disciplines. Nowhere is this schism more apparent than in studies of *Common Sense*, the pamphlet that launched Paine's public career and catapulted America towards Independence. The result of this scholarly disconnectedness is an assortment of theories regarding the origins and significance of Paine's writings. Sadly, these theories do little to advance Paine scholarship; they provide us with more pieces of the puzzle, but no complete portrait to aid in its construction. To advance scholarship on the evolution of Paine's career as a writer, therefore, it is important to begin by establishing the context.

Bailyn (who has come closer than any other scholar to answering this all-important question) correctly hinted that the answer lies in the study of Paine the individual. In a 1973 article on the originality of *Common Sense,* Bailyn argued that "there is something unique in the intellectual idiom of the pamphlet."[5] He further noted that the language of *Common Sense* suggests "deeper elements—qualities of mind, styles of thought, a writer's personal culture."[6] In other words, Paine's revolutionary pamphlet is a reflection of Paine himself: his thoughts, his ideas, his own unique context. Historians who study the Declaration of Independence, for example, are in no way surprised to discover that Jefferson's work closely resembles Locke's *Second Treatise,* because it is well-known that Jefferson was a devotee of John Locke. As Bailyn suggests, understanding an author's work often begins with understanding the author himself; any other method of research (as has been the case with Paine studies) would be placing the cart before the horse. Thus, to correctly assess Paine's writings and their impact, to discover the answer to "why Thomas Paine," scholars must first begin with an understanding of who Thomas Paine was and what he believed. This kind of approach is especially important because Paine had been reared, educated, and lived in England for the majority of his adult life. In fact, it should be noted that the first thirty-seven years of his life were spent in England, and a mere fifteen of his total seventy-two years were spent in America. His "personal culture," therefore, would have been markedly different from the rebellious American colonists he later championed.

The fundamental question this chapter attempts to answer then, is "why Thomas Paine?" by investigating the creation of his watershed pamphlet *Common Sense.* Such a study will also necessarily include a discussion of the contextualization of Paine and his revolutionary work. This new contextualization will not only help to illustrate why Paine wrote the pamphlet, but it will hopefully demonstrate conclusively that Thomas Paine was the only man who could have written *Common Sense.* This new approach will also further shed light on the reasons why Paine's pamphlet was so unique. While in many ways *Common Sense* clearly marked a new beginning for Paine, the evidence will show that its author had to reach back to his past in order to create his future.

THE SUM OF HIS PARTS: PAINE AT THIRTY-SEVEN

Although later in life Paine considered himself to be a citizen of America and the world, he wrote as a man who was English by birth and by education. He was unashamed and unafraid to use his intimate knowledge of his fellow countrymen to attack them and expose their weaknesses. Paine admitted that "it was in a great measure owing to my bringing a knowledge of England with me to America that I was enabled to enter deeper into politics, and with more success, than other people."[7] Shortly before a final peace settlement was reached in 1782, in an attempt to buoy George Washington's spirits, Paine wrote the general that he believed the end was near:

> The British have accustomed themselves to think of *seven years* in a manner different to other portions of time. They acquire this partly by habit, by reason, by religion, and by superstition. They serve seven years apprenticeship—they elect their Parliament for seven years—they punish by seven years transportation, or the duplicate or triplicate of that term—they let their leases in the same manner . . . and this particular period of time, by a variety of concurrences, has obtained an influence in their minds.[8]

The fact that Paine was reared and educated in England is crucial, because it gave the future author of *Common Sense* a more immediate knowledge of King and Parliament which most Americans were not privy to.

Paine's English background is also significant because, as Eric Foner and others have pointed out, Paine did not arrive in America as an idealistic youth. He was thirty-seven years old—beyond middle-age. Therefore "it is not unreasonable to assume that many of his ideas were fixed by the time he arrived in America."[9] In his deist pamphlet, *The Age of Reason,* Paine reminisced about the beginning of his activism in the American Revolution. He professed, "I had no disposition for what is called politics. It presented to my mind no other idea than as contained in the word Jockeyship. When, therefore, I turned my thoughts toward matter of government I had to form a system for myself that accorded with the moral and philosophic principles in which I have been educated."[10] Paine was clearly referring to his upbringing in England and his experiences there. It is essential then to uncover what his life was like in England, and what influence his time there had on his political ideology. A knowledge of eighteenth-century England is likewise necessary in order to place Paine's development in the appropriate context. The years that Paine resided in England, 1737–1774, were marked by nearly continual warfare and political strife. Thus Paine's activities during these years, and the formation of his political and religious ideas, must be set within the context of events like the Jacobite uprising, George III's ascendance to the throne, and the Seven Years' War. Economic class, local politics, and other cultural phenomena that Paine may have been exposed to or participated in should also be included in the investigation.

What should not be included in an investigation of Paine's life in England is a reliance upon suspect biographies like Chalmers or Cheetham. Thomas Paine was a reticent man; he very rarely wrote about his personal life in or out of England. It was not really until the 1790s that Paine offered his readers any real glimpse into his past, and even then he offered very little. Circumstantial evidence may be employed—but carefully. Far too often scholars state as fact what can best be termed conjecture, and conjecture should never give way to suppositions (like his alleged impotence) that add nothing relevant to Paine's contribution to history. This makes a biographer's, or any scholar's job difficult but not impossible. There are available sources which can help put the pieces together, but in the end what evolves can only be a rough portrait of a very public yet very private man.

The most logical place to begin an investigation of Paine's life in England is in his birthplace of Thetford. Thetford is in Norfolk County, located in the southeastern region of England known as East Anglia. The town's name is derived from the fact that it is located on a ford which is situated on the river Thet. During the Heptarchy of the seventh, eighth, and ninth centuries, it was the capital city of the Kingdom of East Anglia. It was therefore a center of commerce, and was at one point the Episcopal See of the Norfolk diocese.[11] Thetford remained a prosperous town through the reign of Henry VIII who often hunted there. His hunting lodge, the "King's House" still stands regally in the city center.

By the time Paine was born in 1737 Thetford had fallen on hard times; it was no longer a jewel of the empire, nor was it the location of the Episcopal See. Norwich, some twenty miles to the east of Thetford, became a much more important city, and the Bishopric was moved there. An account of Thetford, written just two years before Paine's birth, described the city as "a pretty large Place, and hath a good Market weekly on Saturday, and a fair on May 1."[12] In addition to the markets and fairs, the Lent Assizes were also held annually in Thetford. These civil and criminal court sessions were held throughout England and Wales in each county. Because of the yearly assizes, punishments for crimes, such as hangings, would have been a common sight in Thetford. In fact the gaol house (and scaffold) was located on the town's market street, in plain view of any passersby.

At the time of Paine's birth, Thetford was a corporate borough, and subject to all the troubles that such "rotten" boroughs were heir to. In the eighteenth century, corporation boroughs were controlled by wealthy patrons (in Thetford's case, the Duke of Grafton and the Petre family) and only the mayor, aldermen, and the members of the common council could vote to elect Thetford's allotted two members of Parliament. More often than not, these types of rotten boroughs had at one time been very prosperous ancient cities that had since fallen into decay—like Thetford. The central problem in Thetford, and in other places that were likewise so situated, was the political "jockeyship" that corrupted the city. In Thetford, "votes were bought and sold for huge sums, while public benefit and financial propriety were viewed with a profound lack of enthusiasm."[13] The corruption created a political atmosphere in Thetford that was likewise "exclusive, indolent, venal and undemocratic . . . a source of scandal and notoriety, its affairs a synonym for dishonesty."[14] Interestingly, the city was not, like the rest of England, divided bitterly along the national Whig and Tory party lines; Thetford's political difficulties were almost exclusively the result of local rivalries and power struggles.

Thetford remained a rotten borough during Paine's residency in the city—about twenty-one years. It is conceivable, therefore, that he was influenced by the political events he witnessed in his hometown. Perhaps it was these memories of England that led him to declare in 1791 that "an Englishman is not free in his own country: Every one of [these chartered towns] places a barrier in his way, and tells him he is not a freeman—that he has no rights."[15] It is also conceivable that Paine witnessed, more likely as an adult than as a child, the unfortunate outcomes of some of the trials that were held in his hometown. Perhaps this is what led him to ask, later in his life, "Why is it that scarcely any are executed but the poor?"[16] Because of these circumstances, more than one scholar has rightfully declared that "the seeds of Thomas Paine's *Common Sense* were sewn in his native Thetford where he early witnessed the abuses of politics. The people as such had no voice in their own affairs."[17]

In 1734 Joseph Pain, a stay-maker, married Frances Cocke, the daughter of a middle-class attorney. Frances Cocke Pain was eleven years older than her new husband and from a family of considerably higher status (the Pains fwere lower-middle class artisans). These differences were complicated by the fact that Joseph was a Quaker by birth and practice, but his new wife was an Anglican. They had two children: Thomas, born in 1737, and a daughter Elizabeth who was born a year later, but died in infancy.

Historians have debated whether or not Joseph Pain was cast out of the Society of Friends for his marriage to Frances Cocke, but there is no evidence to suggest this. In fact, there is more evidence to suggest that Joseph Pain continued to practice his Quaker beliefs, and to pass them on to his son. Paine later acknowledged that, "My father being of the Quaker profession, it was my good fortune to have an exceedingly good moral education, and a tolerable stock of useful learning."[18] Although it cannot be proven for certain, it seems likely that on occasion Thomas attended Quaker meetings with his father. Bible study, in whatever form it may have taken, would have amounted to little more than a history lesson as the Quakers did not view the Bible as a sacred text. This moral instruction very likely also included an emphasis on the equality of all mankind (a central tenet of Quakerism) and an introduction to Robert Barclay, one of the Quaker's earliest and most significant theologians. Before the Society of Friends embraced quietism, Barclay was also one of England's most outspoken advocates for religious tolerance.

Thomas Paine was the product of an interfaith marriage, and began his life in a home that stressed the importance of Christian worship—albeit in different forms. The role of Paine's mother in the formation of his religious beliefs and moral "principles" should not be discounted, although it all too often has been by scholars. Her husband's Quaker affiliation notwithstanding, Frances Pain insisted that Thomas be baptized in the Anglican church and he attended at least one sermon in the home of a family member. Despite the importance his parents placed upon Christianity, however, Paine admitted later that such efforts were wasted on him. "From the time I was capable of conceiving an idea and acting upon it by reflection," he wrote in *The Age of Reason*, "I either doubted the truth of the Christian system or thought it to be a strange affair."[19] This attitude was no doubt partially the result of a sermon, describing the redemption, that he heard at age seven or eight which shook his nascent faith to its core.[20] Unable to view God as a being who would kill his own son to save humanity, Paine turned his back upon Christianity forever, choosing instead to rely upon his reason and intellect rather than faith.

Young Thomas began his formal schooling at the age of seven when he began attending the Thetford Grammar School. The school was only a short walk from his house on Bridge Street, and he enjoyed learning immensely. From the ages of seven to thirteen Paine studied English, mathematics, science and poetry. His fellow classmates also learned Greek and Latin, but Paine's father's Quaker ethics prevented him from allowing his son to learn the dead languages. (Paine admitted later, however, that he did not let this lack of knowledge deter him from learning the subject matter and the arguments of the books his classmates read.)[21] The young scholar

Why Thomas Paine?

excelled at poetry and mathematics, but science was his favorite subject. Regrettably for Paine, his formal schooling ended abruptly when his father forced him to leave the grammar school to serve as his apprentice. However Paine, ever the consummate scholar, seldom in his life "let a moment pass without acquiring some knowledge."[22] Over forty years later, Paine bitterly observed that "many a youth with good natural genius, who is apprenticed to a mechanical trade, such as a carpenter, joiner, millwright, blacksmith, etc., is prevented getting forward the whole of his life, from the want of a little common education when a boy."[23] Although it was not his choice, Paine began training to follow in his father's artisan footsteps.

Because the corset was required dress attire for women in England, stay-makers were gainfully employed in every town. It was not a craft that ensured great wealth, but rather a comfortable living. The vocation of stay-maker was a complex one. The trade required great physical strength for the bending and inserting of the whalebone into the fabric to make the stays for the corsets, but it also required a man to be delicate "[because] he approaches the Ladies so nearly."[24] It also required a gentle touch (and often a great deal of discretion) when fitting the customer with her new garment. Still, it was an occupation that held no attraction for Thomas Paine. Although he dutifully obeyed his father and became a diligent apprentice, he never gave up on the idea of seeking a different life elsewhere. Like so many restless young men in the eighteenth century, Paine decided that as soon as he was old enough he would run away to sea.

By the time Paine's seven-year apprenticeship came to a close, England again went to war against France. 1756 was the beginning of the Seven Years' War for Britain and Europe, even though by that time Britain's American colonists had been engaged in the fight against the Indian allies of the French for two years. During Paine's youth, England had already fought in two wars and quelled a significant national uprising. In 1739, just two years after Paine's birth, England declared war against Spain in what became known as the War of Jenkins' Ear; two years later Britain was at war against France in the War of the Austrian Succession, which lasted until 1748. In the midst of the latter conflict, the English had to fend off its domestic enemies in Scotland as well, as "Bonnie" Prince Charlie attempted to reestablish the Stuart monarchy in the Jacobite rebellion of 1745. This rebellion, and the Jacobite threat, finally ended with the Battle of Culloden in 1746. Thus England had finally achieved some semblance of peace around Paine's eleventh birthday. It was short-lived.

Whatever plans Joseph Pain may have had for his son to join him in his Thetford business, or even perhaps take it over someday, the Seven Years' War irreparably altered. Twenty year-old Thomas had been heavily influenced by the stories of his former schoolmaster, Reverend William Knowles, and decided that he desired a life of adventure.[25] Paine completed his apprenticeship and he decided to go to London and become a privateer. The renewal of conflict meant that licensed (or unlicensed) piracy could prove to be quite lucrative, so he enlisted on *The Terrible,* whose captain was ironically named William Death. Fortunately for the impetuous youth, his devoutly pacifist father discovered his plans and persuaded him not to board the vessel. This proved to be fortuitous, because *The Terrible* sank weeks later and all hands were lost. Decades later, Paine recalled his near-miss, giving credit to "the affectionate and moral remonstrance of a good father."[26] He further added that his father, "being of the Quaker profession, must have begun to look upon me as lost. But the impression, much as it effected me at the time, began to wear away...."[27] Soon after his brush with near-disaster, Paine shipped aboard the *King of Prussia* and finally joined the conflict as a privateer.

Paine served aboard the prosperous vessel for six months, then returned to London as a journeyman working under a master stay-maker. London was the perfect place for the twenty year-old, because it afforded him the opportunity to indulge in intellectual pleasures. Paine regularly attended scientific lectures where he heard Benjamin Martin and James Ferguson deliver addresses that aimed at popularizing Newtonian physics for the layman. He also became friends with Dr. Bevis, an astronomer of the Royal Society. Paine became engrossed in the study of physics, purchasing equipment to teach himself the basic principles of the universe.[28] His examination of Rittenhouse's orrery led to a powerful conversion experience to the rational belief of deism. Paine's conversion was the culmination of his rejection of Christianity as a youth, and his reliance upon his own reason and scientific study. Although his parents had provided him with a strong Christian ethic, ultimately Paine's own questioning, thought, and study prevailed. He discovered that science was the "true theology" and that "it is through that medium that man can see God, as it were, face to face."[29] This new creed of deism instructed Paine that the laws governing the universe—and mankind—were systematic, ordered, rational, and simple. Furthermore, Paine learned that his duty to God required him to "imitate Him in everything moral, scientific and mechanical."[30]

It was probably during this period in London, moreover, that Paine began to read various magazines and newspapers that further fed his appetite for knowledge. Most scholars believe that Paine "read few books of any kind, customarily gleaning his knowledge ... from conversation, newspapers, and magazines."[31] This is possible, as Paine referenced very few works throughout his lengthy career. However, the best, most accurate, conclusion that can be reached about Paine's reading habits is that while he may not have read original works in their entirety, he surely read excerpts of them in magazines and newspapers. There is plenty of evidence to suggest that while Paine may not have been well-read in the traditional sense, he managed to acquire enough knowledge through popular publications to be conversant on any number of subjects. One particular favorite of Paine (which he read even after he left England) was *The Universal Magazine of Knowledge and Pleasure*. It was a monthly publication aimed at "Gentry, Merchants, Farmers, and Tradesmen."[32] It cost an affordable sixpence and covered a wide variety of topics including "Letters Debates Poetry . . . History . . . Criticism [and] . . . Chemistry."[33] An example of the kinds of things Paine read can be discerned from a sampling of the 1770 July issue list of topics:

- Dr. Goldsmith, "the Life of Thomas Parnell D.D."
- Thomas Hunter, "Review of Lord Bolingbroke's Philosophy"
- Uses of the Looking-Glass transl. from Levinus Lemnius on the Occult Miracles of Nature (Latin)
- view of Lord Bolingbroke's Moral Character
- Proceedings in Parliament
- History of England
- Brief Observations on Reason and Revelation and their Use, in Matters of Religion[34]

This is only one publication of many that Paine read while in England. He also read *The Gentleman's Magazine, Reviews and Parliamentary Debates*, and the *Court Register*.[35] He evidently kept a watchful eye not only on science, but also politics as well. Perhaps this sort of broad reading led his friends and companions to note frequently that "his mind was a storehouse of facts and useful observations; he was full of lively anecdote and ingenious, original, pertinent remarks upon almost every subject."[36]

Paine's time in London was brief; by 1758 he had moved to the county of Kent where he was once again employed as a stay-maker. He was first engaged as a journeyman in Dover, then finally as Master with his own shop in Sandwich. There he met and married his first wife, Mary Lambert, who was employed as a lady's maid. (Evidently it was not a marriage arranged for either party's financial betterment.) The two wed in St. Peter's Church, Sandwich, on September 27, 1759. Very little is known of Mary Lambert Paine. Apparently she was the daughter of an excise officer, and as her own signature appears below that of the bridegroom's on the marriage banns, she was evidently literate.[37] The newlyweds moved to Margate in Kent where Paine set up shop as a master stay-maker. Sadly, their union did not last very long; Mary Lambert Paine died less than two years after they were married. No records have been found indicating her exact death date nor is there any evidence to show the cause of her death. Until recently most historians speculated that she died in childbirth (as so many women did) sometime in late 1760 or early 1761. However, recently evidence has been found by an Australian researcher, Hazel Burgess, to indicate that Mary Paine did in fact give birth to a daughter named Sarah who was baptized on December 7, 1760.[38] According to parish records found in Thanet, near Margate, Sarah Paine died in infancy on September 12, 1761; she was nine months old.[39] Within two years Paine had suffered not only the loss of his wife, but also his child whom he possibly reared, for a time at least, on his own.

In 1760 Paine was a twenty-three year-old widower and master of a craft he disliked. Possibly influenced by his former father-in-law, he decided to change careers and try for a position as an officer of the Excise—a tax collector. In order to be appointed, he had to pass a rigorous examination and obtain personal letters of recommendation. Paine returned to his parents' house in Thetford for solace and a quiet place to study. He passed his examination and finally, in 1762, was awarded a temporary position in Lincolnshire on the North Sea. After two years as a temporary officer there he was awarded a permanent position in that district.

After serving only one year, on August 27, 1765 Paine was dismissed from the excise without cause. For whatever reason Paine did not immediately apply for reinstatement. (It is possible that he did not like the low pay—he earned a mere £50 a year which barely kept him out of debt.) Paine instead moved to Diss, in Norfolk, to work again as a stay-maker. Soon afterwards he moved to London in 1766 where he began a brief career as a teacher in a private academy. He worked at a school in Leman Street, run by a Mr. Noble, where he was paid a pittance of £25 for his year's worth of work.[40] While at Noble's academy, Paine applied for reinstatement to the excise maintaining to the Board that "no complaint of the least dishonesty or intemperance ever appeared against me."[41] The Board met the day after Paine's letter arrived and restored him at the next available vacancy. That vacancy opened in 1768 in Lewes, Sussex—a town approximately twice the size of Thetford. His residence in Lewes from 1768–1774 marked a watershed for Paine, because "it was in Lewes that he came to adopt the political and social consciousness which would manifest itself later in his actions during his first years in America."[42]

In Lewes, Paine rented lodgings from Samuel Ollive and his family at their home known as Bull House. The house was adjacent to a dissenter's chapel. Ollive and his wife Esther operated a tobacco and grocery store on the ground floor of Bull House. In addition to his mercantile duties, Ollive was a Constable of Lewes and a Headborough and was therefore active in the governance of the town as well. Samuel Ollive died in 1769 leaving the shop for his wife and daughter Elizabeth (then twenty) to manage. Upon Ollive's death, Paine moved out of the Bull (most likely for reasons of propriety). Paine helped Ollive's widow Esther operate the family business, and in 1771, at the age of thirty-four, he married Elizabeth and moved back into the Bull. Apparently Paine was happy enough in Lewes to decide to settle there permanently.

Paine took great advantage of the opportunities which awaited him in Lewes. One of the first things he did was to join a debating club at the White Hart Inn aptly named the White Hart Club. Members of the club were working class Britons, artisans, and commoners—like Paine himself. In this environment—and speaking as one of them—Paine learned to articulate the views of the masses as he debated the issues of the day. Moreover, during Paine's stay in Lewes (1768–1773) there was quite a lot to debate about. The country was in the middle of a political crisis both at home and abroad. Domestically, 1768 was the peak of the Wilkite movement in England. That year John Wilkes had been elected to Parliament for the prosperous county of Middlesex while he was technically "an outlaw," because of his prior conviction for sedition against the king.[43] Parliament thus refused to seat Wilkes causing a furor among his popular followers who voted for him despite his exile. For many ordinary Britons, "Wilkes became the personification of liberty," and they rallied around him.[44] They admired his boldness and viewed him as a champion of the time-honored English right to free speech.

Wilkes was aided in his efforts to claim his seat in Parliament by the fact that the majority of Britons did not like their new king. In 1760 George III became King of Great Britain. Interestingly, the man that Paine would one day refer to as "the sullen-tempered Pharaoh of England" was only a year younger than he was.[45] Not only had the young king failed to capture the affections of his people, he had not even managed to command their respect. According to Linda Colley, there is ample evidence that "the king was widely and actively disliked, not just in radical London . . . but throughout the provinces as well."[46] In fact, during the Wilkite movement, rioters had been so bold as to "[drive] a hearse into the grounds of St. James's Palace to remind its royal occupant of the fate of tyrants."[47] Moreover, the Reverend John Wesley, upon returning from one of his circuit rides, noted in his journal, "[the people of England] do not so much aim at the ministry . . . but at the King himself . . . They heartily despise his Majesty, and hate him with a perfect hatred."[48]

King George and his Parliament's difficulties were complicated by the fact that by 1768 the tight bond that had once held the American colonies to Mother England proved to be illusory. In 1766 the colonists' vigorous protests successfully forced the repeal of the hated Stamp Act which was passed the previous year. In an effort to reign in their colonies, Parliament then passed a number of other tax measures proposed by Charles Townshend, the Exchequer. This further fanned the flames of resistance resulting in a national nonimportation movement in America, the quartering of British troops in Boston, and, tragically, the Boston Massacre. By putting economic pressure on the merchants of England, the colonists struck another blow for liberty, forcing the repeal of the all of the Townshend duties save one: the tax on imported tea. Newspapers everywhere were teeming with discussions of the rights of Englishmen (inspired by Wilkes) and the rights of the British colonists in North America. By 1773, the year that Paine left Lewes, the remaining tax on tea sparked a whole new colonial and parliamentary crisis which ultimately resulted in the formation of the United States of America. This is the political climate in which Paine's activism in politics first began and where his skills were first honed.

Paine and the other members of the White Hart Club were certainly aware of these and other events, and undoubtedly debated the issues raised by these tumults. Given his economic status, his following, and his future lobbying efforts in England, it is most likely that Paine argued as a Whig, rather than as a Tory. He participated in a number of debates where he made his opinions known, and his voice usually emerged as the loudest. The club had a tradition whereby the morning after a debate they would send "The Headstrong Book" (an old copy of Homer) to the most intractable member of the group; it was a prize and a jest all wrapped in one. The book was passed to Paine so often that the inscription of the book was changed to read,

THE HEADSTRONG BOOK;

or,

THE ORIGINAL BOOK OF OBSTINANCY,

written by

****** ****, OF LEWES, IN SUSSEX,

and revised and corrected by

THOMAS PAIN.[49]

All of this proves two very important things about Paine's tenure in Lewes: (1) that he immersed himself in the political affairs of England and (2) that he knew how to garner attention and make his views the center of that attention. This latter skill would prove to be one of the strongest weapons in his arsenal as he grew to become one of the world's greatest polemicists.

It should also be noted that while in Lewes Paine did more than just talk about politics. In Sussex he gained a practical knowledge of government by becoming a vestryman in 1769. One of Paine's responsibilities was the auditing of the town's accounts. In the Lewes *Town Book* there are numerous entries for the years 1769–1773 bearing the signature "T. Paine."[50] This calls into question the statements of many historians who have claimed for decades that one of Paine's shortcomings was his lack of experience in government. Scholars often point out that Paine's lack of "reality" with regard to politics was due to his lack of any practical knowledge of government. One historian avers that Paine's understanding of politics was "rooted not in experience nor even in the real world."[51] He further argues that "for all his political activity and pretended wisdom he was sorely lacking in real political experience or responsibilities."[52] Perhaps the best response to such charges comes from Michael Kiley who wonders,

> Had Paine no political experience? He had been a Lewes Vestryman, a civil servant under the Crown, a labor spokesman and lobbyist, and had flourished in the face-to-face politics of the English pub. Paine served in the Lewes Committee of Twelve from October, 1769 until July, 1772, dealing with taxation, elections and auditing the Constables' and Headboroughs' accounts.[53]

Clearly these activities demonstrate that Paine made a name for himself and garnered the trust of many in his new home. Unfortunately for the new bridegroom and his wife, he was not as astute a shopkeeper as he was a politician and the shop failed miserably. He did have his income as an exciseman to rely upon, but at £50 a year it was barely enough to support one person, let alone two.

Paine's fellow excise officers in Lewes undoubtedly heard him argue and debate in the pubs and knew him as a local merchant and office holder. They also would have known that, if anyone, Paine understood well the plight of His Majesty's Officers of Excise. The salary for excise officers had been fixed at £50 per year—with no possible adjustments for cost-of-living increases or other hardships. There was also no system for rewarding faithful officers with bonuses or pay raises. This caused tremendous hardship for men like Paine. After paying housing costs, taxes, and travel expenses (which were not tax deductible), an exciseman was lucky to break even. For men with families this situation often led to debt and abject poverty, which in turn led to many instances of "stamping." Stamping was essentially bribery. An exciseman would agree to stamp a cargo as "taxes paid" in exchange for a bribe from the cargo's owner. This type of smuggling was rampant in England, which meant that excise officers like Paine who did their duty without accepting bribes were quite unpopular with local merchants.

In 1772, a year after Paine married Elizabeth Ollive, he was approached in Lewes by his fellow excise officers. They asked him to argue their case before Parliament by writing a pamphlet that could be circulated to that body's members, thus hopefully sparking a debate or petition in the House of Commons. The fact that Paine was chosen to write the pamphlet—rather than volunteering—is significant. It demonstrates that in his brief time in Lewes he must have been known as a man of great abilities, both intellectual and literary. He must also have been known to be a man who had enough self-confidence to take on the British government. It was a challenge that Paine happily accepted.

In the *Case of the Officers of Excise,* Paine put forth an emotional plea for increasing the salaries of excise officers. He appealed to the simple principle of fairness. Because of the fixed wages, revenue officers were, he wrote, "shut out from the general blessing—they behold it like a map of *Peru*. The answer of Abraham to Dives is somewhat applicable to them, '*There is a great gulf fixed.*'"[54] His central thesis was simple: if officers were paid a living wage, then the practice of stamping and other crimes of theft would cease. He argued that "The tenderness of conscience is too often overmatched by the sharpness of want; and principle, like chastity, yields with just reluctance enough to excuse itself."[55] The *Case of the Officers of Excise* is an important work in the study of Paine's political activism. Largely because it "reflects that deep disaffection from eighteenth-century English society which would characterize so much of his subsequent writing."[56]

William Lee, a Lewes publisher and member of the Headstrong Club printed 4,000 copies of Paine's work. Three thousand copies were for excise officers, the rest were Paine's to distribute as he saw appropriate. Paine went to London to distribute them to draw attention to the cause of his fellow officers. He overflowed with self-confidence. He had enough aplomb to send a copy of his work to the noted author and distinguished courtier Oliver Goldsmith and invite him for a drink to discuss the pamphlet. In his letter he confessed, "I have received so many letters of thanks and approbation for the [pamphlet], that were I not rather singularly modest, I should insensibly become a little vain."[57] Whether or not their meeting took place is unknown, but it does demonstrate that Paine was obviously generating a lot of positive feedback and a degree of notoriety.[58]

Paine divided his time in 1772 and 1773 between his excise post in Lewes and time in London working to have the case of the officers heard before Parliament. While in London in 1773 one very auspicious event occurred: Paine met Benjamin Franklin. The two met through a mutual friend, George Lewis Scott, F.R.S., who was also a Commissioner on the Board of Excise.[59] It was Benjamin Franklin who, recognizing how talented Paine was, persuaded him to leave England and seek a better life in America. He even offered to write a letter of introduction for him to ensure that he would find employment and be well taken care of if he undertook the journey.

All three gentlemen shared a love of science (Scott was the author of a two-volume work on scientific matters), and Paine was very fond of Scott.[60] He noted that Scott was "one of the most amiable characters I know of."[61] Scott had also served as a sub-preceptor (tutor) for young George III. In listening to Scott's stories of their king's youth, Paine "obtained the true character of the present King . . . and . . . of the present ministry."[62] Paine, having lived in England at a time when George III was perceived as incompetent at best and tyrannical at worst, probably did not need any further evidence to persuade him that the English people were right to loathe their sovereign. Nonetheless, the information he gleaned from Scott undoubtedly meant that Paine would never be able to view his sovereign with much reverence. Thus once in America he was stunned to find that "the people of this country were all wrong, by an ill-placed confidence."[63]

After nearly two years of trying to get the Parliament to take action, Paine's words simply were not persuasive enough—nothing happened, and the excise officers had lost their battle. This defeat was still with Paine years later when he wrote his great tract, *The Rights of Man*, denouncing the British government: "Among the claims that justice requires to be made, the condition of the inferior revenue-officers will merit attention. It is reproach to any government to waste such an immensity of revenue . . . and not allow even a decent livelihood to those on whom the labor falls."[64] To make matters worse, Paine was dismissed from his post on the grounds that he was absent without permission. The shop in Lewes failed, as did his marriage. Divorce was a difficult and costly process in eighteenth-century England, so the Paines opted instead for a legal separation.[65] This left Paine with enough money to start a new life in America (they divided the proceeds from the sale of the remaining items in the shop between them) and— perhaps most importantly—"unhampered mobility."[66] Yet again he was free to choose his own path wherever it might lead him. Paine sought refuge in the colonies, away from "towns in which the inequities of the system of Parliamentary representation and the dominance of the landed aristocracy in political life were all too apparent."[67]

Nearly a decade of resistance had transpired in America when Paine arrived jobless, homeless, and with little knowledge of the colonial situation. When he left England to avoid the inequities of parliamentary representation, he likely had no idea he would find precisely that when he arrived in America. Whatever knowledge he had acquired about American politics—first perhaps from Franklin, later from American associates—would have been secondhand. The fact that Paine was an outsider has been too long overlooked by scholars. Perhaps Paine's own description of himself as an American and his pivotal role as one of America's Founding Fathers has caused historians to overlook the fact that he was new to America's shores. As an outsider, and one who had not suffered along with the colonists, Paine's perspective would have been markedly different from that of Americans at large. For example, Paine had not had to worry about the presence of British soldiers walking and living among him and his neighbors. He did not have to endure their hostility towards Americans or the economic constraints of possibly losing employment because of moonlighting Redcoats. Paine did not have to live with the sight of angry mobs looking for the next victim to tar and feather because of a broken boycott or questionable loyalties. Paine's decision of whether or not to drink tea or coffee while safe in England was little more than a simple matter of taste preference—in America it was nothing less than a choice between freedom and slavery. Paine had been spared all of the anxieties and tensions and fears and frustrations that the colonists had endured for a decade. When the American colonists united to resist the Stamp Tax in 1765, Paine was in England studying for his excise exam. Two years later when the colonists organized to protest against the hated Townshend taxes, Paine was traveling the southeast coast of England collecting them. Although he had been a vestryman in Lewes, Paine had also never known the kind of local government autonomy that the American colonists had taken for granted for over a century. In his hometown of Thetford—where political corruption was the norm and even freemen were denied the right to vote—Paine directly experienced the might and power of King and Parliament. Ironically, the "rights of Englishmen" that so many colonial leaders were fighting to uphold would have been unfamiliar to Paine.

Paine brought with him to America a lifetime of experiences that separated him from the American colonists. The almost thirty-eight years he had spent in England molded him in a way that defined his character and shaped his destiny, distinguishing him from the colonists he later embraced as his brethren. Paine's entire belief system—both political and religious—had been created and nurtured in England—not America. All of the heartaches, joys, frustrations, and anxieties that Paine experienced while in England he brought to bear when he confronted the American situation. Thomas Paine produced *Common Sense,* but it was England that produced Thomas Paine.

In 1776 Paine's literary juggernaut *Common Sense* burst forth from the press, instantly becoming the continent's first best-seller, creating a flood of inquiries about its anonymous author. So many were moved by Paine's' rhetoric—most of them to the Patriot cause—or stunned by his blunt words that people were naturally curious about the mysterious author himself. Ironically, the man who changed America's political landscape and wooed Americans to rebellion was not one of them. He was a middle-aged, expatriate Englishman who knew little of America's struggle with Great Britain. Years of political, social, and military turmoil had wreaked havoc upon American lives, and countless articles, pamphlets, and political tracts had been written to document and defend America's struggle. Yet none of these works even came close to the impact of *Common Sense;* none had transformed the American people from resisters to revolutionaries; that accomplishment belonged to Thomas Paine alone.

Paine summoned all of his knowledge and experience from his life in England when he broached the subject of independence in *Common Sense.* His reliance upon reason and God's laws of nature he used to put forth a rational argument for independence. His thorough knowledge of scripture as an historical chronicle is clearly evident when he discussed the origins of monarchy and their sinful nature. His contempt—indeed his nation's contempt—for George III is palpable in the language Paine uses in *Common Sense* to describe his sovereign. Paine's insistence that simplicity and order should be the basis for a system of government are reflections not only of his commitment to reason, but his devout deism which taught him the importance of those guiding principles. The emotions expressed by Paine in the pamphlet—anger, sorrow, dread, urgency—can all be better understood as an expression of his own resentment towards the nation that caused him such misery and that promised to create the same misery in his adopted land. In the winter of 1776 *Common Sense* was a reflection of everything that Thomas Paine was. More importantly, its publication marked the beginning of everything he was to become.

Chapter Four
The Origins and Significance of Paine's Religious Beliefs

The popularity of *Common Sense* and its role in America's quest for independence have been well documented by historians and scholars alike, thus such a study is not warranted here. What is missing from the historical record, however, is a study of the impact the famous work had upon its author. Of the many holes in Paine scholarship, this is perhaps the most ponderous because *Common Sense* not only marked the beginning of Paine's career as a revolutionary pamphleteer, but it fostered the ideological motive for his political activism for the next thirty years. This new direction in Paine's political career following *Common Sense* was largely the result of Paine uniting his religious convictions and his political aspirations in one global mission to spread the gospel of deism to the world. The goal of this chapter will be to explore how Paine developed this mission by obtaining a better understanding of how Paine's political ideology was shaped almost exclusively by his belief in deism.

Because Paine's religious beliefs were the core of his political ideology and the root of his activism, a thorough examination of Paine's religious beliefs and their origins will be explored here for the first time. Although the basic tenets of Paine's deism have been alluded to previously in this work, to fully comprehend the scope and significance of his theology, a fuller explanation is essential. Moreover, this chapter will demonstrate conclusively that the core of Paine's religious beliefs and his theology were readily apparent as early as 1776, not later as many historians have asserted. Also, a clear connection will be made between his religious beliefs and his political ideology. Paine's hidden agenda will finally be revealed, and with it the discovery that for Paine political revolution was only the beginning.

THE PROBLEM OF HISTORIOGRAPHY

To date, only one study (unpublished) has undertaken to objectively uncover why the son of a Quaker and an Anglican adopted the unorthodox creed of deism.[1] This is particularly surprising in light of the fact that Paine scholars agree almost universally that the pamphleteer's politics "can only be viewed within the context of his theology."[2] There is, nonetheless, considerable debate over what exactly Paine believed, why, and when.

Paine's reticence about his early life and influences presents one problem for scholars; another is the prevalence of historians who have attempted to reduce the origins of his beliefs to one single influence or another.[3] These "all or nothing" hypotheses have hampered efforts to uncover the true origins of Paine's beliefs and have failed to adequately answer the question. Paine's first modern biographer, Moncure Conway, researched heavily into the primary sources both in America and abroad and, in 1892, produced a two-volume biography of the Revolutionary figure. Conway concluded that it was Paine's fathers' Quakerism that was the primary influence on his later beliefs.[4] Harry Hayden Clark attributes the origins of Paine's beliefs largely to Newtonian Science, and denounces the Quaker influence almost entirely.[5] Thus in his zeal to refute Conway's simplification of Paine's early influences, Clark commits the same fallacy.

Although fifteen biographies of Paine followed Conway's, it is clear that the interpretations of these two scholars have dominated the academic study of the origins of Paine's beliefs. These attempts by Clark and Conway to quantify Paine's early influences, and attempts to circumscribe those influences to simply Quakerism or science has prohibited a truly objective study of the genesis of his beliefs. Unfortunately, this "tunnel vision" has also led to a number of errors in the interpretation of Paine's beliefs, despite the clarity of Paine's writing.[6]

Objectivity is yet another historiographical problem with relation to studies of Paine. Upon reading scholarship about the origins of Paine's beliefs it is evident that there is also an undercurrent of timidity; historians are wary of crediting the Quakers or Newton as a primary influence lest it make Paine seem less of a deist.[7] John Keane, Paine's latest biographer is by far the most objective in his study of the origins of Paine's deism. (Keane's primary focus is on the political life of Paine, not his theology, so Keane only superficially studies the origins of his subject's beliefs.)

Thus the purpose of this chapter will be to attempt an objective, in-depth study of the origins of Paine's religious beliefs as expressed in *The Age of Reason*. It will also attempt to show that the ideas Paine expressed in *The Age of Reason* in 1794/5 actually date back as far as his days in England before he left for America in 1774. All conclusions will be based on what Paine himself wrote or implied, and all speculation will be clearly specified. Evidence provided by Paine suggests that the two principal influences on the formation of his deism were Christianity and science. This study seeks not to determine the proportion of influence of these two areas, but rather to discern their impact on the formation of Paine's own religion as expressed in *The Age of Reason*.

THE ORIGINS OF PAINE'S DEISM

When Moncure Conway wrote in 1892, "Had there been no Quakerism there had been no Thomas Paine," he launched a debate among historians which still wages today.[8] However, Paine scholars universally agree (and rightly so) that Paine's strong philanthropic motivation was partially derived from his exposure to a religious group who "pioneered in many enterprises, including anti-slavery, women's rights, and prison reform."[9] In point of fact, many historians are convinced that "it is as a humanitarian reformer that Paine most of all shows Quaker influences."[10] The mere fact that Paine devotes attention to the Society of Friends in *The Age of Reason* and other writings, bears a certain significance and should command attention.

The Society of Friends was founded by George Fox in 1652 in Lancashire, England. Known more colloquially as "Quakers" or "Children of the Light," these dissenters became an organized, politically active body that was a driving force behind the movement for religious toleration in England. In order to be a Quaker one had to believe that the "Inner Light" of Christ dwelled in all humankind, and it was this light that divinely revealed to man Christ's teachings. It was because of the highly introspective nature of Quakerism that by the time of Paine's birth, the Friends had become "quietistic:" all outward displays of ornate clothing, elaborately decorated churches, hymns, and elegant speech were viewed as distracting.[11] Complete silence and absolute simplicity were required to ensure the Friends that they were proper vessels to receive Christ's revelation, and to be able to distinguish the divine message from their own. Quakers also placed a strong emphasis on humanitarian causes, education, and the sciences. In fact, Friends became members of the Royal Society as early as 1663.[12]

The year 1737 was an auspicious time for the Pain family as well as the Quakers. That year, Joseph Pain was made a Freeman of Thetford, their only son was born, and the Society of Friends established the policy of birthright membership. According to this policy, any immediate family member of an existing member would automatically become a member of the sect as well. Therefore Thomas, his sister Elizabeth, and their mother Frances all became birthright members of the Society of Friends because of their relationship to Joseph Pain. It is therefore not a falsehood to state that Paine "was a member from early life" of the Society of Friends, or that the Friends were a group "to which . . . he officially belonged."[13] It would be erroneous, however, to conclude that Paine was a life-long practicing member of the sect based on his birthright admittance to the Society. Paine, and others like him, "grew up a class of habitual birthright Quakers, distinguished by adherence rather than commitment."[14] Other than possibly attending meetings with his father as a child, there is no evidence to suggest that Paine ever truly espoused the official doctrines of the Quakers.

Joseph Pain, despite marrying a staunch Anglican, was a practicing Quaker. There has, however, been some dispute among historians about his official status within the organization. Conway and others assumed that Pain had been censured or "excommunicated" by the Quakers because of his marriage to Frances Cocke by an Anglican priest. This is simply not true; Paine's words clearly suggest that Joseph Pain was a practicing Quaker all of his life. While he never mentioned his mother in his writings, Paine always spoke affectionately of his father. It was his father—the pacifist—who persuaded his son not to ship out on the *Terrible*. Moreover, Paine wrote in *The Age of Reason:* "My father, being of the Quaker profession, it was my good fortune to have an exceedingly good moral education."[15] He further noted, "I did not learn languages . . . because of the objection the Quakers have against the books in which the language is taught."[16] This strongly suggests that Paine's education was controlled by his father and his father's Quaker ethics.

When Paine wrote about the Quakers and their teachings, he wrote with confidence and as an insider: "[The Quakers] are remarkable for their care of the poor of their society. They are equally as remarkable for the education of their children. I am a descendent of a family of that profession; my father was a Quaker; and I presume I may be admitted an [sic] evidence of what I assert."[17] The Quakers were well-known for their philanthropy, but the fact that Paine deemed it important to stress his admiration for their educational contributions is worth further analysis. The Quakers, because they dissented from the established church in England, were excluded from universities like Oxford and Cambridge. Friends thus compensated for this by forming their own schools, which "predisposed Friends to a certain degree of innovation in curriculum, notably the importance many attached to the study of nature and what useful skills could be derived from the science of the time, like the practical applications of mathematics."[18] Thus by Paine stating that he himself was the beneficiary of a Quaker education (at least in part), and the expression of his obvious pride at being taught such strong morals by the Friends through his father, suggests that their teachings would indeed be a factor in the formation of his own beliefs. This is not purely speculation; Paine declared in *The Age of Reason*, "The religion that approaches nearest of all others to true Deism, in the moral and benign part thereof, is that professed by the Quakers."[19] Hence, in the midst of his greatest deist polemic, Paine retained a link to the Quakers of his youth. One could speculate that his attraction to deism was, in part, stimulated by its similarity to the Quaker ethics which Paine knew so well.

The Quakers also bequeathed another legacy to Paine—a thorough knowledge of the Bible. Even as late as 1802, a friend and observer was amazed that "the Bible is the only book which he has studied, and there is not a verse in it, that is not familiar to him."[20] Still, Paine's bold statement in *The Age of Reason* that the Quakers "do not believe much about Jesus Christ, and they call the Scriptures a dead letter," has led many scholars like Robert Falk to assert that Paine "speaks out in bold ignorance of the Quaker attitude toward the Bible."[21] Paine's further conviction that the Society of Friends "do not hold the Bible to be the Word of God. They call it *a history of the times*," convinced many scholars that Paine knew nothing at all about the Quakers.[22] This is unfortunate because Paine was in fact correct on all accounts.

Robert Barclay, when he set forth the Quaker creed in his *Apology for the True Christian Divinity* in 1678 declared that "the *Spirit* and *not the scriptures, is the rule.*"[23] He further argued that the scriptures "are only a declaration of the fountain, and not the fountain itself, therefore they are not to be esteemed the principal ground of all truth and knowledge."[24] In essence, Barclay and the Friends believed that the words themselves meant nothing; it was the Spirit of God behind the words that gave them their meaning. Without the Spirit, they were in fact a "dead letter." Barclay moreover wrote that the Bible was "A faithful historical account of the actings of God's people in divers[e] ages, with many singular and remarkable providences attending them."[25] In other words, "a history of the times." Perhaps Quaker historian Douglas Gwyn best summarized this concept when he wrote, "God was the Word, and the scriptures were writings; and the word was before the writings were."[26] It would seem that Paine's supposed ignorance has been the invention of historians who failed to trust in Paine's knowledge, or who failed to accurately assess the Friends' attitude toward the Bible. Scholars have likewise failed to acknowledge that Quakerism varies by sect—it is in fact a very individualistic religion with the common link of the belief in the Inner Light. It is therefore possible that the Quakers of Thetford did indeed instruct their congregation that the Bible was not a sacred text and that Jesus the Man was not as important as the teachings provided by the Son of God.

Two scholars have recently argued that by adhering to the Quakers' repudiation of the Bible as a sacred text, Paine was able to view the Bible more critically than contemporary scholars: "Although his adherence to his early Quaker training seems to have been brief, it not only made the Bible familiar to him, but also may have provided him with . . . authorization to speak about the Bible, especially later in life, when he needed to find some such enablement for assailing Scripture itself."[27] In fact, Paine's view of the Bible was perhaps more radical than even the most radical of deists, for Paine saw portions of the Bible as being truly expressive of his own natural religion:

> Almost the only parts of the [Old Testament] that convey to us any idea of God are some chapters in Job and the 19th Psalm; I recollect no other. Those parts are true *deistical* compositions, for they treat of the *Deity* through His works. They take the book of the creation as the Word of God, they refer to no other book, and all the inferences they make are drawn from that volume.[28]

The Nineteenth Psalm also garnered equal respect from Paine; so much so that he inserted all three stanzas of Joseph Addison's version of it from memory. At first glance, Paine's analysis of the Scriptures as "deistical" seems at once original and heretical. To attempt a connection between his unorthodox views and those of an established religious sect seems unfeasible; but it should be remembered that the Quakers encouraged the study of Nature, and the Nineteenth Psalm's first line "The heavens declare the glory of God; and the firmament sheweth his handywork" would have been in accordance with Quaker ethics.[29] Paine's admiration for these two Old Testament passages has also been largely ignored by scholars, much to their discredit. Another unexplored area by scholars is Paine's connection to Quaker theologian Robert Barclay.

The lives of Robert Barclay (1648–1690) and Thomas Paine were similar in many respects. Each suffered imprisonment for their convictions, neither accepted any money for their religious works, and both men shared a keen awareness of how to best reach their respective audiences. Paine always wrote his pamphlets using plain language to reach the masses, while Barclay "used Latin because it was the one sure way of reaching the best-educated minds regardless of geographical location."[30] In his fight against monarchy and tyranny, Paine believed that the people were the only true effective agents of change. Barclay knew that if he wanted to change England's intolerance of the Friends and other dissenters, he would have to win the respect of the nation's clergy and scholars. Hence Paine helped start a revolution from the grass-roots level, and Barclay gained respect for the Society of Friends during an era of religious persecution. D. Elton Trueblood's description of Barclay as a man who "had an excellent mind, which he used effectively; he entered into public life; he engaged in controversies; he spread the gospel," could just as easily describe Thomas Paine.[31]

Barclay's *Apology* (English version 1678) was "the most widely read and distributed of all the many volumes of Quaker literature in three hundred years."[32] Barclay intended the work to be a thorough explication of Quaker beliefs in order to quell the rumors circulating at the time about the Society of Friends. He wrote it primarily for scholars and clerics to enhance their understanding in an effort to provoke them to espouse the Friends' cause of religious toleration. The *Apology* became "the standard exposition of the Quaker faith" and its author "was the only systematic theologian the Society of Friends has produced."[33] The Quakers have never had a set creed, but Barclay's work "was often the final court of appeal."[34] Moreover, the Quaker scholar Rufus Jones asserts that "The *Apology* is beyond question the primary influence which made Friends quietistic."[35] We know that Paine was familiar with Barclay's work because of a lengthy footnote that Paine included in his "Epistle to the Quakers" (1776) (his appendix to *Common Sense*). Paine inserted the following passage from Barclay's "Address to Charles II," his introduction to the *Apology*:

> Thou hast tasted of prosperity and adversity; thou knowest what it is to be banished thy native country, to be over-ruled as well as to rule, and sit upon the throne: and being *oppressed* thou hast reason to know how *hateful* the *oppressor* is both to God and man; If after all these warnings and advertisements, thou dost not turn unto the Lord with all thy heart, but forget him who remembered thee in thy distress, and give up thyself to follow lust and vanity, surely, great will be thy condemnation.—Against which snare, as well as the temptation of those who may or do feed thee, and prompt thee to evil, the most excellent and prevalent remedy will be, to apply thyself to that light of Christ which shineth in thy conscience, and which neither can nor will flatter thee, nor suffer thee to be at ease in thy sins.[36]

Since quotations from other authors are comparatively rare with Paine, the fact that he quotes Barclay at some length is significant. The source of this quotation is a matter of debate among scholars. A. Owen Aldridge contended that Paine knew about the address from Voltaire, not Barclay.[37] A careful textual analysis of the versions of Paine, Barclay, and Voltaire reveal that Paine's version (italics and punctuation included) is nearly identical to that of the early Friend.[38] It is most likely that Paine's "moral education" involved readings in or lessons from Barclay's famous tract.

Barclay instructed his brethren not to accept money for their ministry, with the exception of those occasions when a Friend's duties called him away from his regular employment. Even in such a case, Barclay insisted that a Friend should receive only enough money to afford the necessities of life. Paine concurred with Barclay; he never took pay for "preaching, praying, politics or poetry," but rather insisted that the profits from his writings be donated to the causes he espoused.[39] The only time Paine insisted on being paid for his work was when he incurred expenses from his travels as a secretary to the Committee of Foreign Affairs or other such non-literary occupations.

Another view that both Paine and Barclay shared was the belief that the Bible portrayed God negatively. Paine's contention that the redemption of Christ seemed to make "God Almighty act like a passionate man who killed His son when He could not revenge Himself in any other way" is remarkably similar to Barclay's assertion that the redemption "*is highly injurious to God,* because it makes him the author of sin" by virtue of the Lord's "demonstrating of the glory of his justice."[40] Paine clearly agreed with Barclay's declaration that the redemption "makes the coming of Christ an act of wrath."[41]

The two polemicists also demonstrated that they were receptive to Enlightenment ideas in their recognition of the importance of reason. Barclay maintained that man, using reason, could "apprehend in his brain . . . a knowledge of God and spiritual things," and that "God . . . hath given man . . . the light of reason to rule him in things natural."[42] Paine likewise believed that man could discover God "only by the exercise of reason," and that reason was "the choicest gift of God to Man."[43]

Yet another characteristic that both Barclay and Paine shared was their use of science and scientific examples as demonstrations of their beliefs or illustrations of their theories. Barclay, in a section of the *Apology* entitled "Natural demonstrations from astronomy and geometry," attempted to prove to his readership that one of the uses of Scripture was to provide proof of Christ's message to those who had not experienced his revelation directly.[44] He used the example of an astronomer or a "geometer" who knew the rules and formulas of his discipline by rote, and accepted them as infallible, but when he attempted to explain an eclipse or a right triangle to "an ignorant rustick," he had to physically demonstrate that knowledge to the inquirer.[45] The geometer is obliged to "certify some ignorant man concerning the certainty of his art, by condescending to measure it, and make it obvious to his senses."[46] Trueblood argues that for Barclay "it was soon evident that the logic of religious experience follows the same identical form as does the logic of scientific experience. Both are empirical and both require verification."[47] In much the same way, Paine believed that for those who could not see evidence of God's existence in the Creation, the study of science would provide the necessary proof. For Paine, "the principles of science are in the creation, and are unchangeable and of divine origin."[48] Moreover, according to Paine, science was the only "true theology" because subjects like astronomy "study of the works of God, and of the power and wisdom of God in His works."[49] The alarming similarity between the writings of Barclay and Paine raises an interesting question: were the Quakers a dominant influence on the beliefs of Thomas Paine? Unfortunately, because Barclay is the only Quaker author that Paine cited in his writings (or even referred to), influence is difficult to prove. However, there are striking similarities between the doctrines of the Quakers and Thomas Paine. Perhaps when Paine remarked "the seeds of good principles, and the literary means of advancement in the world, are laid in early life," he was giving due credit to his father and the Society of Friends.[50]

There remains one final note about the Quakers and Thomas Paine that should be mentioned. In Paine's Last Will and Testament he requested to be buried in a Quaker cemetery. Paine wrote, "I know not if the Society of people called Quakers admit a person to be buried in their burying ground, who does not belong to their Society, but if they do, or will admit me, I would prefer being buried there; my father belonged to that profession, and I was partly brought up in it."[51] The Quakers denied his request, and many scholars concluded that it was because of *The Age of Reason* and Paine's deist beliefs. These same scholars failed to recognize that it was Friends who took care of Paine in his last days—in fact, he died in the home of a well-respected Quaker. The consensus among recent historians is that the Quakers denied Paine's final request because they feared Paine's followers would want to erect a monument to his memory at his final resting place, and this was strictly against Quaker principles. However, the fact that Paine's last thoughts were of his father and the Quakers raises an interesting question: Why would a man who firmly declared before the world his belief in deism, want to be buried among the Society of Friends? Perhaps the answer is simply this: that the Friends made a significant impression on him—so much so that Paine carried a reverence for that society literally to his deathbed. It is also possible that his decision was the result of a fond remembrance for his father. Nevertheless, the final words of Thomas

Paine made in reference to his father and the Quakers are significant. Therefore the possible impact that the Society of Friends had on the formation of his deism must not be discounted or minimized. To do so would be a failure to recognize how important Paine himself considered the Society to his formation as a person and as a polemicist.

The Anglicans also played a fundamental role in the formation of Paine's later deistic beliefs, and the expression of those beliefs. Paine's ties to the Church of England were also rooted in his childhood. He had been baptized and confirmed into the Church of England, and no doubt his knowledge of the Bible was advanced by both his parents' faiths. In *The Age of Reason,* Paine vividly recounted a striking memory about the doctrines of the established church. What is perhaps most intriguing about this disclosure is the rational, intellectual approach used by the author. "From the time I was capable of conceiving an idea and acting upon it by reflection," Paine wrote, "I either doubted the truth of the Christian system or thought it to be a strange affair."[52] He traced the origins of his "reflective mind" and his disbelief of Christianity to the age of seven or eight when he heard a sermon at a maternal relative's home on the redemption by the Son of God.[53] This sermon had a monumental impact on Paine's religious beliefs and contributed, either directly or indirectly, to preparing him for his acceptance of deism over Christianity. Paine's reaction to the sermon, therefore, is worth quoting in full:

> After the sermon was ended, I went into the garden, and as I was going down the garden steps (for I perfectly recollect the spot) I revolted at the recollection of what I had heard, and thought to myself that it was making God Almighty act like a passionate man who killed His son when He could not revenge Himself in any other way, and, as I was sure a man would be hanged who did such a thing, I could not see for what purpose they preached such sermons. This was not one of that kind of thoughts that had anything in it of childish levity; it was to me a serious reflection, arising from the idea I had that God was too good to do such an action, and also too almighty to be under any necessity of doing it. I believe in the same manner at this moment; and I moreover believe that any system of religion that has anything in it that shocks the mind of a child cannot be a true system.[54]

These two short paragraphs speak volumes about the thought process of their author. They also provide a keen insight into the genesis of his future beliefs.

Paine's notion of God's infinite goodness may not have been "childish levity" but it is consistent with the mind of most children. Paine seemed to be particularly sensitive to and aware of the impressionable nature of children. He even took issue with children's stories like Aesop's fables. "Though the moral is in general just," Paine admitted cautiously, "the fable is often cruel; and the cruelty of the fable does more injury to the heart, especially in a child."[55] These passages suggest strongly that at the very least it is consistent with a child who has also been instructed (as per Robert Barclay) that the redemption is *"highly injurious to God."* The passage also shows evidence of Paine's enlightenment rationalist leanings. His statement that he knew a man would be hanged for committing murder reflected an early application of reason in religious matters—perhaps a foreshadowing of his later susceptibility to deistic ideas. Finally, Paine's remembrance of how this idea "shock[ed]" him as a child, led him to conclude as an adult that Christianity was not a "true system." This questioning of Christianity and the outright rejection of its most central tenet as a youth was an unexpected legacy left to Thomas Paine by his Anglican heritage and thereby contributed to his later espousal of deism.

At the age of twenty Paine was a skeptic of revealed religion. He admitted later in *The Age of Reason* that he had always been attracted to scientific study and that he had never been able to understand or accept fully Christianity as a way of belief. In other words, Thomas Paine lacked the one thing necessary to be a Christian: faith. From an early age (seven or eight he claimed) he approached religion with the reason of a scientist rather than the faith of a cleric. It seemed illogical to Paine that an Almighty being would kill his own son. It was irrational to accept that God (whom he believed was a benevolent being) could do such a thing, and, furthermore, that people would simply accept this as a compassionate attempt to save mankind. He had doubts about Christianity and thought it was a "strange affair."[56]

Paine declared in *The Age of Reason* that from an early age "the natural bent of my mind was to science," and he apparently took great pleasure in having the opportunity to advance his studies in this area.[57] Shortly after he arrived in London in 1757, Paine "purchased a pair of globes, and attended the philosophical lectures of Martin and Ferguson."[58] He also became acquainted with Dr. Bevis, an astronomer of the Royal Society.[59] In addition, Paine purchased and mastered the use of the orrery, a device he described as

> a machinery of clock-work, representing the universe in miniature, and in which the revolution of the earth round itself and round the sun, the

revolution of the moon round the earth, the revolution of the planets round the sun, their relative distances from the sun, as the center of the whole system, their relative distances from each other and their different magnitudes are represented as they really exist in what we call the heavens.[60]

In *The Rights of Man,* written three years before *The Age of Reason,* Paine insisted that "the mind, in discovering truth, acts in the same manner as it acts through the eye in discovering objects; when once any object has been seen, it is impossible to put the mind back to the same condition it was in before he saw it."[61] In 1757 Thomas Paine purchased and mastered the orrery—a model of the universe in miniature. His study of natural philosophy in general and of the orrery in particular forever changed the way Paine conceived the universe, God, and his obligations as a human being. His mind could not return to thinking as it had before because his eyes had seen a new truth—a truth unveiled to him by Newtonian science. Through Ferguson and his exposure to Newtonian science, Paine had developed a clear emphasis on the primacy of reason and, perhaps most importantly, formed his own concept of the "true theology" and "true religion": deism. The significance of the orrery and what it taught Paine cannot be overestimated. It was here, in studying gravitation, planets, and orbits that Paine was able to form (at least partially) his own system of theology based on his scientific studies. The device, according to Paine, taught him five very important things:

1. Space is infinite.
2. Matter is indivisible.
3. God created a plurality of worlds—not just the Earth and its inhabitants.
4. God created the laws which govern the universe.
5. In studying science we study God, the Creator of science and the universe.[62]

These five principles are at the very core of Paine's deism which he revealed in *The Age of Reason* in 1794. Science led Paine to the belief that "our ideas, not only of the almightiness of the Creator, but of His wisdom and His beneficence, become enlarged in proportion as we contemplate the extent and the structure of the universe."[63] Because of his scientific investigations he came to view the world and God in a fresh new way which created an indelible impression upon the mind of the young stay-maker. He arrived at these conclusions from the study of his orrery, and the result was that Paine underwent a kind of religious awakening which can best be described as a conversion experience.

Paine related this conversion experience in the concluding paragraphs of Part II of *The Age of Reason*. As Paine made a final and powerful attempt to convert his French readers to his creed of deism, he abandoned his scathing critique of the Bible and its contents and his vitriolic attack on Christianity. Instead he chose to focus on the positive rather than the negative; he tried to find a way to bring people to a belief in his God. Paine sought a way, in those last paragraphs, to demonstrate to his readers the purity and righteousness of his deism by detailing his own experience. For Paine, there was one certain way to accomplish his goal: encourage his readers to engage in scientific study. In the conclusion Paine reiterated to his readers the dangers of revelation, or false theology. He reasserted that the Creation was the only true Word of God and that therefore the Bible was itself blasphemous. He insisted that "We can know God only through his works . . . The principles of science lead to this knowledge; for the creator of man is the creator of science."[64] The easiest way, therefore, for humans to discover God was by studying God's creation in totum. He argued,

> Could a man be placed in a situation . . . to mark the movements of the several planets, the cause of their varying appearances . . . their connection and dependence on each other, and to know the system of laws, established by the Creator, that governs and regulates the whole, he would then conceive, far beyond what any church theology can teach him, the power, the wisdom, the vastness, the munificence of the Creator. . . . His mind exalted by the scene, and convinced by the fact, would increase in gratitude as it encreased [sic] in knowledge. His religion or his worship would become united with his improvement as a man; and any employment he followed, that had connection with the principles of the creation . . . would teach him more of God, and of the gratitude he owes to him.[65]

In other words, the simplest way to demonstrate God to mankind was space travel. Could a person stand among the stars, look down upon the Earth and behold other galaxies, their conception of God's power and benevolence would at once be perfectly grasped and understood. Never again would mankind need the intervention of priests, rabbis, or ministers. This heavenly sight alone would teach mankind their duty to this benevolent infinite Creator. This was Paine's purpose in writing *The Age of Reason*; this was his deism.

Well aware that such travels were impossible (even Paine never foresaw such advancements), he took heart in the fact that "though man cannot arrive, at least in this life, at the actual scene I have described, he can demonstrate it."[66] He reminded his readers that since Newtonian science had given mankind knowledge of the laws which governed the universe, "we know that the greatest works can be represented in model, and that the universe can be represented by the same means."[67] And what was the best model? According to Paine, "Could a model of the universe, such as is called an orrery, be presented before him and put in motion, his mind would arrive at the same idea."[68] In other words, man could arrive at the true theology of deism simply by studying science and the orrery. The orrery had given him a new conception of God, thus it is almost certain that when Paine left London for Sandwich in 1758 he left as a man with a strong inclination towards deism.

After recounting his childhood "garden experience" and his exposure to scientific lectures in *The Age of Reason,* Paine revealed,

> After I had made myself master of the use of the globes and of the orrery, and conceived an idea of the infinity of space, and the eternal indivisibility of matter, and obtained at least a general knowledge of what is called natural philosophy, I began to compare, or, as I have before said, to confront the eternal evidence those things afford with the Christian system of faith.[69]

Paine's word choice provides an important insight into how he attempted to reconcile Newtonian science with revealed religion. Paine declared that he "confronted" this new scientific information suggesting that his experiences with the orrery had been positive enough to take root in his mind but that they did not provide all the answers he was searching for. Despite his skepticism Paine had been raised by devout Christians and it would have been natural for him to retain some interest (if not attachment) for that system of beliefs. It would also have been natural for Paine, a man obviously enamored with the scientific method to study Christianity and religion scientifically. In other words, to "confront the eternal evidence" and draw his own conclusions based thereon. It seems that Paine embarked upon a mission to uncover the truth about God and Christianity scientifically; he had all the evidence he needed to support the Enlightenment conception of a deist God, but not that of a Christian God. Perhaps his experimentation with Methodism was an attempt to reconcile his Christian upbringing with his new empirical impulses.

The Methodists began preaching in England in 1739—just two years after Paine's birth. They were a sect within the Church of England itself, not a separate body. The Methodists were, according to Elie Halévy, "a Nonconformist sect established to remain faithful to the Church of England."[70] Paine, having been partially raised as an Anglican, would therefore have been familiar with their basic ideology, if not their evangelicalism. Being familiar with the rhetoric of the Church also allowed Paine to discern how the Methodists differed in their interpretations of Scripture and in their oratorical style. It was perhaps these differences that attracted Paine to this radical sect.

In 1758 Paine was living in Sandwich, England in the County of Kent. It was here, in 1759, that accounts of Paine's Methodist preaching surface. Paine was an artisan at a time when John Wesley's fiery preaching converted many of Paine's brethren into the Methodist fold. Wesley did in fact lead many revival meetings in Kent, particularly in Sandwich, at the time that Paine resided there. Therefore the likelihood that Paine did attend a revival (or meeting) or was familiar with Methodism and Methodist doctrine is very high indeed. If, as some scholars would have it, Paine did in fact preach as a Methodist in Kent he would have to have been a lay preacher—not an ordained minister. The Anglican Church required knowledge of Latin for ordination (which Paine did not possess), while the Methodists had no such formal education requirements for their evangelists.

Nonetheless, the scholarly evidence for Paine's alleged preaching is tenuous at best. The source most historians rely upon heavily is an editorial footnote in Nehemiah Curnock's 1916 edition of John Wesley's journals. Curnock insisted that in 1759 Paine "was so far trusted as to be requested to conduct a service in default of the appointed preacher."[71] The source for this information, Curnock revealed, was an article in *The Methodist Recorder* in 1906. The article entitled "The White Cliffs of Dover: Methodism in a Great Fortress," was written by an anonymous author, "The Visitor." (Curnock was himself editor of the *Recorder* until he became seriously ill in 1906.) In the article, the mysterious author declared that in Sandwich in 1759

> A class-leader, perhaps the first, was Mr. Grace, by trade a stay-maker. The building in question, now a public house, has one queer association. Tom Paine, author of 'The Age of Reason,' read a sermon there one day. He was apprenticed to Mr. Grace, and went with him to class and to chapel. He professed to believe, and was so far trusted that when a minister failed one day Tom Paine took the service.[72]

"The Visitor" gave no source for this information. George Hindmarch, who has done the most extensive writing by far on Paine's connection to Methodism, also relies heavily on Curnock's note, asserting confidently that Curnock "would not have repeated the report unless he was sure it was an authentic record."[73] Sadly, Hindmarch's evidence also hinges upon Chalmers' questionable biography of Paine, which again calls into question the accuracy of Hindmarch's evidence. Furthermore, and by far the most damaging component of Hindmarch's study, is that the bulk of his evidence rests upon numerous articles published in the *Lewes Journal* which he claims to have been written by Thomas Paine. It has since been proven conclusively by George Spater that these articles were in fact not authored by Thomas Paine, but rather by a clergyman named Richard Nichell.[74]

John Keane's study (1995) also used Curnock as his principal source to assert that Paine preached in Sandwich. Moreover, Keane refers to an inscription on the inside front cover of a 1746 edition of Wesley's *Sermons on Several Occasions* (volume one). According to Keane, the volume was owned by the English father of noted Methodist preacher Albert Nash (1812–1900). The inscription reads, "Out of this volume Thomas Paine, author of the Age of Reason, used to read sermons to the Congregations at the Methodist Chapel in Dover when they were disappointed of a Preacher. At that time he belonged to the Methodist Society in that place."[75]

There is some question as to who wrote this inscription and when—Keane does not say. (The spelling of Paine's name—with an "e"—may shed some light on the date. Paine did not likely add the "e" to his name until some time during or after his stay in Lewes, which is a decade after he allegedly preached in Sandwich.) Nevertheless, the inscription does add credence to Curnock's assertion. However, it should be carefully noted that there is a difference between preaching an impromptu sermon and reading one. The possibility that Paine attended Methodist meetings has already been conceded, and it is just as easy to concede that he may have been called upon—as surely others were—to read sermons when the circuit rider was not available. This does not necessarily mean that Paine was a preacher; all that can really be ascertained is that Paine seemed to be a favorite orator among his Methodist companions. The question of literacy is also valid. While it would be wrong to overgeneralize and assert that the majority of English Methodists were illiterate, it would not be incorrect to assert that the possibility existed that Paine read sermons because he may have been one of a select few who could.

Historians have usually argued that Paine's attraction to Methodism revolved principally around the ability of that sect to attract large crowds with their persuasive oratory. Yet there were other doctrinal similarities

The Origins and Significance of Paine's Religious Beliefs

between Paine and the Methodists. For example, "Utilitarians and [Methodists] agreed to work together for commercial freedom, the abolition of slavery, and the reform of criminal law."[76] Paine was a champion of many of these causes and he wrote about them in his pamphlets *Agrarian Justice*, and *The Rights of Man*. Historians have further argued that these qualities (along with Methodism's democratic elements and its similarity to Quaker egalitarianism) were adopted by the future revolutionary to persuade two nations to strive for independence.[77]

It is entirely possible that Paine was able to temporarily bridge the gap between deism and Christianity by focusing on their commonalities. There are four principal components of Paine's beliefs as expressed in *The Age of Reason* which were shared by the Methodists as well. The first was the belief in a benevolent, democratic God. The second was the Arminian belief in salvation by works. Paine believed that doing unto others and endeavoring to better the conditions of one's fellow man was not only man's duty to God, but also the means of securing rewards in the hereafter.[78] Paine also readily declared in *The Age of Reason* his reverence for the teachings of Jesus Christ and his benevolent morality.[79] Finally, there were the numerous charitable activities that the Methodists engaged in which would have appealed to Paine's humanitarian Quaker upbringing.

It makes perfect sense, then, that Methodism might have been attractive to a young and very curious Thomas Paine. However, by the end of his year in Sandwich the experiment had apparently run its course because there is no evidence that Paine ever preached or read a sermon outside of Sandwich. In fact all the evidence (even Curnock's tenuous secondary source) points to one year and one location: Kent, 1759. Paine was certainly not known to any of his friends as a "preacher" or a "Methodist," or the evidence would bear that out. It seems likely then that his flirtation with Methodism was brief and his fascination with that religion never left Kent. The very fact that there is no evidence outside of Sandwich strongly supports the conclusion that Paine's skepticism about Christianity and his exposure to Newtonian science had left an indelible impression upon him which did not allow him to fully espouse the tenets of Methodism. "It has been by rejecting the evidence that the world or works of God in the creation afford to our senses, and the action of our reason upon that evidence," Paine argued, "that so many wild and whimsical systems of faith and of religion have been fabricated and set up."[80] He further argued that

> There may be many systems of religion that, so far from being morally bad, are in many respects morally good; but there can be but ONE that

is true; and that one necessarily must, as it ever will, be in all things consistent with the ever-existing word of God that we behold in His works. But such is the strange construction of the Christian system of faith that every evidence the heavens afford to man either directly contradicts it or renders it absurd.[81]

Apparently Paine, who had long been suspicious of Christian dogma, discovered in Sandwich that while Methodism may have been a morally good religion, ultimately it was still Christianity and therefore a false system. For Paine the only true religion was deism, and he outlined his beliefs in his most personal work *The Age of Reason*.

The Age of Reason

For the great majority of his political career Paine avoided religious discussions and topics except on rare occasions. However, in 1794 while in Paris during the French Revolution, Paine startled the world by writing an exhaustive treatise divulging his own personal religious beliefs and championing deistic theology. He opened the work by declaring that "it has been my intention, for several years past, to publish my thoughts upon religion" and further added, "I intended it to be the last offering I should make to my fellow-citizens of all nations."[82] The French Revolution proved to be the catalyst for *The Age of Reason*. In a letter to John Inskeep in 1806, Paine explained his motivation for shifting from political discourse to religious didacticism: "my motive and object in all my publications on religious subjects . . . [has] been to bring man to a right reason that God has given him; to impress on him the great principles of divine morality, justice, mercy, and a benevolent disposition to all men and to all creatures. . . ."[83] The pamphlet has widely been regarded by many as the "Deist Bible."[84] Kerry S. Walters affirms that it is "probably the best-known treatise in the history of American deism."[85] In the pamphlet Paine revealed his personal thoughts on the Bible, Christianity, and deism. His purpose in producing the work was to counteract the potentially ill effects of the "abolition of the whole national order of priesthood" in France by attempting to attract his readership to natural theology.[86] Paine feared that the weakening of Catholicism in France would lead to atheism and the French people would "lose sight of morality, of humanity and of the theology that is true."[87]

Another motivation was Paine's concern about the uncertain future of France, as well as his own personal well-being. Aware that his opinions had become unpopular with the leaders of the revolution, Paine rushed to finish the work. He wrote to Samuel Adams in 1803,

> In the first place I saw my life in continual danger. My friends were falling as fast as the guillotine could cut their heads off, and as I every day expected the same fate, I resolved to begin my work. . . . In the second place, the people of France were running headlong into atheism, and I had the work translated and published in their own language to stop them in that career, and fix them to the first article . . . of every man's creed who has any creed at all, *I believe in God*.[88]

His suspicions were correct; in December 1793, within hours of completing the work, he was arrested and incarcerated in Luxembourg Prison where he remained until November of 1794. Paine left a copy of his manuscript with the noted American author Joel Barlow before he was imprisoned, but he wrote the introduction and dedication to the work from his cell at the Luxembourg. Barlow disseminated copies of the treatise and it was published while its author awaited execution. After he escaped the guillotine and recovered from a severe illness contracted at the Luxembourg, Paine began Part Two of *The Age of Reason,* and completed the work while further recuperating at the home of James Monroe. It went to press in 1795.

Part One of the work (composed without a Bible at his disposal) attacked Christianity and the Scriptures directly. The Bible, according to Paine, was a book replete with "rapine, cruelty, and murder" and the only true Word of God was the Creation.[89] The Bible, "too ridiculous even for criticism," was to Paine the root of all of mankind's rejection of the true theology of deism, for it led people to believe it contained the Word of God.[90] The author refused "to believe any book that ascribes cruelty and injustice to God . . . therefore I reject the Bible as unworthy of credit."[91] It disturbed Paine greatly to know that

> People in general do not know what wickedness there is in this pretended Word of God. Brought up in habits of superstition, they take it for granted that the Bible is true, and that it is good . . . Good heavens! it is quite another thing; it is a book of lies, wickedness and blasphemy; for what can be greater than to ascribe the wickedness of man to the orders of the Almighty?[92]

Furthermore, Paine maintained that "it is a duty incumbent on every true Deist, that he vindicate the moral justice of God against the calumnies of the Bible."[93]

For Paine, the belief in one God was a purely rational act. According to the author: "[one] arrives at the belief of [God] from the tenfold greater difficulty of disbelieving it."[94] He also wholeheartedly rejected the Bible's portrayal of God as a "changeable, passionate, vindictive being" when the Creation gave evidence of "a contrary idea—that of unchangeable and of eternal order, harmony and goodness."[95] With regards to man's duty to God, he believed that "religion consists in contemplating the power, wisdom and benignity of the Deity in His works," and in "doing justice, loving mercy, and endeavoring to make our fellow creatures happy."[96]

Part Two of the pamphlet was partially a response to criticisms of Part One, but more specifically it was a book-by-book critique of the Bible. Using the Bible as a reference, Paine systematically examined each book of the Old and New Testaments for falsehoods. He also attacked biblical chronology and the authenticity of the authorship of the Scriptures. Beginning with the Old Testament, the author sought to remove the reverence of biblical figures like Moses, who was to Paine, "among the detestable villains that in any period of the world have disgraced the name of man."[97] The Old Testament was for Paine simply "a history of wickedness that served to corrupt and brutalize mankind," and, he averred, "I sincerely detest it as I detest everything that is cruel."[98]

Paine's next target was the New Testament: "The New Testament! that is, the *new will*, as if there could be two wills of the Creator."[99] He further argued, "What is it the Testament teaches us?—to believe that the Almighty committed debauchery with a woman engaged to be married, and the belief of this debauchery is called faith."[100] For Paine, "THE WORD OF GOD IS THE CREATION WE BEHOLD and it is in *this word* which no human invention can counterfeit or alter that God speaketh universally to man."[101] However, the author's primary purpose for his critique of the New Testament was "the fable of Jesus Christ, as told in the New Testament, and the wild and visionary doctrine raised therein."[102] The story of Christ's birth was "blasphemously obscene" but as for the character of Jesus, "he was a virtuous and an amiable man. The morality that he preached and practised was of the most benevolent kind."[103] Nonetheless, regarding Jesus' divinity, Paine contended "there is nothing in the works of God that is evidence that he begat a son . . . and therefore, we are not authorized in believing it."[104]

"The Christian religion," which "begins with a dream and ends with a murder," was abhorrent to Thomas Paine.[105] He declared that Christianity "appears to me a species of Atheism—a sort of religious denial of God. It professes to believe in a man rather than in God . . . and is as near to Atheism as twilight is to darkness."[106] Moreover, he blamed Christianity for contributing to the rise of atheism and a denial of true theology:

> Of all the systems of religion that ever were invented, there is none more derogatory to the Almighty, more unedifying to man, more repugnant to reason, and more contradictory in itself, than this thing called Christianity. Too absurd for belief, too impossible to convince, and too inconsistent for practise, it renders the heart torpid, or produces only atheists and fanatics.[107]

True theology for Paine meant "the belief of one God, and an imitation of his moral character, or the practice of what are called moral virtues."[108]
Across the Atlantic in America, Paine's treatise was devoured by the buying public. It was inexpensively priced (like all of Paine's previous works) and there were eight editions published in 1794, seven in 1795 and two in 1796. There were 100,000 copies of the pamphlet sold in 1797 alone.[109] It was evident that Paine had written yet another best-seller, and in general Paine scholars and historians agree that there were two primary reasons why the pamphlet sold in such voluminous numbers: First and foremost because it was written by Thomas Paine. The buying public was well aware of the author's reputation and his previous works. Secondly, it sold well because of the nature of the pamphlet itself. For the first time Biblical criticism and the tenets of deism were written specifically for the layman and made accessible to him by an inexpensive price. A subject that had once been the private domain of clerics, scholars, and elites, was now a matter of public debate. According to Eric Foner, "Paine's *Age of Reason* ridiculed for a mass audience the divine inspiration of the Bible, a cardinal precept of Protestant Americans."[110]

Although Paine wrote *The Age of Reason* in 1794, he became a deist much sooner. The basic tenets of Christianity were something that Paine, even before he ever saw an orrery, had never been able to reconcile with his own personal beliefs about God. Paine had never been able to accept the divinity of Jesus Christ, much less his role as Redeemer. It seems clear that some time between 1759 and 1776 reason triumphed over revelation, and Paine was free to practice—and later preach—his deism. There is, moreover, plenty of evidence to support this conclusion.

In the beginning of Part I of *The Age of Reason* Paine confessed that "It has been my intention, for several years past, to publish my thoughts upon religion."[111] This suggests at the very least that his conversion to deism occurred long before the French Revolution. He further added that he intended his treatise on religion "to be the last offering I should make . . . and that at a time when the purity of the motive that induced me to do it could not admit of question."¹¹² Paine clearly had thought carefully and for a considerable time about exactly how and when to produce his final composition, and the fact that he wrote it so quickly, and under so much pressure, indicates how clear and entrenched his deist beliefs were.

In his *Autobiography*, written in 1802, John Adams recalled an evening in 1776 when Paine paid him a visit at his Philadelphia lodgings. According to Adams, Paine was angry at him for writing against *Common Sense* in the public papers. The two engaged in a debate about Paine's incendiary pamphlet, with Adams castigating Paine for his use of the Old Testament in his call for Independence (Adams called Paine's reasoning "ridiculous").¹¹³ Their conversation then turned to religious matters and Paine, according to Adams, "expressed a Contempt of the Old Testament and indeed of the Bible at large, which surprized me."¹¹⁴ When Paine noted Adams' reaction, Paine "check'd himself, with these Words 'However I have some thoughts of publishing my Thoughts on Religion, but I believe it will be best to postpone it, to the latter part of my Life.'"¹¹⁵ Adams then assured his readers that they spent the evening together "in good humour" with no resentment expressed by either participant.¹¹⁶

Scholars like A. Owen Aldridge and others have dismissed Adams' statements as those of an angry, senile old man, striking out at someone he believed below contempt since the publication of his unchristian tract. It is true that Adams developed a healthy (bordering on obsessive) loathing for Paine—but not in 1794. Adams had not been an admirer of Paine since *Common Sense*. It is no secret that Adams was jealous of the fact that the Englishman had managed in one stroke to garner attention for a cause he himself had been championing in vain for years. Nevertheless, Adams respected Paine as an intelligent and committed man, but as a man whose political views were far too liberal to be comforting to the conservative from Massachusetts. He lashed out at Paine publicly and privately during the course of the American Revolution and throughout Paine's European career. Thus Adams' statements about Paine in his *Autobiography* would not have surprised anyone—least of all Thomas Paine. Still, many Paine scholars dismiss Adams as a man with a motive; as a bitter man who sought to trample Paine's reputation. This reasoning is illogical. In 1802 when Adams' autobiography was written, Paine had no reputation left to damage. He was already considered to be a drunken infidel by many Americans and therefore Adams could not have caused Paine any further harm. He could, however, have written this passage to dissociate himself from the vilified Paine in 1802. However, had that been Adams' motive, why make the point that however unorthodox Paine's opinions were in 1776, they were not radical enough to cause Adams to end their relationship? Rather,

Adams insisted that he and Paine spent the rest of the evening together pleasantly, suggesting that Paine's views caused him no great concern. Thus the most logical deduction is that Adams wrote about this incident in his *Autobiography* with the purpose of informing his readers that Paine's deism was apparent long before the French Revolution and the appearance of *The Age of Reason*. (In other words, it was a not-so-nice way of telling the world that his former colleague had always been an infidel.)

This is particularly significant because many of Adams' contemporaries (and some scholars today) believe that the French Revolution was critical to the formation of Paine's beliefs. Adams' statements in his autobiography suggest otherwise, as do Paine's own statements in *The Age of Reason*. Referring to his conclusions in Part I, Paine averred "the opinions I have advanced in that work, are the effect of the most clear, and long established conviction, that the bible and the testament are impositions upon the world ... that the only true religion is deism. ..."[117]

Paine also provides similar early glimpses into his later religious views in his writings before *The Age of Reason*. Paine rarely referred to religious matters in his political writings, but when he did he was very consistent and bold. In a 1777 letter to the *Pennsylvania Journal*, Paine declared that "a man may be religiously happy without *modes* [of worship]"[118] One year later in the fifth number of his "Crisis" essays, Paine warned his readers about the stubbornness of the British commander Howe: "to argue with a man who has renounced the use and authority of reason ... is like administering medicine to the dead, or endeavoring to convert an atheist by scripture."[119] In *The Rights of Man* Paine refers to the Mosaic account of the creation as being "merely historical."[120] Surely these remarks would not have been made by someone who was a Christian? However it was Paine's reaction to the success of *Common Sense* that provided the clearest proof of the establishment of his deism by 1776, and the significance of his convictions.

MIGHTIER THAN THE SWORD

When *Common Sense* debuted on January 10, 1776, it became a runaway bestseller. Scholars estimate that by the end of 1776 at least half of all the colonists had either read *Common Sense* or were familiar with Paine's arguments. There have been other estimates made of the number of copies published and purchased, but none are completely accurate. This is due in large part to the fact that many who read *Common Sense* either borrowed copies, had it read to them, or purchased cheaper, unauthorized, versions. Quantitative studies aside, Paine had not only captured the attention of the

American colonists, but he also amassed a considerable following in France, and attracted admirers as far away as Holland and Germany. In its first year of publication alone there were twenty-five editions published.[121] Paine had successfully converted Americans to his doctrine of Independence, as colonists everywhere clamored for revolution.[122] During his tenure at *The Pennsylvania Magazine,* Paine declared, "there is nothing which obtains so general an influence over the manners and morals of a people as the Press."[123] *Common Sense* was clearly proof of that assertion. Paine had discovered a potent ally in his use of the popular press; it became the principal organ for all of his future political action. Paine's arguments persuaded the colonists to revolt from Britain, and within six months of *Common Sense*'s publication, the Continental Congress declared American Independence from Great Britain. Paine's victory was complete.

Paine's motives for writing *Common Sense* were simple and clear: his adopted home had been turned into a war zone where he once again found himself battling an unfeeling Parliament and a despised king. It was what he observed in the wake of that bloodshed, however, that truly made Paine a republican who sought to destroy tyranny wherever it existed. "Both prior to and at the breaking out of hostilities," Paine wrote, "I was struck with the order and decorum with which everything was conducted."[124] He was "impressed" by the fact that the colonial assemblies and local governments easily stepped into the void created by the loss of royal authority, which demonstrated to him that "monarchy and aristocracy were frauds and impositions upon mankind."[125] These observations left an indelible mark upon Paine which led him to the conclusion that "a little more than what society naturally performed, was all the government that was necessary."[126] Lexington and Concord had convinced Paine that colonial independence was not only necessary but just; America's response to the growing crisis convinced him that they would be successful. The only thing left for Paine to do was to convince the colonists that he was right. It was "on these principles" that Paine published *Common Sense*.[127]

Paine's methodology was as simple as his motive. In an effort to persuade the colonists to revolt from England, *Common Sense* condemned monarchy as an evil, blasphemous institution. Paine also instructed the colonists that they needed to use their reason to see the truth and establish a government based upon the laws of nature—God's laws—and destroy British tyranny. "Reason and Ignorance," Paine observed, "influence the great bulk of mankind."[128] He believed strongly that "if either of these can be rendered sufficiently extensive in a country, the machinery of government goes easily on. Reason obeys itself, and Ignorance submits to whatever is dictated to it."[129] Reason was the key to establishing a true republic, thus Paine's rhetorical style and arguments forced the colonists to consider the subject of independence from a more rational, scientific perspective. Paine's goal in *Common Sense*, then, was to convince Americans to overthrow a monarchy built upon ignorance and fraud and establish a republic governed by the reason of its citizens. Clearly, as one scholar has noted, "Paine saw the revolutionary process as a dialectical one, demanding a transformation in thinking as well as in institutions and forms of power."[130]

According to Paine's credo it was therefore essential that in order to establish governments based upon first principles (in accordance with God's laws) freedom of worship was critical. "Certain as I am, that when opinions are free, either in matters of government or religion," Paine later declared, "truth will finally and powerfully prevail."[131] There could be no mingling of statecraft and religion in a true system of either worship or politics. This had of course been a central argument in *Common Sense:* monarchy was a blasphemous institution and America would have to abolish it to end God's wrath. Separating church and state in the new republic would incur the Creator's good will because "God reigns more benevolently in America because unmediated by intervening kings."[132] If that meant that the bonds between church and state had to be forcibly broken through bloody revolution, then so be it—without the use of its reason, mankind was doomed to an oppressive, Godless existence. In choosing Independence, America had returned to first principles of both politics and religion.

As a devout deist Paine was the natural enemy of churches that insisted upon the necessity of intermediaries to establish a relationship with God. The Church of England and its rival the Roman Catholic Church were both such institutions. Paine believed that an individual could only discover God through reason and scientific study, therefore any other method used to establish a relationship with God was heretical. In Paine's theology, established churches were engaged in a fraudulent conspiracy, and the sins of both the English and Catholic Churches were compounded when they mingled religion with politics: "It has been the scheme of the Christian church . . . to hold man in ignorance of the Creator, as it is of governments to hold him in ignorance of his rights. The systems of one are as false as those of the other, and are calculated for mutual support."[133] Paine believed that nations like Britain and France used religion as a means of social control, and their established churches regulated the behavior of their citizens through priests and rituals. Once a people's ability to reason had been stripped away by the Church, Paine concluded, they were more easily manipulated by their government. No longer thinking for themselves or questioning policies, people blindly followed the dictates of priests and bishops.[134]

Perhaps because his motives had been so clear and his methodology so scientific, Paine could not have predicted the complex reaction of Americans to *Common Sense*. When Paine freed American minds from the chains of monarchy through his arguments in *Common Sense,* not only did Americans choose a true system of government, but they opened themselves up to new possibilities of spiritual exploration as well. In *Common Sense* Paine had stressed the need for religious freedom and the separation of church and state in the new republic.[135] Yet even Paine was surprised when America's independence from Britain led to the disestablishment of the Church of England and a national push for religious freedom. The new southern states immediately severed their ties with the Anglican Church, and five of the thirteen colonies adopted new state constitutions in 1776 that contained Bills of Rights guaranteeing liberty of conscience to their citizens.[136] For Paine, these new changes in America were clear evidence of the power of reason.

These new changes in the religious and political landscape of America was nothing short of miraculous to Paine. He had not foreseen the potential of *Common Sense* to work such a powerful transformation upon the minds of his readers, nor had he envisioned the powerful impact his success would have upon his own political philosophy. In fact, the success of *Common Sense* yielded for Paine a third and final life-altering epiphany. In his introduction to *The Age of Reason,* Paine's "Profession of Faith" ended with the following statement of purpose:

> Soon after I published the pamphlet 'Common Sense,' in America, I saw the exceeding probability that a revolution in the system of government would be followed by a revolution in the system of religion. The adulterous connection of church and state, wherever it has taken place, whether Jewish, Christian or Turkish, has so effectually prohibited by pains and penalties every discussion upon established creeds, and upon first principles of religion, that until the system of government should be changed, those subjects could not be brought fairly and openly before the world; but that whenever this should be done, a revolution in the system of religion would follow. Human inventions and priest-craft would be detected; and man would return to the pure, unmixed and unadulterated belief of one God, and no more.[137]

Here, in this confession from *The Age of Reason,* is the sum of Paine's political career following *Common Sense*. From the moment he realized that it was possible to bring people to a correct understanding of politics and religion, Paine's mission was clear: to return mankind "to the pure, unmixed and unadulterated belief of one God, and no more" through political revolution. By severing the "adulterous connection" between church and state through political rebellion, allowing people to reason freely, Paine believed that mankind would naturally revert to deism. This became his quest: to convert people to deism by "liberating humanity from ages of oppressive control by the despotic triumvirate of scripture, church, and state."[138] In his latter years Paine proudly asserted that "My motive and object in all my political works, beginning with *Common Sense* . . . have been to rescue man from tyranny and false systems and false principles of government and enable him to be free."[139] Thus the ultimate motive and direction of Paine's political activism changed dramatically following *Common Sense*. This change in Paine's philosophy has been best summarized by R.F. Smith: "Revolution was to be the salvation of the world."[140]

The significance of Paine's revelation in *The Age of Reason* is manifold. In a broad sense it completes the ideological and philosophical portrait of Paine that scholars have been attempting to paint for centuries. The pieces of the puzzle are all finally in place, and a number of startling, historically significant discoveries have been revealed. Perhaps the simplest, most immediate deduction from Paine's statement in *The Age of Reason* is the fact that it can be clearly discerned that he was a deist in 1776. He confessed that in 1776 he wanted to return mankind to the "pure, unmixed and unadulterated belief of one God and no more." Paine's deist beliefs were therefore present at the time he wrote *Common Sense*. Finally, and most importantly, Paine's admission officially links his religious beliefs with his political activism beginning with *Common Sense*. As he declared in the second *Crisis* paper in 1777, "What I write is pure nature, and my pen and my soul have ever gone together."[141]

Chapter Five
"One God and No More": The Strange Mission of Thomas Paine

No one, especially Thomas Paine, could have predicted the profound impact *Common Sense* would have upon the American psyche in January 1776. In a matter of weeks, the pamphlet set the colonies aflame with its dramatic and urgent call for revolution. After he published *Common Sense* Paine's initial shock regarding its success was replaced by the knowledge that he had the power to change the way that people thought with mere words. Not only that, but he believed that his success was the result of Americans using their capacity for reason to recognize the irrationality of remaining in the British Empire. This triumph of reason, as Paine perceived it, worked a curious and significant change upon Paine's own mind: he determined that it was possible to create entire nations of devout, democratic, deists through political revolution.

Paine's missionary zeal was cleverly disguised to his readers (he did not publicly admit his goals until 1794) yet his political writing from 1776 until his death in 1809 bear witness to the fact that Paine never strayed from this ultimate purpose. Most polemicists, it would be fair to argue, change their style or content over time either consciously or sub-consciously as a response to any number of personal, rhetorical, or political changes at work around them. This is simply not true of Paine. His arguments were an attempt to convert his readership to a new truth; a truth that embraced both republicanism and deism. The result of Paine's new focus was a remarkable, unmistakable continuity in his writing. In fact, Paine's confession in *The Age of Reason* "establishes a continuum unifying his career as a political writer from 'Common Sense' to [*The Age of Reason*] in terms of distinguishing between false connections and true connections."[1] Paine's style was so consistent that Cecilia Kenyon argues, "One of the remarkable things about *The Rights of Man,* written almost fifteen years after *Common Sense,* is that . . . it could just as easily have been written in 1776."[2] Without a doubt this continuity of Paine's thought and rhetoric in his works from *Common Sense* to *The Age of Reason* is the clearest proof of his mission to instigate revolution and spread deism throughout the western world. This immutability was largely due to the fact that, as Eric Foner astutely observes, "from the end of 1776 to the end of his life, the hallmarks of Paine's political and social outlook remained remarkably constant."[3] Whether he was advocating a tax in Rhode Island, fomenting revolution in France, or denouncing paper currency, his methods and arguments were always the same. Many of Paine's political works are essentially rhetorical echoes of *Common Sense,* and are evidence of Paine's steadfast devotion to a single cause; a reflection of his singular devotion to one omnipotent God. This simple piety led Paine to instigate one historically significant revolution and become the tireless defender of another.

During the French Revolution Paine declared, "when a man in a long cause attempts to steer his course by any thing else than some polar truth or principle, he is sure to be lost."[4] Paine's polar truth was his deism; it taught him not only how to correctly conceive his relationship with God but also how to properly worship Him. Religious worship for a true deist, according to Paine, "consists in contemplating the power, wisdom and benignity of the Deity in all His works, and in endeavoring to imitate Him in everything moral, scientific and mechanical."[5] Paine's personal contemplation of God's power through his study of the sciences eventually led him to adopt the belief system he outlined in *The Age of Reason*. His imitation of his Creator led him to form a political ideology that mirrored his deist theology. It was these polar principles of his deism which Paine used to guide him in his attempt to "return mankind to the pure, unmixed unadulterated belief of one God and no more."[6]

Paine's religious principles have been discussed at length throughout this work, but it is important to remember that for Paine reason was essential to discovering God. Reason was also the foundation of science and scientific study which taught mankind the true theology. This theology in turn instructed mankind that the Creation was simple, ordered, universal, egalitarian, and a reflection of God's benevolence. Paine's political philosophy also embraced these concepts. Just as mankind could not discover false theology without reason, neither would they be able to distinguish between a false monarchical government and a true republican one. Paine likewise challenged his readers to study politics scientifically; to understand that simple, ordered, rational governments were best and that the struggle for universal equality was mandated by God. Moreover, God's "benignity," according to Paine, required reciprocation. Man's duty to God was simple: as God was benevolent to mankind, so should mankind should be benevolent to one another. Ultimately Paine came to the conclusion that political revolution was the most benevolent act of all. Replacing false systems with true ones, encouraging mankind to use their reason to discover not only the truth about politics, but also the truth about God—this was his mission.

"It is only by the exercise of reason that man can discover God." [7]

In Paine's system of beliefs, reason was the cornerstone upon which his deism was built. Reason was God's gift to man, thus Paine placed his unconditional trust in its ability to show him—and all of mankind—right from wrong. "Take away that reason," Paine insisted, "and [man] would be incapable of understanding anything."[8] This included, of course, the ability to distinguish between false political systems and true ones. According to Paine, "the most formidable weapon against errors of every kind is reason. I have never used any other and I trust I never shall."[9] In *The Rights of Man* Paine reiterated that when it came to politics, he "neither read books, nor studied other people's opinions. I thought for myself."[10] Because reason was essential in politics, Paine's rhetoric instilled in his readers the necessity of placing reason above all things. Doing so would remove any ingrained "prejudices" or other irrational thought processes and awaken mankind to a new way of thinking. Once Paine taught men to think rationally, he surmised, they would use reason as their guide and revolt against false governments and false religion.

To change the way his readers thought, Paine first had to demonstrate that their current method of deliberation was in fact irrational and illogical. In *Common Sense,* Paine helped to bring about this change in thinking habits by informing the colonists, "I bring reason to your ears, and, in language as plain as A, B, C, hold truth to your eyes."[11] In order to detect a false system of government, it was critical for people to first "trace to the root and origin of things."[12] "If we reason to the root of things," Paine argued in the first *Crisis* paper, Americans "shall find no difference" between an army of murderers and one "brutish" king.[13] Just as he had beseeched Americans to seek the root cause of their oppression, Paine instructed his French audience over a decade later to "lay the axe to the root" and form a new, more humane system of government.[14]

When individuals permitted their emotions to rule, or strayed from their reason, trouble ensued. "When men have departed from the right way," Paine declared in 1776, "it is no wonder that they stumble and fall."[15] The same could be said of governments. Writing about Britain's new Coalition Parliament a decade later, Paine observed that it appeared to him to be "a nation under the government of temper, instead of a fixed and steady principle."[16] However, if an individual "permits his reason to act," Paine declared, "his rule of moral life will follow of course."[17] By exercising their reason and reasoning to the root cause of problems, mankind would never be led astray in the quest for political and religious liberty: "when precedents fail to spirit us, we must return to first principles of things for information, and *think,* as if we were the *first men* that *thought.*"[18] The same was equally true for governments that had strayed from the correct path. Great changes could be made by introducing reason into politics. Paine argued, "the greatest forces that can be brought into the field of revolutions, are reason and common interest."[19] Reason was therefore more than a mere thought process for Paine; it was perhaps the most potent ammunition people could employ in the fight for their rights.

Perhaps more practically, by using "reason and discussion" as "weapons," a rational mind would be able to see through the social and political controls imposed upon it by monarchy and an established church.[20] It was of course in the interest of governments who controlled their citizens through tradition and religion to keep them from thinking independently. In Paine's view, eliminating these controls by relying upon reason would allow people to distinguish between false systems and true ones. The first step in this process was to remove the veils of national tradition and religious indoctrination in order to shed the light of reason upon them. In 1776 Paine warned the American colonists that they suffered under the national delusion that monarchy was worthy of reverence and obedience. Paine bemoaned, "Alas! we have long been led away by ancient prejudices and made large sacrifices to superstition."[21] This left Americans vulnerable to oppressive parliamentary measures and warfare by the very monarch the colonists had been taught to revere. "I know it is difficult to get over local or long standing prejudices," Paine empathized, but pleaded with his reader to "divest himself of prejudice and prepossession, and suffer his reason and his feelings to determine for themselves."[22] Once divested of such predilection, his audience would understand that "a long habit of not thinking a thing *wrong,* gives it a superficial appearance of being *right,*" and they would be better able to choose between the false and the true.[23] During the French Revolution, Paine again argued that the monarchical system would crumble if people would only analyze it rationally. "The hazard to which this office is exposed in all countries is not from anything that can happen to the man," Paine insisted, "but from what may happen to the nation,—the danger of its coming to its senses."[24] "It is time that nations should be rational," Paine avowed, "and not be governed like animals for the pleasure of their riders."[25]

In his *Letter to the Abbé Raynal* (1782), a refutation of Raynal's history of the American Revolution, Paine explained that putting an end to such detrimental habits ultimately led to American Independence: "As the mind closed itself toward England, it opened itself toward the world, and our prejudices like our oppressions, underwent, though less observed, a mental examination; until we found the former as inconsistent with reason and benevolence, as the latter were repugnant to our civil and political rights."[26] Paine's *Letter*, written before the Revolution officially ended, further argued that "our style and manner of thinking have undergone a revolution of the country."[27] Free from monarchical rule and established church doctrine, Americans "see with other eyes . . . hear with other ears; and think with other thoughts."[28] Paine explained to the French historian that the United States had become so enlightened that "we are really now another people, and cannot again go back to ignorance and prejudice."[29] "We can look back at our own prejudices, as if they had been the prejudices of another people," Paine proudly proclaimed, because "the mind once enlightened cannot again become dark."[30] Paine again echoed this sentiment in another revolt against monarchy, the French Revolution. "No man is prejudiced in favor of a thing, knowing it to be wrong," he declared in *The Rights of Man*, "he is attached to it on the belief of its being right; and when he sees it is not so, the prejudice will be gone."[31] In 1791 Paine looked forward to a time when, like the Americans and the French, the rest of mankind would achieve enlightenment, and "have pride or shame enough to blush at being thus imposed upon."[32] When mankind began to use reason as their guide they could be assured of both political liberty and religious freedom.

Paine had already witnessed how dramatic an effect the employment of reason had upon one nation, the United States. Two years after the publication of *Common Sense* Paine wrote, "it is the practice of the new world, America, to make men as wise as possible, so that their knowledge being complete, they may be *rationally* governed."[33] Paine was pleased that the same changes wrought in Americans' manner of thinking also seemed to occur in France. The French Constitution in Paine's estimation, reflected "a *rational* order of things."[34] As in the American Revolution, this new method of governing by reason meant that "principles humanize with forms," and "forms grow out of principles," ensuring the growth of a truly democratic republic in France.[35] Great changes had been wrought in the world since Paine had brought reason to the ears of Americans and the world in 1776, and he was pleased that in 1791 "The insulted German and the enslaved Spaniard, the Russ and the Pole are beginning to think."[36] Everywhere men were beginning to use their reason, and Paine welcomed the possibility of future revolutions. "The present age will hereafter merit to be called the Age of Reason," he believed, "and the present generation will appear to the future as the Adam of the new world."[37] "Reason and discussion will soon brings things right," Paine confidently boasted, "however wrong they may begin."[38] Paine had already witnessed two nations employ their reason to establish true systems of government; he rejoiced at the example they provided for the rest of mankind: "the peoples of France, England and America, who are at once enlightened and enlightening, will be able to serve as models of good government to the universe and will also have sufficient influence to compel the practical enforcement of it everywhere."[39] With reason as their guide, mankind would be receptive to the concepts of both republicanism and deism. Perhaps more significantly—for the purpose of creating a religious revolution—mankind would now be able to comprehend science. Without reason man could not comprehend science, and without science there would be no theology: "that which is called natural philosophy . . . is the study of the works of God, and of the power and wisdom of God in His works, and is the true theology."[40]

"for the creator of man is the creator of science, and it is through that medium that man can see God, as it were, face to face"[41]

Paine always viewed politics and political situations scientifically and encouraged his readers to do the same. Like so many Enlightenment thinkers of his day, the laws of science and nature were God's laws, and Paine's writings attest to this fact. For example in his earliest work, the *Case of the Officers of Excise,* Paine declared "No laws compel like nature."[42] Likewise in *Common Sense,* Paine made several appeals to natural law affirming that "he who takes nature for his guide, is not easily beaten out of his argument."[43] Ever the radical empiricist, Paine challenged Edmund Burke to produce the British Constitution. "If he cannot," Paine argued, "we may fairly conclude, that though it has been so much talked about, no such thing as a constitution exists."[44] Moreover, Paine also employed scientific imagery or scientific language to illustrate his points. In *Common Sense* he argued that people were naturally inclined to be social because individuals could not provide for all of their needs. "Necessity, like a gravitating power," created a compulsion for individuals to seek the company of others.[45] Paine made the same argument over a decade later during the French Revolution, arguing that the compulsion to form society operated upon individuals "as naturally as gravitation acts to a center."[46] Such use of scientific language and imagery was meant by Paine to be an effective teaching tool. Imitating God in all things "scientific" meant for Paine applying God's laws to temporal as well as spiritual matters. This was true most specifically in the realm of politics—Paine's chosen profession.

He purposely designed his political ideology and prose to reflect God's laws as demonstrated to him through science and expressed so plainly in *The Age of Reason*. The five most significant principles that Paine drew from his studies of science were embodied in both his theology and his political philosophy: order, simplicity, egalitarianism, universality, and humanitarianism.

"The Plan and Order of the Universe"[47]

Paine's demands for a political system that was ordered (ordered according to God's laws) were characteristic of many Enlightenment thinkers. According to Eric Foner, "Like the Newtonian universe, the natural state of society was harmony and order. It was government . . . which deranged this natural order."[48] Paine blamed monarchical government—an unnatural system—for corrupting not only politics but also religion. To return mankind to a natural state of order, Paine began by deposing kings. His personal quest for order and simplicity began with America and *Common Sense*. He described independence as the path of least resistance for the colonists, and therefore the correct one. "The more simple any thing is," Paine explained, "the less liable it is to be disordered."[49] He further added that "independence, being a single simple line" was preferable to "reconciliation, a matter exceedingly perplexed and complicated."[50] The reason for Paine's faith in simplicity in matters of government was because he believed simplicity was a "principle in nature" and therefore an appropriate model for politics.[51] The same was true for the concept of order.

Order meant more than simply God's natural order; for Paine, it also entailed the need for people to develop a "system" that would both maintain order and keep the system from becoming disordered. Finding the root cause of problems, for example, was "the only way to become right, when we are got systematically wrong."[52] Ever the scientist, in the tenth number of the *Crisis* papers, Paine was moved to remark, "I love method, because I see and am convinced of its beauty and advantage."[53] Without method, "everything becomes embarrassed and difficult."[54] This was true not only in large matters like revolution, but also in smaller affairs like taxation. In 1782 Paine attempted to simplify for Americans the new nation's pressing economic concerns by explaining that "we must come down to order, system and method."[55] Unfortunately, as Paine lamented five years later, "right by chance and wrong by system are so frequently seen in the political world."[56] The danger of disorder was obvious for Paine: political upheaval and turmoil. The American Revolution provided clear proof of this:

> The American war was prosecuted at a great expense, on the publicly declared opinion that retaining America was necessary to the existence

of England, but America being now separated from England, the present politics are that she is better off without her than with her. Both these cannot be true, and their contradictions to each other shows want of system.[57]

Paine similarly warned the people of Britain in *The Rights of Man* that social reform would not be enough: "the defect lies in the system. The foundation and superstructure of the government is bad."[58] Correcting the underlying problems would mean aligning them with the natural order that God intended.

Because Paine was "confident" that "God governs the world," he insisted that governments imitate that divine stewardship.[59] Paine warned Americans in *Common Sense* that they had incurred the wrath of God because they supported monarchy—a system of government in defiance of God's natural law. Paine therefore applauded the French in *The Rights of Man* for revolting against their king. "It is by distortedly exalting some men, that others are distortedly debased," he argued, "till the whole is out of nature."[60] It was this "unnatural" element of monarchy that Paine had condemned during the American Revolution, and likewise during the French Revolution. "Nature is orderly in all her works," Paine insisted, "but [monarchy] counteracts nature."[61] The purest, most natural form of government for Paine was a republic, because "the representative system is always parallel with the order and immutable laws of nature."[62] Moreover, he characterized the political revolutions in both America and France as "a renovation of the natural order of things."[63] Revolt from monarchy and restoration of the natural order included for Paine restoring the principle of equality to mankind.

"I believe in the equality of man"[64]

Paine's fight for equality included both a recognition of the equality of individuals as well as a fight for equal political rights. The equality of individuals required no proof; for Paine it was enough to remind his readers that "all men are born equal," because "every child in the world must be considered as deriving its existence from God."[65] It was on this principle that he opposed the institution of monarchy during both the American and French Revolutions. In *Common Sense* Paine argued that "no truly natural or religious reason" could justify "the distinction of man into KINGS and SUBJECTS."[66] "Nature" had separated individuals by gender, and "heaven" differentiated between "good and bad;" all other distinctions were human constructs.[67] Paine reiterated this argument in *The Rights of Man* when he declared, "whether in heaven or in hell . . . the good and the bad are the only distinctions."[68]

Because individuals were created equal, it followed necessarily for Paine that according to God's laws they were entitled to equal rights. Equality of rights, according to Paine, was a self-evident truth: "There are points so clear and definitive in themselves that they suffer by any attempt to prove them. He who would suffer to prove the being of a God, would deserve to be turned out of company for insulting his maker. Therefore what I have or may yet offer on the equality of rights is not by way of proof but illustration."[69] Written in 1778, Paine's "Serious Address to the People of Pennsylvania" forcefully argued that rights and freedoms existed in "perfect equality," and this equality guaranteed "security to all and every part of society."[70] However, Paine reserved his most thorough explication of equality and political rights for his discussion of the French Revolution in the aptly titled pamphlet *The Rights of Man*. It was in this work that Paine laid bare his notions of equality and the connection between political rights and divine inheritance. Countering Edmund Burke's historical justification of monarchy in *Reflections on the Revolution in France* (1790) Paine argued, "The error of those who reason by precedents drawn from antiquity, respecting the rights of man, is that they do not go far enough into antiquity."[71] According to Paine, men were created by God as perfect equals, with equal natural rights. This "divine principle" could not be altered by men, no matter how far they had strayed from the original intent of "the Maker of man."[72] Paine fought the oppression of man's equal rights because he believed that what affected one man, affected all mankind. As James Betka observes, "his 'natural equality' of all men which had dictated a need for government due to a common propensity for sin, was also the basis for universal natural rights."[73] It was this broad worldview—this universality—that led to Paine's involvement in two world revolutions.[74]

"God speaketh universally to man"[75]

Paine's belief in the principle of universality was directly tied to his deist beliefs. Paine objected to the Bible's designation as the Word of God and instead believed that "THE WORD OF GOD IS THE CREATION WE BEHOLD."[76] Because the Bible had been transcribed by men and translated into a select few languages, Paine refused to consider it as holy writ. Moreover, such a book was necessarily subject to human error, therefore its contents could not be trusted. Paine believed instead that God had directly revealed his Word to all of his creation in a language all could understand. The Creation "is an ever-existing original which every man can read," Paine insisted.[77] He further asserted that "The Creation speaks a universal language" which "preaches to all nations and to all worlds."[78] Much of this attitude toward the Bible and the Creation was due, of course, to

Paine's study of the sciences and the orrery. His study of a miniature universe and the laws which governed it led to Paine's belief that everyone could study the Creation in a similar fashion and reach the same conclusions. It was a "language" that "all nations and all worlds" could comprehend equally. As he expressed in his *Letter to the Abbé Raynal*, "Science, the partisan of no country, but the beneficent patroness of all, has liberally opened a temple where all may meet."[79] In his "imitation" of God's universal revelation and natural laws Paine attempted to tailor his rhetoric and arguments to reach as broad an audience as possible. He likewise engaged himself in any cause that he considered to be the cause of all mankind.

In his introduction to *Common Sense*, Paine presented the colonists' struggle as not merely a local rebellion but a global fight for the rights of all mankind. "Many circumstances have, and will arise, which are not local, but universal," Paine wrote, "and through which the principles of all lovers of mankind are affected."[80] He expressed a similar sentiment two years later in his seventh *American Crisis* paper. Addressed to "the People of England," Paine clarified for his international audience the reason for his involvement in the revolution: "Perhaps it may be said that I live in America, and write this from interest. To this I reply, that my principle is universal. My attachment is to all the world, and not to any particular part."[81] "Universal empire is the prerogative of the writer," Paine argued, because "his concerns are with all mankind."[82] Paine was drawn to the American struggle because of the "universality of their cause" and the "universal foundation" of equal rights he hoped to establish through revolution.[83]

Paine's convictions about universality led him to conclude that a broader worldview was a necessary component for the creation of a true system of government. For example, the United States had undergone a complete "renovation" and shed itself of limiting prejudices to embrace a more enlightened global perspective and destiny. France had also adopted a more enlightened form of government complete with "a system of principles as universal as truth and the existence of man."[84] America's former colonial ruler, England, had not—and thus remained in the dark politically. "A total reformation is wanted in England," Paine proclaimed in 1782.[85] England "wants an expanded mind—a heart which embraces the universe."[86] Britain's failure to embrace the universe exposed a deeper, spiritual flaw for Paine: "The true ideas of a great nation, is that which extends and promotes the principles of universal society—whose mind rises above the atmosphere of local thoughts, and considers mankind, of whatever nation or profession they may be, as the work of one Creator."[87] Clearly not only was universality a key component of political systems, but also a further reflection of Paine's deist beliefs. Religion was, as Paine explained to Raynal, the process by which the "universal family of mankind" directed its worship "to the divine object of all adoration."[88] Paine's own worship of God (as defined by his deism) proved to be the primary motivating factor behind his reluctant entrance into public life and his push for political revolution.

"the only idea we can have of serving God is that of contributing to the happiness of the living creation that God has made. This cannot be done by retiring ourselves from the society of the world and spending a recluse life in selfish devotion."[89]

Paine's political life and mission was driven by his confirm belief that "religious duties consist in doing justice, loving mercy, and endeavoring to make our fellow creatures happy."[90] For Paine, practicing humanitarianism was more than a political tool; it was a mandate from God: "It is as if He had said to the inhabitants of this globe that we call ours, 'I have made an earth for man to dwell upon, and I have rendered the starry heavens visible, to teach him science and the arts. He can now provide for his own comfort, AND LEARN FROM MY MUNIFICENCE TO ALL, TO BE KIND TO EACH OTHER.'"[91] Although this particular component of Paine's political ideology was not explicitly outlined until *The Age of Reason* in 1794, Paine's humanitarianism and his attempt to properly worship his God were clearly evident decades earlier. In fact, the above quotation closely resembles a passage from the eighth number of the *Crisis*, written fourteen years earlier:

> In addition to this, it may be remarked, that men who study any universal science, the principles of which are universally known, or admitted, and applied without distinction to the common benefit of all countries, obtain thereby a larger share of philanthropy than those who only study national arts and improvements. Natural philosophy, mathematics and astronomy, carry the mind from the country to the creation, and give it a fitness suited to the extent. It was not Newton's honor, neither could it be his pride, that he was an Englishman, but that he was a philosopher: the heavens had liberated him from the prejudices of an island, and science had expanded his soul as boundless as his studies.[92]

Quite obviously, as Harry Hayden Clark observed, "scientific deism directly motivated [Paine's] vast humanitarian interests."[93]

Because of Paine's deist beliefs he abhorred any system, government, or individual that he considered to be unjust or unfeeling. In his political career he sought to expose such flaws and "teach governments humanity."[94] Paine's first political work, the *Case of the Officers of Excise,* was motivated by this simple principle. Paine tried to communicate to Parliament the way "the language of poverty strikes the heart."[95] Both the American and French Revolutions provided Paine with the opportunity to rid the world of compassionless monarchies and replace them with republican governments that acted with their hearts, rather than their heads. During the American Revolution Paine insisted that he was motivated by "a fixed, immovable hatred I have, and ever had, to cruel men and cruel measures."[96] He similarly confessed in both the *Crisis* and *The Rights of Man* that "It is the nature of compassion to associate with misfortune."[97] It was Edmund Burke's complete lack of empathy for the French cause which prompted Paine to inquire in *The Rights of Man,* "Is this the language of a rational man? Is it the language of a heart feeling as it ought to feel for the rights and happiness of the human race?"[98] Appealing to his readers' feelings and generating their contempt or anger at cruel men and cruel measures was a key component in Paine's goal to create more human governments. There was however, another (more significant) practical component as well.

Merely exposing corruption and hardship was not enough for Paine. In order to truly perform his obligations as a deist, Paine had to actually work for the greater good. Paine's political activism therefore contained more than mere philosophy; it usually involved working to make changes for the better, or giving his readers the tools or blueprints to make those changes themselves. This aspect of Paine's philanthropy prompted historian Darrel Abel to assert that Paine was "impatient of theory unless it could be made of immediate service to men."[99] *Common Sense* provided Americans with all the information they needed to see the evil of monarchy and the righteousness of republicanism. Paine used *Common Sense* to instigate revolution to ensure that monarchy and the injustices it had created in America were abolished. During the Revolution and the years immediately following Independence, Paine expressed a need for humanitarianism in government and clearly defined the role of a republic.

In his pamphlet "Public Good," published late in 1780, Paine argued that ratification of the Articles of Confederation was critical to maintaining unity during the revolution and a necessary step towards refocusing the energies of the Continental Congress on the long war. Ratification was also important because it had the potential to create a government that could secure "the mutual happiness and united interests of the States of America."[100] The United States needed to stop debating ratification and adopt the articles because "the governing rule of right and of mutual good must in all public cases finally preside."[101] The disunity and disharmony created in the wake of the debates surrounding ratification threatened the welfare of the citizens of the United States, therefore adopting the articles was the best solution, no matter the consequences to individual states.[102]

In political struggles like the Confederation ratification debate, Paine almost always fought for Americans as a whole, rather than individuals or states. In 1783, shortly after the Treaty of Paris was negotiated, Paine wrote "it is the general good, the happiness of the whole, that has ever been my object."[103] A few years later Paine clearly defined the concept of "public good." He explained that public good was "the good of every individual collected."[104] In his article "Dissertations on Government" Paine argued that "the foundation-principle of public good is justice, and wherever justice is impartially administered, the public good is promoted."[105] As a deist Paine was obligated to secure the happiness of his fellow man; he thus promoted the concept of public good because "as it is to the good of every man that no injustice be done to him so likewise it is good that the principle which secures him should not be violated in the person of the other."[106] It was the violation of this foundation-principle and a fundamental inattention to public good by the British government that led Paine to demand humanitarian reform on an unprecedented scale.

During the American Revolution Paine expressed his demands for humanitarianism in government, but it was not until the French Revolution that he organized his desires into a cohesive program. What Paine demanded in *The Rights of Man* was nothing less than the creation of the welfare state in Great Britain. Paine's ambitious program of social reform, designed to completely restructure the function of Parliament, is perhaps the best example of the influence of Paine's religious worship on his political activism. In fact, before he professed his religious beliefs in *The Age of Reason*, Paine declared in Part I of *The Rights of Man*, "The duty of man ... is plain and simple, and consists but of two points. His duty to God, which every man must feel; and with respect to his neighbor, to do as he would be done by."[107] While the first part of *The Rights of Man* was largely a critique of Edmund Burke and an explanation of natural rights and natural law, Part II "marked a turning point in the history of English radicalism."[108] Eric Foner argues that "Paine was the first to provide a social program for the English reform movement" which made the movement "meaningful to the daily lives of the middle class and workingmen."[109] It was in fact Paine's concern for what Norman Sykes called "the condition of the people" that motivated him to approach humanitarian reform more aggressively during the French Revolution.[110]

The birth of viable republics in America and France that operated according to natural law was further evidence for Paine that monarchy was an evil institution. Paine distinguished for his readers the difference between the newly formed virtuous republics of America and France and their profane counterparts (chiefly Great Britain). According to Paine, the existence of these ancién regimes could not have begun "by any other means than a total violation of every principle, sacred and moral."[111] "The horrid scene that is now acting by the English Government in the East Indies," Paine wrote, "is fit only to be told of Goths and Vandals."[112] "Destitute of principle," the Goths—like the English—"robbed and tortured the world which they were incapable of enjoying."[113] The obvious solution to ridding the world of such inhumanity was political revolution. "Revolutions," Paine instructed his readers, "have for their object a change in the moral condition of governments."[114] It was "government founded on a moral theory, on a system of universal peace" that he saw reflected in America and hopefully France.[115] He reminded his readers that it was for this reason that he became involved in politics: "I saw an opportunity in which I thought I could do some good, and I followed exactly what my heart dictated."[116] Paine's heart led him to France where he again found an outlet for his humanitarian impulses. Paine avowed, "Independence is my happiness . . . my country is the world, and my religion is to do good."[117]

For Paine, the best expression of his "religion" was to propose a complete reformation of England along humanitarian guidelines. Part II of *The Rights of Man* contained a comprehensive program of tax reform and government spending which were designed to enhance the lives of the most wretched in Britain while also securing the future of generations as yet unborn. Paine had himself been a victim of Britain's socioeconomic strictures, and sought to eradicate what he deemed inherent and dangerous flaws in that system. He hoped that by attacking the English system of government, he could set an example for the nascent French republic. Paine argued, "it is not worth making changes or revolutions, unless it be for some great national benefit."[118] Reminiscent of his argument in "Public Good," Paine informed his readers in *The Rights of Man* that a republican government was "government established and conducted for the interest of the public, as well individually as collectively."[119] Its sole object was "the general happiness."[120] England had instituted a constitutional monarchy which supported the happiness of its sovereign and aristocracy while ignoring the needs of the majority of its citizenry. For Paine, there was no better example of this flaw in Britain than the king's salary: one million pounds per year, paid by his subjects. "It is inhuman to talk of a million sterling a year," Paine scolded, "while thousands who are forced to contribute thereto, are pining with want, and struggling with misery."[121] Government should concern itself with the welfare of its people, "making provisions for the instruction of youth, and support of age."[122] Humanitarian aims should be of primary importance to governments because they had the power to end "profligacy," "despair," and to produce "general happiness."[123] In *The Rights of Man* Paine attempted to demonstrate how a nation like Britain could reorganize itself fiscally to benefit the nation both morally and socially.

Having already established the ideological principles necessary in a republic, Paine proceeded to outline in *The Rights of Man* "the ways and means of rendering them into practise."[124] Paine mathematically calculated (using published data) the population of Great Britain, the national revenue from taxation, and national expenditures. He then proceeded to demonstrate how, by a reallocation of funds, it was possible for England to provide for the welfare of its citizens and rid itself of its considerable national debt:

> The plan is easy of practise. It does not embarrass trade by a sudden interruption in the order of taxes, but effects the relief by changing the application of them; and the money necessary for the purpose can be drawn from the excise collections, which are made eight times a year in every market town in England.[125]

Paine also proposed—for perhaps the first time in England's history—a progressive income tax.[126] He conceded that his calculations for the new tax would not generate considerable funds, but was instead motivated primarily by "the justice of the measure."[127] Paine bemoaned the fact that "the aristocracy has screened itself too much" and hoped that the new tax scheme would "restore a part of the lost equilibrium."[128] The new progressive tax (based largely on land holdings) plus the reallocation of funds gave Paine enough money to completely restructure public spending.

"The first step" of Paine's new program was "to make a remission of taxes to the poor" and to "abolish the poor-rates entirely."[129] This (according to Paine's calculations) would create a surplus out of which every poor family would receive a stipend of four pounds a year for every child under the age of fourteen.[130] Paine reasoned that so many families were poor because of the financial burden of raising children. "Were twenty shillings to be given to every woman immediately on the birth of a child," Paine posited, "it might relieve a great deal of distress."[131] For those adults who chose to start families regardless of the financial strain, Paine felt the government was obligated to help them. Parents would receive the four-pound stipend on the condition that they sent their children to school "to learn reading, writing, and common arithmetic."[132] "By adopting this method, not only the poverty of the parents will be relieved," Paine contended, but "ignorance will be banished from the rising generation."[133] Moreover, because of this new educated generation of Britons, "the number of poor will hereafter become less, because their abilities, by the aid of education, will be greater."[134] For those families "not properly of the class of poor" who had difficulty providing for their children's education he suggested an annual stipend of ten shillings for six years plus a small allowance for paper and spelling books.[135] This would provide for schooling for six months of the year for England's middling class.

While education was of considerable importance to Paine, providing for the elderly was also a principal concern. Paine divided the elderly into two classes: those who were between fifty and sixty years of age, and those who were sixty or older.[136] (Paine was fifty-five when he published the second part of *The Rights of Man*.) Paine proposed a system of social security, to be paid for by revenue from taxation. He demanded that citizens between the ages of fifty and sixty should be paid an annual sum of six pounds; after sixty it would increase to ten pounds.[137] Paine insisted, moreover, that every Briton—regardless of sex or occupation—should be paid a stipend once they reached fifty years of age. He included in his enumeration "husbandmen, common laborers, journeymen of every trade and their wives, sailors, and disbanded soldiers, worn-out servants of both sexes, and poor widows."[138] Although he feared that his detractors would claim that his pension system was "charity," Paine instead proclaimed it as "a right."[139] "Every person in England, male or female," Paine explained, "pays on an average of taxes, two pounds eight shillings and sixpence per annum from the day of his (or her) birth."[140] Paine simply wanted to return that money to the citizens of Britain when it could be of most use to them, and lessen the burden of the national treasury.

One of the greatest burdens on the national budget was London and the other major cities in Britain. London was England's center of poverty and wretchedness and thus warranted special consideration from Paine. He recommended erecting one or two buildings in the capital and other metropolitan areas that would house the poor in barrack-like conditions. Each building would house no more than 6,000 inhabitants, "without inquiring who or what they are."[141] These were not to be traditional alms-houses; rather there were conditions for habitation designed to help those in need begin to provide for themselves once again:

> that for so much or so many hours work, each person shall receive so many meals of wholesome food, and a warm lodging, at least as good as a barrack. That a certain portion of what each person's work shall be worth shall be reserved, and given to him, or her, on their going away; and that each person shall stay as long, or as short a time, or come as often as he chooses, on these conditions.[142]

Again, Paine also provided for women in his program. To a lesser extent Paine's program also sought to ease communities who were burdened with burial expenses for traveling workers who died away from home; he also demanded an end to the practice of primogeniture.[143] Paine blamed primogeniture for creating classes of poor citizens (disinherited younger sons and daughters, for example) and corrupting government through hereditary power bases. Paine had high hopes for his radical program of humanitarian aid:

> By the operation of this plan, the poor laws, those instruments of civil torture, will be superseded, and the wasteful expense of litigation prevented. The hearts of the humane will not be shocked by ragged and hungry children, and persons of seventy and eighty years of age begging for bread. The dying poor will not be dragged from place to place to breathe their last, as a reprisal of parish upon parish.
>
> Widows will have maintenance for their children, and will not be carted away, on the death of their husbands, like culprits and criminals; and children will no longer be considered as increasing the distress of their parents. The haunts of the wretched will be known, because it will be to their advantage; and the number of petty crimes, the offspring of distress and poverty, will be lessened. The poor, as well as the rich, will then be interested in the support of government, and the cause and apprehension of riots and tumults will cease.[144]

Regardless of whether or not Paine's plan ever came to fruition, he confessed that he was "fully satisfied that what I am now doing, with an endeavor to conciliate mankind, to render their condition happy . . . is acceptable in His sight and being the best service I can perform I act it cheerfully."[145]

FLAWS AND INCONSISTENCIES IN PAINE'S POLITICAL IDEOLOGY

For decades scholars have noted serious inconsistencies and flaws in Paine's attempt to transform the world through political and social revolution. Perhaps the most obvious difficulty with Paine's theory, and most often discussed among scholars, was Paine's trust in humans' capacity to reason. Because of his unwavering faith in mankind, Peter Stanlis concludes that Paine "is therefore unaware of how finite, fallible, and irrational are many of his appeals to reason and logic."[146] Paine was not alone in his misplaced trust in reason; it was characteristic of European Enlightenment thought in general. Paine, like Jefferson, believed that reason could solve everything; if people used their reason they could never be led astray either personally or politically. This is an overly optimistic view of human reason at best, and a gross misunderstanding of human nature at the worst.

Paine seemed to completely discount the fact that while everyone had the capacity to reason, the conclusions people reached about government or society would not necessarily be the same. For example, those who debated in Pennsylvania about the formation of a unicameral or bicameral system of state government undoubtedly thought that both forms were reasonable. It was naive of Paine to assume that "right-thinking men" would "reach agreement with little difficulty."[147] This attitude helps to explain why Paine was taken aback by the formation of political parties in the United States. Paine never considered who would decide what is rational and what is not; he assumed (illogically) that the truth would always be self-evident or easy to uncover. Moreover, even in the best of societies, in the best of all possible worlds, the likelihood that people would always—unfailingly—use reason to make every decision was remote at best. Although he often made appeals to people's emotions, Paine discounted the role of human emotion in decision-making. Paine's faith in human nature and its ability to always place reason above emotion was not only unfounded, it was unwarranted.

Paine's conception of human nature has also been rightfully criticized because Paine never seemed to settle upon one viewpoint. In *Common Sense* Paine argued that mankind lacked "moral virtue" and was thus compelled to form a government to restore order.[148] It was because of this flaw—that men were capable of immoral behavior—that made government a necessary evil. Yet in *The Rights of Man,* Paine contradicted this argument. He declared, "man, were he not corrupted by governments, is naturally the friend of man, and that human nature is not of itself vicious."[149] This suggests that Paine assumed that in the state of nature man's inherent nature was that of goodness, but that government had a degenerating effect upon him. (This argument also meant of course that Paine was unable to explain why governments were formed at all.) Furthermore, because Paine tended to believe that humans were basically good he assumed that humans were naturally altruistic. As Linda Kirk observes, "we smile at his optimism, and indeed his innocence in supposing that setting men free to look after themselves would somehow ensure that they looked after one another."[150]

There are likewise scholars who have difficulty reconciling Paine's deist God with the need for humanitarian philanthropy. Walter Woll wonders, "why should man be obliged to honor this supreme being by doing good to the extent of altruism?"[151] Woll makes an interesting point, but like other scholars, he has confused a theistic God with Paine's deist God. Theism is the belief in a God who is completely transcendent, utterly unknowable, and completely independent of His creation. The God of theism does not intervene in the Creation nor care, therefore the principal difficulty with the theistic deity is that there is no incentive to pray or worship God. In contrast, Paine's deist God was knowable, at least to the point of establishing God's benevolent nature. More importantly, Paine's God both watches and judges mankind and has an active role in His creation. Humanitarianism in Paine's system, therefore, was not only logical, but necessary. Nevertheless, Paine's assumption that once people became deists they would automatically become nicer and unselfish was completely illogical. Not quite as illogical, however, as Paine's notion that once people began to use reason they would automatically (or even willingly) toss aside their previously held religious convictions in favor of deism. Might not people just as easily rationalize that there is no God or that there are a hundred gods?

Another inconsistency often noted by historians is Paine's championing of the cause of religious freedom. He proclaimed in *Common Sense* that government must secure "the free exercise of religion, according to the dictates of conscience."[152] Likewise, in *The Rights of Man* Paine celebrated the fact that "the French Constitution hath abolished or renounced toleration, and intolerance also, and hath established UNIVERSAL RIGHT OF CONSCIENCE."[153] However, Paine's praise of religious freedom, and the acknowledgement of "a diversity of religious opinions" was tempered by his deist impulses.[154] In *Common Sense* he argued ironically that religious freedom "affords a larger field for our Christian kindness," which is a glaring contradiction of the principle of freedom itself.[155] Furthermore, in *The Rights of Man* Paine insisted that "the liberty of conscience which [man] claims, is not for the service of himself, but of his God."[156] Clearly Paine's definition of religious liberty did not extend to atheists. Moreover, Paine's career as a pamphleteer (in which he tried to convert the world to deism) is strong evidence that what Paine really advocated was religious tolerance— not freedom. While Paine was firmly against established churches, he based his support largely upon the fact that they stood in the way of reason and therefore deism. *The Age of Reason* is further testimony that Paine denounced any religion that was not deism. His attempt to turn France from Catholicism (or atheism) to deism is perhaps the best evidence of all that Paine never truly espoused the cause of religious freedom. While he acknowledged that he lived in a world of religious pluralism, he insisted that there was only one religion that was true—and only one religion that honored the Creator.[157]

The overarching flaw in Paine's system of beliefs, notably, was his reliance upon established Enlightenment doctrine. As Harry Hayden Clark observed,

> These major premises involve the belief . . . that an attempt to re-establish in politics and religion a lost harmony with this uniform, immutable, universal, and eternal law and order, and to modify or overthrow whatever traditional institutions have obscured this order and thrown its natural harmony into discord, will constitute progress, will radically decrease human misery.[158]

Paine's adherence to these beliefs prevented him from recognizing the complexity of human nature, the limits of reason, and the complicated nature of politics and governing. Paine naively thought that merely changing the way mankind thought would create a chain reaction whereby everything else that was wrong in a nation or a person would automatically fix itself. Republics that were always responsible and honest, nations that were all deists, and people that were always philanthropic, would be the natural result of returning mankind to first principles and God's natural order. The practical reality of life in the eighteenth-century, however, belied these assumptions. America had become a republic, and had returned to a natural form of government by the consent of the governed. Yet slavery still existed (wholly against the equality Paine advocated so eloquently) and whole segments of the population were denied the right to vote. Things had not worked themselves out naturally at all, either in America or in France. Progress had been made, but it was not the sort of progress Paine hoped for; perfection had not been attained.

The principle difficulty for Paine was that he was a "big picture" person. His focus was always upon the larger issue, or the central overarching dilemma facing mankind at any given moment. Paine believed that if the larger issue or problem could be fixed, then everything else would either fall into place, or work itself out according to the natural order. In America in 1776, for example, the larger issue was the oppression of the colonists by King and Parliament. The solution was simple: declare independence. For seven years Paine worked to achieve independence, being always sure to maintain that as his primary goal. When Pennsylvania had difficulties forming a new state constitution and it threatened the unity of the colonies, Paine urged the voters to choose the proposed constitution. Whatever flaws or problems the politicians had with the draft were irrelevant; ratification was necessary so they could get back to the business of conducting the war. Paine rarely turned his attention to the more detailed questions of governance (slavery? voting rights?) but rather left those to be discussed after the war was over. Once America achieved independence Paine sometimes—but not often—engaged in the minutiae of daily political issues in the United States. He wrote occasionally against issues like paper currency (he preferred God's natural minerals like gold and silver) but in general was dismayed by the fact that America had not become the republican utopia that he predicted.

Perfecting English society had also been a concern of Paine's, as his social welfare program in *The Rights of Man* illustrates. However, even that plan was contingent upon Britain completely restructuring its government. As Paine had pointed out to his readers, "the defect lies in the system," and until Britain changed its government (hopefully through revolution) there would be no progress on the issue of human rights. Perhaps the reason for this and so many other inconsistencies in Paine's thought (and the same could be said of many other followers of the Enlightenment) has to do with the reliance upon self-evident truths. Because, in Paine's view, when man employed his reason, the truth about God and politics was so clearly obvious it defied questioning. It was obvious to Paine that God had created man equally in nature therefore questions concerning individual voting rights, for example, were irrelevant. Similarly, since government by consent of the governed was a natural right, so long as that right was firmly established the actual composition of the government and how it functioned was immaterial.

The real tragedy of Paine's often limited perspective and attention to short-term solutions is that scholars will never know how Paine might have succeeded had he turned his potent pen to such issues as slavery, women's rights, or universal suffrage. Nevertheless, it cannot be denied that Paine's activism (however flawed his reasoning) influenced the minds of his readers who, among other things, helped to found the United States of America. Although Paine had failed in his personal mission to create a world of deists, his indomitable will and his tireless crusade for justice and human rights ensured him of a success unequaled by any other writer of his time.

Conclusion

In the Autumn of 1783, as the American Revolution was concluding, the Continental Congress proposed the appointment of Thomas Paine to the position of "Historiographer of the Continent."[1] It was to be a paid position complete with an annual salary for the duration of Paine's research and writing. His task: to write a history of the American Revolution. In his written reply to the Congress Paine thanked them respectfully for the honor, but declined the offer on several grounds.

Paine was leery of the fact that writing a history of the Revolution would entail more time and research than the Congress conceived. "The matters which unite themselves in this Revolution are so various and numerous, so extensive and complicated," Paine discerned, "that to gain all the necessary information will be exceedingly difficult."[2] He cited the fact that the Revolution concerned matters "made up of public and private" as well as the transcontinental affairs between America, England, France, and Spain.[3] As early as 1779 Paine cautioned that "a proper history cannot even be begun unless the secrets of the other side of the water can be obtained."[4] In order to do the subject justice the research would be so extensive, Paine warned the Congress, that it "will be a work of almost endless observation."[5] Such an undertaking would likewise be prohibitively expensive:

> The expense of collecting materials and information from the different parts of America and abroad (for a man cannot do it effectually unless he does it personally), the time it will take to digest and arrange them and the charge of printing the work and engraving the plates necessary or ornamental to it will amount to several thousand pounds before any part could be reimbursed.[6]

Paine was also sensitive to the question of historical integrity. While recognizing that the cooperation of the Continental Congress would be necessary to writing a complete history of the Revolution, such cooperation had the potential to create bias. Having access to Congressional papers was essential, but "for Congress to reserve to themselves the least appearance of influence over an historian, by annexing a yearly salary subject to their own control, will endanger the reputation of both the historian and the history."[7] History as a matter of personal profit, Paine argued, "will subject the character of the present age to various and hazardous representations."[8] Paine proposed instead an honorary appointment which would "facilitate the collection of materials and give the work the foundation of impartiality."[9]

Paine expressed his most significant objection to writing a history of the Revolution a year earlier in his *Letter to the Abbé Raynal;* a refutation of Raynal's history of the conflict. He informed the Abbé and his readers that "it is yet too soon to write a history of the Revolution."[10] "Whoever attempts it precipitately," Paine cautioned, "will unavoidably mistake characters and circumstances, and involve himself in error and difficulty."[11] Not enough time had passed for the Revolution to be properly understood, because "things, like men, are seldom understood rightly at first sight."[12] Paine argued well that time, careful research, and context were all necessary to understanding the full significance of the American Revolution; the same could easily be said of Paine himself.

Time has sufficiently elapsed, but two centuries of scholarship surrounding Paine and the Revolution has resulted in a quagmire of interpretations yielding a fragmented portrait of the famous pamphleteer. Scholars have consumed themselves with various historiographical questions, including the originality of Paine's works, his contribution to literature and history, and his influence on America's Declaration of Independence. Historians have, however, added considerably to knowledge of Paine and his historical significance. The importance of works like *Common Sense* and *The Rights of Man,* for example, have been firmly established in the arenas of political history and rhetoric. Likewise, *The Age of Reason* has found a place among historians of American religious history (indeed world religious history) and has been discussed and debated for its contribution to a knowledge of the eighteenth-century mind. However these studies, usually self-contained within separate disciplines, have raised significant questions which can only be answered by an interdisciplinary approach. Putting together the pieces of the historiographical jigsaw puzzle yielded surprising results about the unanswered questions surrounding Paine and his place in the Revolution.

Conclusion

There has been, for some time now, nearly universal agreement among historians about the influence of Paine's religious beliefs upon his political ideology. However, until now no study has yet undertaken a full exploration of the connection between Paine's deism and his political activism, drawing upon both prevailing historiography, new research, and new interpretations. Similarly, scholars for decades (if not centuries) have pondered why Thomas Paine was so successful in his political career—that question too has finally been investigated. There were also lingering questions regarding when Paine became a deist, the origins of those beliefs, and how they contributed to his political development. Again, those questions too have been finally given full attention. Perhaps Paine was correct in his assessment that, given enough time, history would yield a more complete harvest of information.

As so many scholars have indicated throughout the years, the best way (indeed for many the only way) to understand Paine's work, his significance, and his contribution to history is by studying the man himself. This particular study evolved very much from that approach. It is an intellectual history of Thomas Paine. It is a history of the evolution of his thoughts, his beliefs, and their expression. This study is also, however, an attempt to finally bring closure to the way studies of Paine had proceeded in the past in order to encourage a more accurate, interdisciplinary approach in the future. Hopefully new avenues of Paine's role in history may be explored as the old questions need no longer occupy scholars' attention.

Since Paine was very forthright in his disclosure of the history of his intellectual development, all that was left for this study was to highlight that history, place it in context, and analyze the significance of Paine's thought and its expression. In studying Paine with this new focus and using an interdisciplinary approach several new facets of Paine's development emerged. With respect to Paine's rhetoric, the significance of *The Pennsylvania Magazine* and its role in Paine's nascent political career have been given a new emphasis and analysis. Avoiding the historiographical pitfall of attempting to ascertain the authorship of articles attributed to Paine has allowed for a more general study of the broader significance of Paine's work at the magazine. Likewise a more thorough evaluation of the language in *Common Sense* reveals a previously unexplored connection to John Milton. Finally, a continuity in rhetorical style and argument has been uncovered, providing proof of the life-long importance of Paine's beliefs in his political writing.

The study of Paine's religious beliefs has also been enhanced by fully examining the origins of his deism. Moreover, once the origins of Paine's beliefs had been fully established, their role in the development of his political ideology was better understood, and revealed a significance previously missed by historians. This was accomplished largely as the result of a new approach to Paine in which attention to context was given central importance. This attention to context likewise unveiled the answers to the more pressing historical questions of the past century. The reason why Thomas Paine was the man who wrote *Common Sense*, for example, has been revealed almost exclusively by studying Paine's personal context. The role of England in Paine's development has taken on new significance; one which Paine himself readily admitted. He "observed that in writing *Common Sense* . . . the necessity of knowing both countries was so material, that no person who had reflected only on one could have sufficiently succeeded in a proposition for their political separation."[13] Similarly, by studying the political context of America, the nagging question of Paine's role in the Declaration of Independence has also (hopefully) found resolution.

Paine's dual mission to spread both political revolution and deism throughout the western world is a prime example of the information that can be gleaned by approaching Paine's work with a fresh, interdisciplinary perspective. The confluence of his religion and concomitant political ideology created a rhetorical style that was both recognizable and immutable. Paine's mission led him to a degree of success unparalleled in his day. According to Sean Wilentz, "Paine's immediate impact on his time was far greater than that of any number of his more celebrated English and European cohorts, including . . . Rousseau, Voltaire, Kant and (for that matter) Burke."[14] Not only that, but Paine "served in the army; he served in civil life; he labored for the good of humanity."[15]

Paine's involvement in the American Revolution as writer, soldier, and civil servant warrants closer examination. It is in fact the sincere hope of this study that Paine's involvement in the Revolution will help to redefine the concept of "Founding Father" to be more inclusive. Social historians have cautiously avoided including Paine too much in their studies lest he contribute to the "Great White Male" school of history. This is unfortunate, because if this study demonstrates anything, it demonstrates that Paine was an ordinary man who accomplished extraordinary things by appealing to other ordinary men. He was a founder of this country, but a founder nonetheless who counted himself no different from those who fought on the battlefields or strengthened the homefront. Perhaps Paine and others like him can build a bridge between social and political history with the larger aim of creating a more inclusive synthesis of American history.

Paine never had a chance to write his history of the American Revolution. After the ratification of the Treaty of Paris, Paine opted instead (understandably so) for a quiet life and scientific pursuits. He was still

Conclusion

intrigued by the idea of writing a history of the Revolution, but his proposal included not one, but three histories:

> one that should state fully all the leading principles, policy and facts of the revolution, so as not only to inform posterity but to confirm them in the true principles of freedom and civil government; a second, being rather an abstract of the first cast into easy and graceful language to be used as a standing school-book, and a third for Europe or the world.[16]

Paine believed that all three approaches were necessary to "give the present Revolution its full foundation and extent in the world."[17] Apparently Paine intended to write an intellectual and political history of the Revolution and to make that work accessible to the general public. How appropriate given Paine's own intellectual and political contributions to the Revolution, and his emphasis on making his arguments accessible to all Americans.

Perhaps the only question that remains is what Paine might have said about himself in his history; what he considered significant about his contribution to the cause of Independence. By far, Paine was proudest of his writing. He was content that he had "added something to the reputation of literature" and "arrived at an eminence" in that genre.[18] He credited his success to his singular ability "to make a reader feel, fancy, and understand justly at the same time."[19] "To call three powers of the mind into action at once, in a manner that neither shall interrupt, and that each shall aid and invigorate the other," Paine boasted, "is a talent very rarely possessed."[20] Moreover, it was a talent that "aristocracy, with all its aids, has not been able to reach or to rival."[21] Just as Paine sought to invigorate the mind by appealing to all of its many facets, perhaps it is time for social history to find new life in a more interdisciplinary approach. As Paine's life and career demonstrate, placing him in the pantheon of Founding Fathers need not deter social historians from viewing him as an example of the triumph of the ordinary man. After all, it was Paine the ordinary man whose pen helped start the American Revolution.

Appendix
Common Sense: An Historiographical Essay

Although a lengthy, detailed study of the scholarship surrounding *Common Sense* is beyond the scope of this study, a general survey of the literature is warranted and necessary.

By far, the most prevalent studies of *Common Sense* are those written by scholars of rhetoric. This should come as no surprise—the dazzling language and altogether unique style of Paine's early work makes *Common Sense* an easy target for literary criticism and interest. From dissertations entitled "The Rhetoric of Revolution: an Analysis of Thomas Paine's *Common Sense*" to articles like Bruce Woodcock's "Writing the Revolution: Aspects of Thomas Paine's Prose," English scholars have eagerly scrutinized Paine's revolutionary pamphlet.[1] Like Bernard Bailyn, literary critics have been captivated by the aspects of *Common Sense* that set it apart from other pamphlet literature of its day—such as Paine's use of common language (unique for political writing in the eighteenth century) and the fiery tone of his pamphlet. Rhetoricians have spent considerable time debating whether or not Paine's plain style marked the invention of a new mode of American political discourse, or whether he borrowed upon previous literary traditions.[2] Similarly, the violent imagery of *Common Sense*, replete with "images of blood, ashes, suffering, cruelty, corruption, monstrosity, hellishness, and villainy," has received no dearth of attention.[3]

Some of that attention has been garnered by historians, creating some scholarly overlap. Eric Foner argues that the "tone and rhythm" of Paine's work allowed him to convey the idea that "anyone could grasp the nature of politics and government."[4] Bailyn, interestingly, likens Paine's prose to that of Jonathan Swift, "a verbal killer in an age when pamphleteering was important to politics."[5] These are but two of many examples of historians who have been seduced by Paine's riveting discourse. A. Owen Aldridge, Sean Wilentz, and Winthrop Jordan can also number themselves among those who have also attempted a literary analysis of *Common Sense*.[6] The inherent flaw of these literary studies of *Common Sense* is the glaring lack of historical and political context. These studies seem to take place almost in a scholarly vacuum. This is unfortunate because perhaps the clearest explications of Paine's arguments are written by English scholars. One possible exception to this trend is Robert Ferguson's 2000 article "The Commonalities of *Common Sense*."[7]

Of all the literary analyses of *Common Sense*, none are as well-written, concise, well-argued, or insightful as Robert Ferguson's recent work. Ferguson provides—by far—the best summary of Paine's arguments in *Common Sense*. Ferguson offers little in the way of new scholarship or new interpretations but does provide a thorough literary analysis of Paine's unique pamphlet. Interestingly however, Ferguson's approach does not minimize Paine's arguments nor oversimplify them; rather his uncomplicated interpretation echoes Paine's own "plain arguments."[8] Thus Ferguson's work is altogether as accessible to readers today as Paine's pamphlet was to Americans generations ago. In general Ferguson, like others before him, highlights the principal themes in *Common Sense*. Ferguson also expounds upon Paine's often noted denunciation of monarchy. Again, Ferguson offers nothing new in this approach, but he successfully summarizes and clarifies the main points of Paine's argument.

To his credit, Ferguson (more so than any other literary scholar) does attempt somewhat to ground Paine's work in an historical context. For example, it is Ferguson who notes that Paine adroitly straddled two eighteenth-century worlds: one, "steeped in a bible culture" and the other "on the cutting edge of the enlightenment."[9] He perhaps, more than any other literary scholar, comes closest to bridging the gap between disciplines. Still, Ferguson lacks any attention to the historical significance of *Common Sense*. Ferguson is intrigued by the words Paine used to describe his sovereign (a "royal brute" descended from a "bastard") but not by the fact that in the history of the colonies no one had ever dared be so publicly hostile and insulting to the King.[10] Paine's open hostility and contempt for George III had a dramatic impact on the minds of Americans; a consequence missed by English scholars. It has therefore been left to historians like Winthrop Jordan to reveal that Paine was the first person to successfully shift the colonial ire away from Parliament, placing the blame for America's woes squarely upon George III's crowned head.[11]

Where Ferguson and other rhetoricians fail, political scientists and historians excel. At their best, these studies provide considerable insight into Paine's watershed pamphlet; at their worst they are consumed by irrelevant, circular arguments. In general there are three discernible schools of thought that comprise the bulk of historical scholarship surrounding *Common Sense*. One school of thought asserts that Paine's pamphlet was a possible catalyst for the American Revolution. Another, perhaps the most pervasive line of argument, evaluates the originality of Paine's argument. The last focuses on the unique ability of Paine to appeal to a broad segment of the American population. Like other studies of Paine's works they too suffer from a lack of context, but not to the same degree as rhetorical studies.

There is no denying that Paine's purpose in writing *Common Sense* was to move Americans' towards a final separation from Great Britain, and the colonists obligingly devoured his pamphlet and his radicalism. Stuart Andrews attributes the success of *Common Sense* to the fact that Paine's argument "presented independence as the only rational option," but most historians also give credit to Paine's bold rhetoric.[12] His words were so persuasive, James McCormack argues, that Paine was able to "strengthen the believing, confirm the doubting, and convert the unbelieving to the doctrine of independence."[13] Indeed, the American public's reaction to *Common Sense,* and the ensuing agitation for revolution that followed (culminating in the Declaration of Independence) has led many scholars to succumb to the temptation of establishing a direct causal relationship between *Common Sense* and Jefferson's document. Paine's triumph has caused no end of scholarly debate over whether or not the Englishman should be credited with causing the Continental Congress to vote for Independence in July 1776, or whether Paine's pamphlet was simply one of many catalysts in the movement for separation. Complicating the matter is the myriad ways in which individual scholars define "independence." For some it refers to a popular movement; others view it as the Continental Congress' singular political act; still others refer exclusively to Jefferson's legendary draft. This has been a divisive issue among both historians, political scientists, and Paine scholars alike. Therefore, historiographically, scholarly conclusions regarding the significance of *Common Sense* with regards to American Independence vary considerably.

Like the bulk of Paine studies, the scholarly pendulum surrounding this particular debate swings from one extreme to the other. It should come as no surprise that early biographers (clearly biased in favor of their subject) considered *Common Sense* to be nothing less than Jefferson's sole inspiration for the Declaration of Independence. Albert Matthews, an early critic of such theories, likened this phenomena to "the well-known tendency of a biographer to 'claim everything' . . . on behalf of the person whose life he is writing."[14] In Matthews' estimation, the blame for such unfounded claims rests with one of Paine's earliest and most revered biographers, Moncure Conway.[15] It was Conway who first made the suggestion that Paine was a significant influence on Jefferson's thought, and according to Matthews it was only a matter of time before Conway's suggestion, "put forward as a possible, is soon regarded as probable, and finally emerges as a certainty."[16] This led to the inevitable—and altogether baffling—attempt of some early writers to offer "proof" that it was actually Paine and not Jefferson who wrote the now sacrosanct document.[17] The best example of this phenomenon is Joseph Lewis' 1947 study, *Thomas Paine: Author of the Declaration of Independence*.[18] For more than three hundred pages, Lewis attempts to prove not only that Paine wrote the document, but that Jefferson "actually asked him to write [it]."[19] For proof, Lewis offers nothing more than a list of Paine's acquaintances—Jefferson among them—and a few literary similarities between Paine and Jefferson.[20] Such claims, once in abundance, have now rightfully been dismissed as false.

Further towards the center of the pendulum's path are studies by noted historians like Winthrop Jordan, Bernard Bailyn, and Eric Foner. This elite scholarly triumvirate make more plausible (and more relevant) claims than those of Lewis and Conway. Jordan's more modern study of *Common Sense* demonstrates that, according to Jordan, Paine played a significant role in influencing the political beliefs of Americans. Jordan steadfastly claims that "with the possible exception of *Uncle Tom's Cabin*, *Common Sense* was demonstrably the most immediately influential political or social tract ever published in this country."[21] While he stops short of arguing conclusively that Paine was directly responsible for America's separation from Great Britain, Jordan concedes that the influence Paine had upon the minds of Americans was enough to psychologically sever America's ties to Britain, creating a sort of emotional independence. Pauline Maier concurs with Jordan's conclusion, attributing Independence to "a corrosion of American affection for Britain," but stops short of giving Paine all of the credit for this psychological transformation.[22] Bernard Bailyn and Eric Foner also tend to chart a middle course, agreeing that Paine's pamphlet had a significant impact on the formation of the United States of America, but decline to give Paine all of the credit. More recent biographers, historians, and political scientists firmly disagree with the notion that Paine was the cause of the Continental Congress' decision to seek Independence. In fact, the overwhelming relativism that permeates recent studies brings the pendulum to a complete stop; scholars no longer even wish to engage in the "Declaration debate," preferring to dismiss the matter entirely due to a lack of concrete evidence.[23] Perhaps the scholar who comes closest to contributing the most to this discussion is Edward Larkin. Although the "legitimating constituency" he claimed Paine created centered around political awareness among Philadelphia's artisan community was already present, Larkin is not too far wrong. By rallying the American people to the cause of Independence, Paine did in fact create a support base which Continental Congressmen could use to urge the matter forward. Those in Congress who had consistently ignored the minority radical faction were no longer able to do so after *Common Sense;* the American people demanded revolution and their representatives were forced to respond. That response led, ultimately, to the Declaration of Independence.

However lively the debate surrounding *Common Sense*'s contribution to American Independence, it pales in comparison to what can best be termed "the originality trap." Since *Common Sense* debuted over two centuries ago, the praise for Paine's opus has been accompanied by swirling doubts concerning the originality of his argument. Perhaps Paine's earliest critic was his future Congressional patron John Adams. Adams repeatedly insisted that Benjamin Rush "furnished [Paine] with the Arguments which had been urged in Congress an hundred times," (arguments Adams himself had made) and that Paine thus should not be credited with his genius.[24] Since Adams' protestations in the eighteenth century, legions of historians have enlisted their considerable talents to settle the matter of what is—and what is not—original about Paine's arguments in *Common Sense*.

Among those who celebrate Paine's creativity and give his intellect more credit than Adams could muster is Eric Foner. Foner, for example, considers the "leveling spirit" present in *Common Sense* to be noteworthy.[25] In fact Paine provides a stark contrast to Adams' "unmistakable elitist bias," and the more moderate polemics of Paine's contemporaries.[26] Foner further argues that *Common Sense* "was unique in the extent of its readership and its influence of events," and that Paine's denunciation of monarchy was indeed significant.[27] Bernard Bailyn expressed similar sentiments in his earlier work, *The Ideological Origins of the American Revolution*. According to Bailyn, *Common Sense* was a "superbly rhetorical iconoclastic pamphlet" that successfully destroyed the familial ties between Britain and America.[28] While impressed with Paine's "slashing attack upon the English monarchy," Bailyn maintains that "the intellectual core" of *Common Sense* was "its attack on the traditional conception of balance as a prerequisite for liberty."[29] Other historians, like R.F. Smith, attribute the originality of *Common Sense* to Paine's overt militancy rather than his rhetorical subtext. For Smith the very fact that Paine "issued the first unequivocal call for independence some six months before the actual signing of the Declaration" makes *Common Sense* exceptional.[30] In general, however, it should be noted that there is a marked uniformity of opinion in these studies: the style and the sentiments expressed in *Common Sense* set it apart from all other revolutionary pamphlets.

Criticism of the originality of Paine's famous work, by contrast, is not only varied but incongruous. Winthrop Jordan focuses his critique on singular aspects of *Common Sense* like Paine's biblical refutation of monarchy. Sean Wilentz' criticism centers more on Paine's personal intellectual development; in Wilentz' estimation Paine "lacked Madison's realism and originality," as well as Hamilton's "frightening genius."[31] Somewhat less scathing but equally as disparaging is Cecilia Kenyon's article, "Where Paine Went Wrong," published half a century ago.[32] While conceding that Paine's oratory was persuasive, Kenyon argues that Paine's words lacked depth and thoughtfulness. In Kenyon's estimation *Common Sense* was "an eloquent call to action and to sacrifice," but Paine's arguments were too simplistic.[33] For Kenyon, *Common Sense* offered nothing that had not been written before, but Paine played well the part of a polemical Pied Piper: "in times of crisis men will listen to a great exhorter."[34] Once again Paine's rhetorical abilities become the primary focus in a discussion of his historical significance.

Paine's writing skills have led to inconsistent and contradictory conclusions by scholars engaged in the debate concerning Paine's originality. However, where scholars of rhetoric are better able to reach definitive conclusions because of their limited focus and lack of historical context, historians seem unable to draw such conclusions because they know all too well Paine's pivotal role in American history.[35] A prime example of this dilemma is Sean Wilentz, who is already on record as arguing that Paine lacked both realism and originality, admits in the same paragraph that "Paine defined, better than any other Founding Father, the American revolutionary cause as ordinary patriots came to define it—not as a trans-Atlantic tax revolt or struggle for independence but as an effort to give birth to a new social and political world, a cause for all mankind."[36] Furthermore, Wilentz asserts that Paine's "forward-looking republicanism" casts the Revolution "in its full and proper light, as a genuinely radical revolution, a thorough break from the past."[37] Finally, Wilentz claims that "for all their ambiguities, Paine's writings did help to change the world forever. They unleashed ideas about privilege, liberty, and democracy that have resounded ever since."[38] In other words *Common Sense* was not original (or perhaps parts of it are), Paine was not a genius (but he changed the world), and the historical significance of his pamphlet is not in question (or is it?). The debate continues.

Perhaps the one thing that historians and political scientists agree upon was Paine's unique ability to appeal to a broad segment of the population.

There is an element of universalism in Paine's writings which allowed him to influence the minds of Americans who had previously been ignored by colonial leaders.[39] *Common Sense* marked the beginning of this trend in Paine's rhetoric. Political scientist Gregory Claeys observes that "more than anyone else, it was he who transformed the narrow vision of the 'liberties of Englishmen,' which implied no corresponding rights for Frenchmen, and the natural rights of Christians, not shared by infidels, into a cosmopolitan vision which afforded protection and sustenance to all."[40] Likewise, Frank Smith argued that Paine expressed his desire for revolution in *Common Sense* "in terms which are applicable not only to the circumstances of eighteenth-century America, but to all men, in all places, at all times."[41] Because of the unprecedented popularity of *Common Sense*, Paine's success in translating this cosmopolitan vision has led many historians to conclude that certainly the articulation of that vision is worthy of the designation "original" if nothing else.

Paine's attempts to appeal to the entire American populace did not end with a redefinition of natural rights, but rather extended to include a clever appeal to religious unity as well. According to Robert Ferguson, Paine's God in *Common Sense* was also accessible to all.[42] Paine's pamphlet contains more than an "abstract" God and a call for religious freedom; for more than four pages Paine quotes extensively from the Old Testament to bolster his argument.[43] Because of these seemingly contradictory elements at least one historian has wondered (in spite of Paine's later confessed devotion to deism) whether or not Paine was a Christian at the time he wrote *Common Sense*. A. Owen Aldridge boldly declares that "it is obvious that much of *Common Sense* appeals to the authority of scripture, most of it implies that the author is Christian."[44] However, Aldridge curiously insists that "the work is undubitably written from the Christian perspective" but "the conclusion is inescapable that [Paine] did not personally accept the Scriptures as the inspired Word of God at the time that he wrote *Common Sense*."[45] In other words, Aldridge believes that although Paine was a deist, he used Christianity to appeal to his readership and strengthen his argument in *Common Sense*. There are two significant problems with Aldridge's assertions. One is his assertion that Paine's argument is "Christian" and the other is that Aldridge dismisses the possibility that the rhetorical tactic was not Paine's original conception at all.

Aldridge's first claim is easily dismissed: Paine's argument in *Common Sense* cannot truly be termed "Christian" since his biblical evidence comes from the Old Testament. There are only two citations in *Common Sense* from the New Testament, neither of which have any bearing on his historical argument using the book of Samuel.[46] There is no appeal to Jesus Christ, the redemption, or Christ's teachings in *Common Sense*. In fact, one New Testament citation is used as historical evidence to decry monarchy. Paine argues that "*'Render unto Cesar the things which are Cesar's,* is the scripture doctrine of courts, yet it is no support of monarchical government, for the Jews at that time were without a king."[47] Paine's use of evidence from the bible was, in fact, historical. He used it to explain the origins of monarchy and demonstrate God's disapproval of the institution. (Furthermore, Paine's God in *Common Sense*—like the one he worshiped as a deist—was the monotheistic God of Abraham, not the trinitarian God of the New Testament.) Thus, Paine's religious argument in *Common Sense* is not Christian in any sense.

Astonishingly little has been written regarding the religious aspects of *Common Sense*. The only other (and very recent) line of inquiry concerns the possible presence of millennial themes in *Common Sense*. In general, scholars agree that Paine's work should not be compared to other strongly millennial works of its time—albeit for different reasons. In his study of millennialism and *Common Sense*, Jack Fruchtman argues that Paine's calls for a New World Order ring hollow when compared with those of his more pious contemporaries.[48] Fruchtman has difficulty defining exactly what he regards as "millennial," but rather chooses to define Paine by "the other"—in this case devout Christian millenarian Joseph Priestley.[49] In Fruchtman's estimation, Paine's "broad vision of the perfectability that men might experience" should be labeled "'secular millennialism'" to differentiate it from the traditional Christian belief.[50] By contrast, Ruth Bloch, whose definitive work *Visionary Republic: Millennial Themes in American Thought, 1756–1800* was published a year after Fruchtman's study, has no difficulty defining her terms. Bloch bases her argument upon a strict definition of "millennialism": "statements directly referring to the visionary prophecies of the Bible."[51] Using this narrow interpretation, Bloch clearly distinguishes *Common Sense* (which contains no such prophecies) from other contemporary works. Bloch effectively argues that a better label for the religious themes in *Common Sense* is "secular utopian," characterized by "exaltation over the rise of reason" and a denial of the necessity of revelation.[52] Gregory Claeys echoes this conclusion, although he disagrees with Bloch's description of Paine's work as utopian. According to Claeys, "[Paine's] vision was considerably more secular and republican and less apocalyptic, perfectabilist, and Utopian than theirs, and consequently should not be termed 'millenarian.'"[53]

One notable difference between Fruchtman, Bloch, and Claeys is Bloch's knowledge of and attention to context. Both Fruchtman and Claeys base their perception of Paine's millenarianism on comparisons with other famous millenarians, namely Joseph Priestley and (in the case of Claeys) Richard Price. Bloch, on the other hand, focuses her study upon the entire eighteenth century literary, religious, and historical context. "Between 1773 and 1776," Bloch argues, "a fully millennial interpretation of the imperial crisis rose to the fore as American patriots finally moved from resistance to revolution."[54] During the Revolution Bloch asserts that "elements of nationalism and universalism thus were drawn together in a kind of passive political messianism," in which "American principles, not power, would ultimately prevail throughout the globe."[55] This was an unusual time in American history—the Old and New Worlds were colliding and a wide range of ideas became acceptable. It was Bloch, however, who first perceived that

> At a time when Thomas Paine still quoted extensively from scriptural texts and when Thomas Jefferson's draft of the Declaration of Independence emerged from Congress with references to the power of Providence, revolutionary millennialism quite comfortably straddled traditional Protestant and Enlightened world views.[56]

This clash of religious ideologies during the American Revolution was perhaps first elucidated by Catharine Albanese in her 1776 work *Sons of the Fathers: The Civil Religion of the American Revolution*. She concluded (convincingly) that Americans' conception of God changed during the Revolution. According to Albanese, "it was clear that the mental world of the patriots required a double-facing divinity, "one who could be both "Jehovah God of Battles" on the field and "Nature's God" to direct Providence in the Patriots' favor.[57] Albanese argues that Americans became increasingly uncomfortable with the Calvinist God of their past because that arbitrary dictator on High too closely resembled their tyrant foe George III. Thus as the Revolution progressed Americans increasingly turned towards a God that was active (on their side) but Deistic (aloof and non-interfering) at the same time. "Neither anticlerical nor ecclesiastical," Albanese declares, "the deism which permeated the religious structure of the Revolution was one with which a broad spectrum of Americans could be at home."[58] It was certainly a structure which Paine, a deist himself, would have been at home with. While both Bloch and Albanese's studies help clarify the literary and religious context into which *Common Sense* emerged, they can only partially explain the circumstances which produced it. To understand how and why *Common Sense* was written—and why Thomas Paine was its author—requires a better understanding of Paine's "personal culture." Hopefully this study finally answers those important questions.

Notes

NOTES TO THE INTRODUCTION

1. A stay-maker makes stays for women's corsets. They are also alternately referred to as corset-makers, but stay-makers generally were restricted just to the manufacture of the whalebone stays, not the whole garment.
2. A tax collector.
3. At the same time that Paine was awarded his honorary citizenship, George Washington, Alexander Hamilton, and James Madison were also awarded the same honor.
4. Paine felt that King Louis XVI should not have been targeted or blamed for the problems in France. He believed that the institution of monarchy itself was the source of France's problems, and that it had corrupted Louis XVI and his queen. Paine wanted to return the king and queen to life as civilians in exile, hopefully in America. See Paine's speech, "Reasons for Preserving the Life of Louis Capet" in *Complete Writings*, 551.
5. Theodore Roosevelt, *The Life of Gouverneur Morris* (New York: Houghton-Mifflin Co., 1888), 288–289.
6. The titles of some of these works suggest their bias: *Tom Paine: America's Godfather, 1737–1809; Tom Paine: Friend of Mankind; Tom Paine: America's First Liberal*.
7. Jack Fruchtman Jr., *Thomas Paine: Apostle of Freedom*, (New York: Four Walls Eight Windows, 1994) and John Keane, *Tom Paine: A Political Life* (Boston: Little, Brown & Company, 1995). I am not including Eric Foner's book, *Tom Paine and Revolutionary America* (London: Oxford University Press, 1976) as a biography of Paine because it is really more of a social history of Pennsylvania during the Revolution with an emphasis placed on Paine's activities there. I hope Professor Foner does not disagree with my interpretation of his superb work.
8. H.T. Dickinson, review of *Tom Paine: A Political Life* by John Keane and *Thomas Paine: Apostle of Freedom* by Jack Fruchtman Jr., In *History* 81 (262 [1996]): 233.

9. For a detailed listing of the historical errors in both Fruchtman and Keane see Dickinson's excellent review. Perhaps most regretful is the lack of analysis of Paine himself. Neither author can truly explain why Paine became a participant in two of the worlds most significant revolutions, nor do they address the role his religion played in his activism in any meaningful way.
    Of the two works, the most problematic by far is Keane's. There is a serious problem with his sources. Keane claims to have used only original primary documents in his research, painstakingly identifying some six hundred-twenty works of Paine's in the process. Even more astonishing, Keane reveals that he discovered "at least seventy items" which have never been used by or been previously available to Paine scholars. However, in his biography, Keane provided no bibliography nor did he reveal where he found these "undiscovered" sources. Instead, Keane provided only notes, promising to publish the bibliography separately as *The Writings of Thomas Paine, 1737–1809: A Guide*. It has never been published. In addition, there is no separate bibliography for secondary sources either. None of this would matter if the citations in Keane's notes fully disclosed the names of sources, the collections in which they were found, and where those collections are located. Unfortunately—and egregiously—Keane does not provide this information consistently. In some instances, there are no citations given at all for quotations attributed to Paine (or others)—in other instances, no page numbers are given. This lack of disclosure makes his evidence questionable at best and unreliable at worst. In the opinion of this scholar, until Keane fully discloses his sources and gives complete citations, his research should be discounted.
10. This polarization is interesting; it is almost a mirror of Paine's own career. He was viewed almost all of his life as a political figure following his successful career as a revolutionary pamphleteer in two revolutions, but after he published *The Age of Reason* he was associated almost exclusively with his religious principles.
11. Benjamin Rush, "To James Cheetham, July 17th, 1809," in *The Letters of Benjamin Rush*, vol. 2, ed. L.H. Butterfield (Princeton: Princeton University Press for the American Philosophical Society, 1951), 1009.
12. Thomas Clio Rickman, *The Life of Thomas Paine* (London: Thomas Clio Rickman, 1819), 11.
13. Joel Barlow, "To James Cheetham, August 11, 1809," in *Life and Letters of Joel Barlow, Poet, Statesman, Philosopher*, ed. Charles Burr Todd (New York: The Knickerbocker Press, 1886; reprint, New York: Burt Franklin, 1972), 238–239. (page references are to reprint edition).
14. See W.J. Rorbaugh, *The Alcoholic Republic: An American Tradition* (New York: Oxford University Press, 1979).
15. Rickman, *Life of Paine*, 46.
16. Ironically, the man who had been publicly proclaimed as impotent was later accused of fathering an illegitimate child with Nicholas de Bonneville's estranged wife. Madame de Bonneville sued for libel and won the case.

17. Francina Kercheville Hail, "Thomas Paine: An Interpretive Study of the Treatment of Paine by Biographers, Historians and Critics" (Ph.D. diss., University of New Mexico, 1977), 245.
18. Gregory Claeys observes that most scholars assume that Paine was a demagogue, a "vulgarizer of Locke," and "therefore has no proper place beside the great political thinkers." Peter Stanlis further argues that "like the *philosophes* and Encyclopedists of the French Enlightenment, Paine is indeed a highly influential but shallow journalistic ideologue, but not a political philosopher." Similarly, Bruce Woodcock believes that Paine's ideas "certainly were not his invention. What he brought was his skill as a writer or narrator of them." Many scholars have fallen into this "originality trap," trying to either place Paine in the same company as other political theorists like Locke or to denigrate him as simply a popularizer of others' ideas through brilliant new rhetorical devices.
19. Sean Wilentz, review of *Thomas Paine: Collected Writings,* edited by Eric Foner, *Thomas Paine: Apostle of Freedom,* by Jack Fruchtman, Jr. and *Tom Paine: A Political Life,* by John Keane, In *The New Republic* April 24, 1995: 2.
20. Arnold King, "Thomas Paine in America, 1774–1787" (Ph.D. diss., University of Chicago, 1952), 92.
21. Cecilia M. Kenyon, "Where Paine Went Wrong," *The American Political Science Review* 45 (1951): 1086.
22. Thomas Paine, *Common Sense,* in *The Life and Major Writings of Thomas Paine,* (New York:The Citadel Press, 1948) ed. Philip S. Foner., 37.
23. Harry Hayden Clark contends that it was a combination of Paine's father's Quakerism and Newtonian Science. Unfortunately he ignores the influence of Paine's mother's Anglicanism and does not analyze significantly the Quaker contribution to the formation of Paine's deism. See Clark's articles, "An Historical Interpretation of Thomas Paine's Religion," *University of California Chronicle* 35(1933): 56–87 and "Toward a Reinterpretation of Thomas Paine," *American Literature* 5 (March 1933-January 1934): 133–145.
24. Walter Woll, *Thomas Paine: Motives for Rebellion,* Anglo-Saxon Language and Literature Series (Frankfurt am Main: European University Studies, 1992), 193.
25. Wilentz, review, 6.
26. Claeys, *Social and Political Thought,* 179.
27. Clark, "An Interpretation,"86.
28. Robert Francis Smith, Jr., "Thomas Paine and the American Political Tradition" (Ph.D. diss, University of Notre Dame, 1977), 11.
29. Ibid., 10.
30. Foner, *Revolutionary America,* xiii.
31. Ibid.
32. Bernard Bailyn, "The Most Uncommon Pamphlet of the Revolution," *American Heritage* 25(1973): 39.

33. Alfred Young, "George Robert Twelves Hewes: Shoemaker and Patriot," in *The Private Side of American History: Readings in Everyday Life*, vol. 1, eds. Gary B. Nash and Cynthia J. Shelton (Fort Worth: Harcourt Brace Jovanovich College Publishers, 1987), 176.
34. Perhaps we need to change the term to "Founding Patriots," or simply "Founders." Both are more inclusive and more indicative of the Revolution as a whole.
35. Woodcock, "Writing the Revolution," 177.
36. Thomas Paine, *The Complete Writings of Thomas Paine* (New York: The Citadel Press, 1945), and *The Life and Major Writings of Thomas Paine*, (New York: The Citadel Press, 1948) ed. Philip S. Foner. Unlike his compatriot Jefferson, Paine's extant life works fit neatly into two or three volumes.
37. Lindsay Campbell, Local Studies Librarian, Thetford Public Library, Thetford, England. Campbell made this humorous (but all too true) comment to me at the library in Thetford while I was surveying their Paine collection in November 1999.

NOTES TO CHAPTER ONE

1. Sheila L. Skemp, *Benjamin and William Franklin: Father and Son, Patriot and Loyalist* (Boston: Bedford Books of St. Martin's Press, 1994), 86.
2. Ibid., 110.
3. Thomas Paine, "Letter to Henry Laurens, January 14, 1779," in *The Complete Writings of Thomas Paine*, ed. Philip S. Foner (New York: The Citadel Press, 1945), 1161.
4. Benjamin Rush, "Travels Through Life," in *The Autobiography of Benjamin Rush: His "Travels Through Life" together with His Common place Book for 1789–1813*, ed. George W. Corner (New Jersey: Princeton University Press, 1948), 113–114.
5. Eric Foner, *Tom Paine and Revolutionary America*, (London: Oxford University Press, 1976), 38.
6. Ibid.
7. For the best study of this see Gary Nash, *The Urban Crucible: The Northern Seaports and the Origins of the American Revolution* (Cambridge, Massachusetts: Harvard University Press, 1979), 240–246.
8. Foner, *Revolutionary America*, 61.
9. Ibid., 56.
10. Ibid., 62.
11. Thomas Paine, "Letter to Benjamin Franklin, March 4, 1775," *Complete Writings*, 1130.
12. Ibid.
13. Ibid., 1130–1131.
14. Ibid.
15. Ibid., 1131.
16. Ibid.

Notes to Chapter One

17. Ibid.
18. Ibid.
19. Edward Larkin, "Inventing an American Public: Thomas Paine, the *Pennsylvania Magazine*, and American Revolutionary Discourse," *Early American Literature* 33(i3) (Fall 1998): 259.
20. Ibid., 260.
21. Thomas Clio Rickman, *The Life of Thomas Paine* (London: Thomas Clio Rickman, 1819).
22. Frank Smith, "New Light on Thomas Paine's First Year in America, 1775," *American Literature* 1(1929/1930): 348–356.
23. Ibid., 352. Smith gives no citation for the source of this letter; he only indicates that it was noted in an advertisement for a 1797 volume of Paine's collected works. There is no citation for this "advertisement."
24. The publishing dates and pseudonyms for these essays are respectively "Unsigned," January 1775; "Unsigned," January 1775, "Esop," February 1775, and "Atlanticus," July 1775.
25. "P.," "*Trifles, light as air, Are to the jealous confirmations strong*," Supplement to The Pennsylvania Packet and General Advertiser, *The Pennsylvania Packet*, August 30, 1773 and "P.," "Of Love of Country, from the St. James Chronicle," *Pennsylvania Packet*, January 23, 1775.
26. "Pacificus," [untitled], *The Pennsylvania Packet*, November 20, 1773.
27. Jerome D. Wilson and William F. Ricketson, *Thomas Paine: An Updated Edition* (Boston: Twayne Publishers, 1989), 136, n9. For the original article published by Smith, see "The Authorship of 'An Occasional Letter on the Female Sex,'" *American Literature* 2 [November 1930]: 277–280.
28. Foner, *Revolutionary America,*,72.
29. Robert Aitken, "Proposal For Printing by *Subscription*, THE PENNSYLVANIA MAGAZINE, or the AMERICAN REPOSITORY of useful Knowledge," *Pennsylvania Packet*, November 21, 1774.
30. Ibid.
31. Ibid.
32. Ibid.
33. Robert Aitken, "To the Public," *Pennsylvania Packet*, November 21, 1774.
34. see n.32 above
35. Aitken, "Proposal," *Pennsylvania Packet*, November 21, 1774.
36. Paine, "To Benjamin Franklin, March 4, 1775," *Complete Writings*, 1131.
37. Unsigned [attributed to Paine], "Publisher's Preface," *Pennsylvania Magazine*, January 1775, 4–5.
38. Ibid., 5.
39. Ibid.
40. Ibid.
41. Ibid.
42. "Contents," *The Pennsylvania Magazine*, January 1775, 6.
43. Ibid.
44. [unsigned] "Utility of this work evinced," *The Pennsylvania Magazine*, January 1775, 10. Of all of the essays attributed to Paine, I would definitely

argue that this was positively written by him. The style, rhythm, and manner of argument are identical to his later works like *Common Sense*.
45. Larkin, "Inventing an American Public," 261.
46. "Contents," *Pennsylvania Magazine*, February 1775.
47. "Atlanticus" [attributed to Paine], "Useful and Entertaining Hints," *Complete Writings*, 1022.
48. Ibid., 1025.
49. This is another essay which I would positively identify as Paine's. He makes an identical argument in *Common Sense*, and, like "Utility of this work evinced," the style is clearly Paine's.
50. "Atlanticus" [attributed to Paine], "Reflections on the Life and Death of Lord Clive," *Complete Writings*, 24.
51. Ibid., 25.
52. Ibid.
53. "Esop" [attributed to Paine], "Cupid and Hymen," *Complete Writings*, 1116.
54. Ibid.
55. Ibid.
56. Ibid.
57. Ibid.
58. Ibid., 1117. "Esop" was also apparently clairvoyant; America was at war with Britain for nearly seven years as well.
59. "Contents," *Pennsylvania Magazine*, May 1775.
60. "Useful Hints—Curious deception—Query on Salt-Petre," *Pennsylvania Magazine*, June 1775, 269, and "Account on the Manufactory of Salt-Petre," 266.
61. "Elegy on the Memory of American Volunteers, who fell on April 19," *Pennsylvania Magazine*, June 1775, (278) and "The Dream Interpreted," 259.
62. "Bucks County," "The Dream Interpreted," *Complete Writings*, 51.
63. Ibid.
64. Ibid.
65. Ibid.
66. Ibid.
67. "Contents," *Pennsylvania Magazine*, July 1775, 309, 310, 313, and 328.
68. "A Lover of Peace" [attributed to Paine], "Thoughts on Defensive War," *Complete Writings*, 54.
69. "from London, May 26," *Pennsylvania Magazine*, July 1775, 333.
70. Ibid.
71. Ibid., 337.
72. Paine, "To Henry Laurens, January 14, 1779," *Complete Writings*, 1161.
73. Paine, "To Henry Laurens, January 14, 1779," *Complete Writings*, 1161.
74. Paine, "To Benjamin Franklin, March 4, 1775," *Complete Writings*, 1131.
75. "Contents," *Pennsylvania Magazine*, August 1775, 358, 360, and September 1775, 395.
76. "Arabella's *Complaint of the* CONGRESS," *Pennsylvania Magazine*, September 1775, 407.

77. A survey of the contents for October and November are telling: no political content. The magazine had clearly changed focus after Aitken took over as editor.
78. See n.19 above. The article was derived from Larkin's dissertation "Thomas Paine and the New Literature of Revolutionary Politics" (Ph.D. diss., Stanford University, 1998).
79. Ibid., 253.
80. Ibid.
81. Ibid., 252.
82. Ibid., 270.
83. Ibid., 252.
84. Ibid.
85. The principal flaw in Larkin's argument resides in the fact that Larkin is not an historian—he is a scholar of English Literature and Rhetoric. He lacks basic knowledge of the historical context of America in the 1770s in which to ground his argument. Rather, Larkin relies too heavily on secondary sources and a narrowly focused literary analysis to prove his thesis. Unfortunately, the fact that there is very little conclusive proof to link Paine to contributions in *The Pennsylvania Magazine* traditionally attributed to him makes Larkin's conclusions even more precarious.
86. The writing style that Paine used in *The Pennsylvania Magazine,* and the selections he chose may have been unfamiliar to his readers but they were certainly not unfamiliar to Paine. He borrowed on his experience with magazines in England, like *The Universal Magazine,* and tried to reproduce that format in America. After all, the publisher (Robert Aitken) insisted in his 1774 public proposal for the magazine that he planned to use English magazines as a guide for the choices of what was included. In his proposal Aitken announced that he "ordered all the *English* and *Scots* magazines to be regularly sent" to him so that he would "have the advantage of public opinion to assist the choice." Thus Paine's "invention" of a new audience was most likely an accident owing to the fact that he followed the format of magazines in Britain that catered to a readership comprised largely of people who were not politically active because of their economic status.
87. Larkin, "Inventing An American Public," 251.

NOTES TO CHAPTER TWO

1. Thomas Paine, "To a Committee of the Continental Congress, 1783," in *The Complete Writings of Thomas Paine,* ed. Philip S. Foner (New York: The Citadel Press, 1945), 1228.
2. Thomas Paine, *The American Crisis Number VII, November 21, 1778,"* in *The Life and Major Writings of Thomas Paine,* ed. Philip S. Foner (New York: The Citadel Press, 1948), 143.
3. Benjamin Rush, "Travels Through Life," in *The Autobiography of Benjamin Rush: His "Travels Through Life" together with His Commonplace*

Book for 1789–1813, ed. George W. Corner (New Jersey: Princeton University Press, 1948), 113–114.
4. Ibid.
5. Ibid.
6. Ibid.
7. Ibid.
8. Ibid.
9. Ibid.
10. Ibid.
11. Ibid.
12. Ibid.
13. Ibid.
14. John Adams, *The Autobiography of John Adams*, in *The Adams Papers: The Diary and Autobiography of John Adams*, vol.2, ed. L.H. Butterfield (Cambridge, Massachusetts: The Belknap Press of Harvard University Press, 1961), 330.
15. Ibid., and Rush, "Travels," 113–114. The "Common Sense" school of moral and political philosophy was the hallmark of the Scottish Enlightenment.
16. Thomas Paine, *The Rights of Man, Part II, Life and Major Writings*, 406n.
17. Thomas Paine, "To Henry Laurens, January 14, 1779," *Complete Writings*, 1162.
18. Rush, "Travels," 113–114.
19. Ibid.
20. Robert Middlekauf, *The Glorious Cause: The American Revolution, 1763–1789* (New York: Oxford University Press, 1982), 313.
21. Ibid.
22. Paine, *Common Sense*, 4.
23. John Locke, *Two Treatises of Government*, ed. Peter Laslett (New York: Cambridge University Press, 1994), 271.
24. Ibid.
25. Paine, *Common Sense*, 4–5.
26. Locke, *Second Treatise*, 329.
27. Paine, *Common Sense*, 4–5.
28. Ibid., 29.
29. Ibid., 6.
30. Ibid., 7.
31. Ibid.
32. Ibid., 8–9.
33. Ibid., 9.
34. Ibid., 21.
35. Ibid., 24.
36. Ibid.
37. Ibid., 23.
38. Ibid.
39. Ibid., 30.

40. Ibid., 23. The full quotation is "For never can true reconcilement grow/ Where wounds of deadly hate have pierced so deep." John Milton, *Paradise Lost*, Book IV, ll. 98–99.
41. Ibid., 18.
42. Ibid., 20.
43. Ibid., 36.
44. Ibid.
45. Ibid., 18.
46. Ibid., 20.
47. Ibid., 18.
48. Ibid., 20.
49. Ibid.
50. Ibid., 33.
51. Ibid., 42.
52. Ibid., 20.
53. Ibid., 21. Before Adams' drafting of the Model Treaty in 1776, before the Treat of Amity and Commerce with France in 1778, before the divisive Jay Treaty with Britain in 1794, and before George Washington's notorious farewell address cautioning America against entangling foreign alliances, Paine pleaded with Americans to be isolationist.
54. Ibid., 19.
55. Ibid., 36.
56. Ibid., 19.
57. Ibid.
58. Ibid., 22.
59. Ibid., 19.
60. Ibid., 23.
61. Ibid., 35.
62. Ibid.
63. Ibid., 38–39, 39.
64. Ibid., 27.
65. Ibid.
66. Ibid., 28.
67. Ibid.
68. Ibid., 29.
69. Ibid.
70. Ibid., 27.
71. Ibid., 26.
72. Ibid.
73. T.S. Eliot, "The Lovesong of J. Alfred Prufrock," *T.S. Eliot: The Complete Poems andPlays (1909–1950)* (New York: Harcourt Brace & Company, 1980), 4.
74. Paine, *Common Sense*, 7.
75. Ibid., 9.
76. Ibid., 22 and 23.

77. Ibid., 23.
78. Ibid., 30.
79. Winthrop Jordan, "Familial Politics: Thomas Paine and the Killing of the King, 1776," *Journal of American History* 60(September 1973): 298.
80. Paine, *Common Sense*, 5.
81. Ibid., 9.
82. Ibid., 10.
83. Ibid., 13.
84. Ibid., 12.
85. Ibid., 10.
86. Ibid.
87. Ibid.
88. Ibid.
89. Ibid., 11.
90. Ibid.
91. Ibid.
92. Ibid., 12.
93. Ibid.
94. Ibid.
95. Ibid.
96. Ibid., and 10.
97. John Adams, *The Autobiography of John Adams*, in *The Adams Papers: The Diary and Autobiography of John Adams*, vol. 2, ed. L.H. Butterfield (Cambridge, Massachusetts: The Belknap Press of Harvard University Press, 1961), 333.
98. A. Owen Aldridge, *Thomas Paine's American Ideology* (Newark: University of Delaware Press, 1984).
99. Aldridge notes that in John Milton's famous political tract, *A Defence of the People of England* (1658) Milton uses a biblical argument (like Paine) to denounce monarchy as a blasphemous institution. Aldridge even notes that both Paine and Milton use the same line from the New Testament ("Render unto Caesar the things which are Caesar's") as evidence. Aldridge's analysis revealed only this common citation, therefore he dismissed outright any link between Milton's argument and Paine's.
100. Chapter Two of Milton's *Defence*, to be precise.
101. 1 Samuel. According to Milton's *Defence*, "in many places God attests that he was very much displeased because [the Israelites] had asked for a king." (101) This request, Milton argues, made God angry, "not only because they wanted a king on the pattern of the nations and not his own law, but clearly because they desired a king at all."(83) Although the Lord disapproved of monarchy, God bade Samuel to set up a king for the Israelites to teach them a lesson. Kings, established in bold defiance of God's laws, became therefore "vicious," "wicked," and "accustomed to create all annoyance and troubles for their people under the guise of the right of kings." (85 and 87)
102. Ibid., 101. The verses are respectively 8:7; 12:12,17,;13:10,11.

Notes to Chapter Two

103. Ibid., 102.
104. "And the LORD said unto Samuel, Hearken unto the voice of the people in all that they say unto thee: for they have not rejected thee, but they have rejected me, that I should not reign over them."
105. Milton, *Defence*, 94.
106. Ibid.
107. Even so, there is no way to prove conclusively that Paine borrowed his argument directly from Milton. However, it does mean that Aldridge dismissed the possibility of Milton's influence too readily. Adams' recollection and the glaring similarity between Milton and Paine's biblical denunciation of monarchy should at least be enough to cast a reasonable doubt upon the originality of Paine's argument and open the matter for further consideration.
108. Paine, *Common Sense*, 15 and 13.
109. Ibid., 14.
110. Ibid.
111. Ibid., 13
112. Ibid.
113. Ibid., 15.
114. Ibid.
115. Ibid.
116. Ibid., 13.
117. Ibid., 16.
118. Ibid., 30.
119. Ibid., 28.
120. Ibid., 14.
121. Ibid., 29, 41, and 25.
122. Ibid., 41.
123. Ibid., 40.
124. Ibid., 15.
125. See n79 above
126. Paine, *Common Sense*, 24.
127. Ibid., 20.
128. Ibid., 25.
129. Ibid., 21.
130. Ibid., 45.
131. Ibid.
132. Ibid., 23.
133. Ibid., 17 and 23.
134. Ibid., 17.
135. Ibid., 3.
136. Ibid., 31.
137. Ibid., 21.
138. Thomas Paine, *Case of the Officers of Excise, Complete Writings*, 3.
139. Ibid., 3.
140. Ibid., 4.
141. Ibid.

142. Ibid., 10.
143. Ibid., 7.
144. Ibid., 11.
145. Ibid., 7.
146. Ibid., 9.
147. Ibid., 7.
148. Ibid., 11.
149. Ibid., 11.
150. Ibid., 14.
151. Ibid., 8.
152. Paine made monetary calculations of the cost of raising an army in *Common Sense*. See pp. 32–33 in Foner's edition.

NOTES TO CHAPTER THREE

1. Bernard Bailyn, "The Most Uncommon Pamphlet of the Revolution," *American Heritage* 25(1973): 39.
2. Ibid.
3. Winthrop Jordan, "Familial Politics: Thomas Paine and the Killing of the King, 1776," *Journal of American History* 60(September 1973): 294–308.
4. Bailyn, "Most Uncommon Pamphlet," 36 and Jordan, "Familial Politics," 294.
5. Bailyn, "Most Uncommon Pamphlet," 39.
6. Ibid.
7. Thomas Paine, "Letter to Nathanael Greene, September 9, 1780," in *The Complete Writings of Thomas Paine*, ed. Philip S. Foner (New York: The Citadel Press, 1945), 118.
8. Thomas Paine, "Letter to George Washington, September 7, 1782," in *Complete Writings*, 1212. Interestingly, Paine seemed to forget the biggest "7" in recent British history—the Seven Years' War.
9. Eric Foner, *Tom Paine and Revolutionary America*, (London: Oxford University Press, 1976), 3.
10. Thomas Paine, *The Age of Reason, Part I*, in *Life and Major Writings*, 496.
11. A recent excavation revealed a large treasure-horde of Roman gold and coins located in Thetford. Apparently it was prosperous long before the Anglo-Saxons formed the Seven Kingdoms. The treasure is on display at the British Museum.
12. *A Description of the Diocese of Norwich: or, The present state of Norfolk and Suffolk, giving an account of the situation, extent, trade, and customs, of the city of Norwich in particular. And of the several market-towns in those counties . . . By a gentleman of the Inner Temple, and native of the diocese of Norwich* (London: T. Cooper, 1735), microfilm.
13. Alan Crosby, *A History of Thetford* (Sussex: England: Phillmore & Co., Ltd., 1986), 75–76.
14. Ibid.

15. Thomas Paine, *Rights of Man I*, in *The Life and Major Writings of Thomas Paine*, ed. Philip S. Foner (New York: The Citadel Press, 1948), 282.
16. Paine, *Rights of Man II*, in *The Life and Major Writings of Thomas Paine*, ed. Philip S. Foner (New York: The Citadel Press, 1948), 405.
17. James J. McCormack, "The Evolution of Thomas Paine's *Common Sense*" (M.A. thesis, St. John's University, 1947), 13.
18. Thomas Paine, *The Age of Reason, Part I*, in *The Life and Major Writings of Thomas Paine*, ed. Philip S. Foner (New York: The Citadel Press, 1948), 496.
19. Paine, *Age I*, 83.
20. This sermon and its consequences will be fully explored in the next chapter.
21. Paine, *Age I*, 496.
22. John Keane, *Tom Paine: A Political Life* (Boston: Little, Brown and Company, 1995), 61.
23. Paine, *Rights of Man II*, 426.
24. R. Campbell, *The London Tradesman* (London: [publ. unknown], 1747; reprint, New York: A.M. Kelley, 1969), 224. (page citations are to the reprint edition).
25. Paine, *The Rights of Man II*, 405.
26. Ibid.
27. Ibid.
28. Paine, *Age I*, 496.
29. Thomas Paine, *Age II*, in *The Life and Major Writings of Thomas Paine*, ed. Philip S. Foner (New York: The Citadel Press, 1948), 771 and 827.
30. Paine, *Age I*, 498.
31. Aldridge, *American Ideology*, 109.
32. *The Universal Magazine of Knowledge and Pleasure* (London), July 1770, frontispiece, microfilm.
33. Ibid.
34. Ibid.
35. Thomas Paine, "Letter to Benjamin Franklin, June 20, 1777," *Complete Writings*, 1133.
36. Joel Barlow, "To James Cheetham, August 11, 1809," in *Life and Letters of Joel Barlow, Poet, Statesman, Philosopher*, ed. Charles Burr Todd (New York: The Knickerbocker Press, 1886; reprint, New York: Burt Franklin, 1972), 238–239. (page citations are to the reprint edition).
37. "Thomas Paine's Banns of Marriage," original, The Thomas Paine Collection, Thetford Public Library, Thetford, England. According to English law dating back to the thirteenth century, three Sundays prior to the ceremony an announcement (or banns) must be made in the church where the marriage will take place. The bride and groom are also required by law to reside in the parish where they marry. Interestingly, there is currently a movement in England to end the 800 year-old practice.
38. Hazel Burgess, "To Thomas, a Daughter," *Thetford Magazine* 22(Summer 2000): 15. Sarah Paine was baptized fifteen months after her parents' marriage.

39. Ibid. The burial entry reads "Paine: Sarah Dr [daughter] of Thomas and Mary." Burgess speculates that because there is no record of Mary Paine's death she may possibly have lived apart from Thomas for years afterwards. This seems implausible as Paine married again later and such an act would have made him a bigamist. It seems more likely that Mary Paine died immediately following or shortly after the birth of their daughter Sarah.
40. Thomas Clio Rickman, *The Life of Thomas Paine* (London: Thomas Clio Rickman, 1819).
41. Thomas Paine, "Letter to the Board of Excise, July 3, 1766," *Complete Writings*, 1128.
42. William C. Kashatus III, "Thomas Paine: A Quaker Revolutionary," *Quaker History* 73 (1984): 42.
43. Linda Colley, *Britons: Forging the Nation, 1707–1837* (New Haven, Connecticut: Yale University Press, 1992), 108.
44. Ibid., 111.
45. Thomas Paine, *Common Sense*, in *The Life and Major Writings of Thomas Paine*, ed. Philip S. Foner (New York: The Citadel Press, 1948), 25.
46. Colley, *Britons*, 208.
47. Ibid.
48. Ibid.
49. Rickman, *Life of Paine*, 12. William Lee of Lewes was the editor of a newspaper in Sussex and a member of the Club—he passed the book on to Rickman.
50. *The Town Book of Lewes, 1702–1837*, Sussex Record Society, ed. Verena Smith, no. 69 (Lewes, England: The Society of Barbican House, 1972). The first entry for "T. Paine" is on page 57.
51. Robert Francis Smith, Jr. "Thomas Paine and the American Political Tradition" (Ph.D. diss., University of Notre Dame, 1977), 284.
52. Ibid.
53. Michael M. Kiley. "Thomas Paine: An American Founder and Political Scientist," *Biography* 8(1) [1985]: 54.
54. Thomas Paine, *Case of the Officers of Excise, Complete Writings*, 5.
55. Ibid., 8.
56. Foner, *Revolutionary America*, 14.
57. Thomas Paine, "Letter to Oliver Goldsmith, December 21, 1772," *Complete Writings*, 1129.
58. There is no evidence to suggest that Paine and Goldsmith ever actually met, or that Goldsmith responded at all to Paine's invitation. See Chester Chapin, "Oliver Goldsmith and Thomas Paine," *ANQ—A Quarterly Journal of Short Articles Notes and Reviews* 11(2): 22–23.
59. F.R.S. stands for "Fellow of the Royal Society."
60. *Cyclopaedia; or, An universal dictionary of arts and sciences*, published in 1751 and 1752.
61. Thomas Paine, "Letter to Henry Laurens, January 14, 1779," *Complete Writings*, 1162.
62. Ibid.

63. Ibid.
64. Paine, *Rights of Man II*, 441.
65. Divorce was very difficult and costly in eighteenth-century Britain. It was usually reserved for the very wealthy. There were, however, other methods to legally separate from unwanted spouses. The easiest, most common ways were to claim abandonment or adultery. In Paine's case the choice was apparently separation by private deed. In such arrangements both parties mutually agreed to a separation; the husband assured his wife of alimony for life, and in return was free from any debts she incurred. Generally the wife was free to act financially in the capacity of a single woman which gave her a great deal of autonomy. Such agreements also allowed either spouse to remarry or cohabit with others without committing bigamy. Rickman claimed that Paine sent money to his second wife, Elizabeth Ollive, until his death (she outlived him). Legal separation could also be claimed if the marriage had never been consummated either as the result of impotence or frigidity. This claim was less common, but it may shed light on the rumors of Paine's impotence which surfaced later. For more information on marital dissolution in Britain see Lawrence Stone, *Broken Lives: Separation and Divorce in England, 1660–1857* (London: Oxford University Press, 1993).
66. Charles J. Norman, "'The American Crisis' By Thomas Paine: A Rhetorical Analysis" (Ph.D. diss., Lehigh University, 1988), 16.
67. Foner, *Revolutionary America*, 4.

NOTES TO CHAPTER FOUR

1. Vikki J. Vickers, "The Origins of the Religious Beliefs of Thomas Paine" (M.A. thesis, University of Missouri-Columbia, 1996). This chapter has been largely adapted from and based upon that work.
2. Robert Francis Smith, Jr., "Thomas Paine and the American Political Tradition" (Ph.D. diss., University of Notre Dame, 1977), 11.
3. "Some," according to Arnold King, "contend that he simply adapted the Quaker ideas . . . that he absorbed from his father." Others, he argues, "find the key to be scientific-deism." Arnold King, "Thomas Paine in America, 1774–1787" (Ph.D. diss., University of Chicago, 1952), 44.
4. Conway was so convinced of the Quaker influence on Paine that he proclaimed "in a profounder sense, Paine was George Fox [the founder of the Society of Friends]." William Kashatus completely discounts Paine's interest in Newtonian science to insist that he was a Quaker during the American Revolution. Moncure Conway, *The Life of Thomas Paine*, vol. 2, (New York: G.P. Putnam's Sons, 1908), 202.
5. See Harry Hayden Clark, "An Historical Interpretation of Thomas Paine's Religion," *University of California Chronicle* 35(1933): 56–87, and "Toward a Reinterpretation of Thomas Paine," *American Literature* 5 (March 1933-January 1934): 133–145.
6. For example, scholars who are more inclined to believe that Quakerism was the primary influence have a tendency to argue that Paine was some

sort of "rational Christian" or a pantheist. Those who believe that science was the principal influence on the origins of Paine's beliefs tend to place his theology alongside those of the seventeenth-century English deists like Lord Herbert of Cherbury—the founder of English deism. Lamentably, none of these interpretations are correct; the truth lies in the confluence of these extremes—the one place scholars have not looked.

7. Robert Falk's article, "Thomas Paine: deist or Quaker?" is a prime example of this type of thinking.
8. Moncure Conway, *Life of Paine,* vol. 1, (New York: G.P. Putnam's Sons, 1908), 11. Since Conway, those who have attempted to qualify or quantify this influence have traditionally been extremists. On one end of the spectrum are scholars like W.E.Woodward who devoted one entire chapter of his biography to "The Little Quaker Boy," and Mary Agnes Best who asserted that "some regard [Paine] as the father of the Hicksite Quaker movement." On the opposite end of the spectrum are historians like Harry Hayden Clark who argued that Quakerism had very little influence on Paine, and that it was Newtonian science that ultimately led to the formation of his deism. Clark maintained that "Paine pushed the argument to extremes certainly not typical of the Quaker faith in the divinity of the Redeemer." Few, like Robert Falk, chose a middle course. W.E. Woodward, *Tom Paine: America's Godfather, 1737–1809* (New York: E.P. Dutton and Co., 1945) and Mary Agnes Best, *Thomas Paine: Prophet and Martyr of Democracy* (New York: Harcourt, Brace, and Co., 1927), 406.
9. Ira M. Thompson, *The Religious Beliefs of Thomas Paine* (New York: Vintage Press, 1965), 61.
10. Falk, "deist or Quaker?" 63.
11. Frederick B. Tolles, *Quakers and the Atlantic Culture* (New York: The Macmillan Co., 1960).
12. Ibid.
13. Hesketh Pearson, *Tom Paine: Friend of Mankind* (New York: Harper and Brothers, 1937), 2, and Jack Fruchtman Jr., *Thomas Paine and the Religion of Nature* (Baltimore:The Johns Hopkins University Press, 1993), 60.
14. John Punshon, *Portrait in Grey: A Short History of the Quakers* (London: Quaker Home Service, 1984), 135.
15. Thomas Paine, *The Age of Reason, Part I,* in *The Complete Writings of Thomas Paine,* ed. Philip S. Foner (New York: The Citadel Press, 1945), 496.
16. Ibid.
17. Thomas Paine, "Worship and Church Bells: A Letter to Camille Jordan, 1797," *Complete Writings,* 759.
18. Punshon, *Portrait in Grey,* 87.
19. Paine, *Age I,* 498.
20. Henry Redhead Yorke, *Letters from France, 1802,* vol. 2 (London: Bye and Law, 1804), 365.
21. Thomas Paine, *The Age of Reason, Part II, Complete Writings,* 183, and Falk, "deist or Quaker?" 56.

22. Thomas Paine, "The Prospect Papers, 1804" *Complete Writings*, 817.
23. Robert Barclay, *An Apology for the True Christian Divinity: Being an Explanation and Vindication of the Principles and Doctrines of the People Called Quakers* (London: Thomas Tegg, 1825), 69.
24. Ibid., 5.
25. Ibid., 4.
26. Douglas Gwyn, *Apocalypse of the Word: The Life and Message of George Fox (1624-1691)* (Richmond, Indiana: Friends United Press, 1984), 118.
27. Edward Davidson and William J. Scheick, *Paine, Scripture, and Authority: The Age of Reason as Religious and Political Idea* (Bethlehem, Pennsylvania: Lehigh University Press, 1994), 28.
28. Paine, *Age I*, 484.
29. Nineteenth Psalm, King James Version.
30. D. Elton Trueblood, *Robert Barclay* (New York: Harper and Row, 1968), 55.
31. Ibid., 17.
32. Ibid., vii.
33. Punshon, *Portrait in Grey*, 122.
34. Trueblood, *Robert Barclay*, 8.
35. Rufus M. Jones, *The Later Periods of Quakerism*, vol.1, (London: Macmillan and Co., Ltd., 1921), 59.
36. Thomas Paine, "Epistle to the Quakers, 1776," *Complete Writings*, 57n (author's note).
37. Alfred Owen Aldridge, *Thomas Paine's American Ideology* (Newark: University of Delaware Press, 1984), 90. It is true that Voltaire printed this passage from Barclay in his *English Letters* (first English translation 1733), but the likelihood of Paine encountering Barclay from Voltaire instead of the author himself is slight given Paine's background.
38. Compare Paine's citation with that of Barclay. It seems apparent that Paine probably copied from (or memorized) Barclay's text:

    Paine: Thou hast tasted of prosperity and adversity; thou knowest what it is to be banished thy native country, to be over-ruled as well as to rule, and sit upon the throne: and being *oppressed* thou hast reason to know how *hateful* the *oppressor* is both to God and man; If after all these warnings and advertisements, thou dost not turn unto the Lord with all thy heart, but forget him who remembered thee in thy distress, and give up thyself to follow lust and vanity, surely, great will be thy condemnation.— Against which snare, as well as the temptation of those who may or do feed thee, and prompt thee to evil, the most excellent and prevalent remedy will be, to apply thyself to that light of Christ which shineth in thy conscience, and which neither can nor will flatter thee, nor suffer thee to be at ease in thy sins.

    Barclay: Thou hast tasted of prosperity and adversity; thou knowest what it is to be banished thy native country, to be overruled, as well as to rule, and sit upon the throne; and being *oppressed*, thou hast reason to know how *hateful* the *oppressor* is both to God and man: if after all these warnings and advertisements, thou dost not turn unto the Lord with all thy heart, but forget him, who remembered thee in thy distress, and give up thyself to follow lust and vanity: surely great will be thy condemnation.

Against which snare, as well as the temptation of those that may or do feed thee, and prompt thee to evil, the most excellent and prevalent remedy will be, to apply thyself to that *Light of Christ*, which *shineth in they conscience,* which neither can nor will flatter thee, nor suffer thee to be at ease in thy sins; but doth and will deal plainly and faithfully with thee, as those that are followers thereof have also done.

39. Thomas Paine, "To the Citizens of the United States, November 19, 1802," *Complete Writings*, 917.
40. Paine, *Age I*, 83, and Barclay, *Apology*, 107.
41. Barclay, *Apology*, 110.
42. Ibid., 137–138.
43. Paine, *Age I*, 484 and 482.
44. Barclay, *Apology*, 61–62.
45. Ibid.
46. Ibid.
47. Trueblood, *Robert Barclay*, 136.
48. Thomas Paine, *The Age of Reason, Part II*, in *Thomas Paine: Collected Writings*, ed. Eric Foner (New York: Literary Classics of the United States, 1995), 771.
49. Paine, *Age I*, 487.
50. Paine, "Worship and Church Bells," *Complete Writings*, 759.
51. Thomas Paine, "The Will of Thomas Paine, January 18, 1809" *Complete Writings*, 1500.
52. Ibid.
53. Thomas Paine, "To the Right Honorable Marquis of Lansdowne, September 21, 1787," *Complete Writings*, 1265.
54. Paine, *Age I*, 497.
55. Paine, *Age II*, 763.
56. Paine, *Age I*, 497.
57. Ibid., 496.
58. Ibid.
59. Ibid.
60. Ibid., 498n (author's note).
61. Thomas Paine, *The Rights of Man, Part I*, in *Life and Major Writings*, 320.
62. Paine, *Age I*, 499 and *Age II*, EF, 827.
63. Paine, *Age I*, 503.
64. Paine, *Age II*, EF, 827.
65. Ibid.
66. Ibid.
67. Ibid.
68. Ibid., 829.
69. Paine, *Age I*, 499.

Notes to Chapter Four 161

70. Elie Halévy, *The Birth of Methodism in England,* trans. and ed. by Bernard Semmel (Chicago: The University of Chicago Press, 1971), 51.
71. John Wesley, *The Journal of the Reverend John Wesley,* vol. 8, ed. Nehemiah Curnock (London: The Epworth Press, 1938), 31n.
72. "The Visitor," "The White Cliffs of Dover: Methodism in a Great Fortress," *The Methodist Recorder and General Christian Chronicle* (August 19, 1906), 9.
73. George Hindmarch, "Thomas Paine: The Methodist Influence," *Thomas Paine Society Bulletin* 6(3) (1979): 62. Hindmarch, "The Methodist Influence," 60.
74. Spater made a significant discovery: "A few years ago a gentleman in England thought he had found the answer. He announced that he had discovered 'more than forty varied articles' written by Paine that had appeared in the local newspaper published in Lewes, Sussex, where Paine had lived from 1768–1774. They were signed 'A Forester,' and we know that several articles Paine later published in America were signed '*The* Forester' . . . . I read beyond the point where the discoverer had stopped, and I found an article in that paper seventeen years later which announced that 'On Tuesday last, after a few days' illness, died, the Rev. Richard Nichell, of East-Dean, author of the many letters that have appeared in this paper, under the signature of 'A Forester. . . .'" George Spater, "The Author of 'A Forester' Article," *Bulletin of the Thomas Paine Society* 7 (1992): 53–56.
75. John Keane, *Tom Paine: A Political Life,* (Boston: Little, Brown and Company, 1995), 544, 29n.
76. Ibid., 27.
77. Hindmarch, "The Methodist Influence," 60.
78. Thomas Paine, "My Private Thoughts on a Future State, 1807" in *The Complete Writings of Thomas Paine,* ed. Philip S. Foner (New York: The Citadel Press, 1945), 893.
79. Paine, *Age I,* 467.
80. Ibid., 504.
81. Ibid.
82. Ibid., 463–464.
83. Thomas Paine, "Letter to John Inskeep, February 1806," *Complete Writings,* 1480.
84. James Turner, *Without God, Without Creed: The Origins of Unbelief in America* (Baltimore: The Johns Hopkins Press, 1985), 74.
85. Kerry S. Walters, *The American Deists: Voices of Reason and Dissent in the Early Republic* (Lawrence, Kansas: University Press of Kansas, 1992), 209.
86. Paine, *Age I,* 464. Paine exaggerated in his assertion that the priesthood and been abolished in France during the Revolution. What Paine is most likely referring to is the radical restructuring of the Catholic Church in France which, among other things, reduced the number of bishops to 83 and allowed parishes to choose their own priests. An oath of loyalty to the republic was also required of the clergy. The controversy over the oath led

to a dramatic reduction in the number of bishops and priests—but they did not disappear entirely.

87. Ibid.
88. Thomas Paine, "Letter to Samuel Adams, January 1, 1803," *Complete Writings*, 1436.
89. Thomas Paine, *The Age of Reason, Part II*, in *Thomas Paine: Collected Writings*, ed. Eric Foner (New York: Literary Classics of the United States, 1995), 822.
90. Ibid., 779.
91. Paine, "To Anonymous, May 12, 1797," *Complete Writings*, 1398.
92. Paine, *Age II*, EF, 747.
93. Ibid., 740.
94. Paine, *Age I*, 484.
95. Paine, "To Anonymous," 1397.
96. Paine, *Age I*, 498.
97. Paine, *Age II*, EF, 746.
98. Paine, *Age I*, 474.
99. Ibid., 477.
100. Paine, *Age II*, EF, 822.
101. Paine, *Age I*, 482.
102. Paine, *Age II*, EF, 792.
103. Paine, *Age I*, 467.
104. *The Complete Religious and Theological Works of Thomas Paine*, unknown editor, (New York: Peter Eckler, N.D.), 399.
105. Thomas Paine, "To Andrew Dean August 15, 1806," *Complete Writings*, 1484.
106. Paine, *Age I*, 486–487.
107. Paine, *Age II*, EF, 825.
108. Ibid., 806.
109. John Keane, *Tom Paine: A Political Life* (Boston: Little, Brown, and Company, 1995), 396.
110. Eric Foner, *Tom Paine and Revolutionary America* (New York: Oxford University Press, 1976), 118.
111. Paine, *Age I*, 463–464.
112. Ibid.
113. John Adams, *The Autobiography of John Adams*, in *The Adams Papers: The Diary and Autobiography of John Adams*, vol. 2, ed. L.H. Butterfield (Cambridge, Massachusetts: The Belknap Press of Harvard University Press, 1961), 333.
114. Ibid.
115. Ibid.
116. Ibid.
117. Paine, *Age II*, EF, 827.
118. Thomas Paine, "Candid and Critical Remarks on a Letter Signed Ludlow, June 4, 1777," *Complete Writings*, 276.

119. Thomas Paine, The American *Crisis* Number V, March 21, 1778, 'To Sir William Howe,' in *Complete Writings*, 106.
120. Paine, *Rights of Man I*, 275.
121. Foner, *Revolutionary America*, 79.
122. There have been many excellent and very detailed histories of the publication of *Common Sense* and its effect upon the American masses, but such an examination is not warranted here. For the best history of the publication of *Common Sense* and the feud between Paine and his first publisher, Robert Bell, see Richard Gimbel, *Thomas Paine: A Bibliographical Check List of Common Sense with an Account of Its Publication* (Port Washington, New York: Kennikat Press, 1956). Other studies worth noting include: Bernard Bailyn, "The Most Uncommon Pamphlet of the Revolution," *American Heritage* 25(1973): 36–41, 91–93; Winthrop Jordan, "Familial Politics: Thomas Paine and the Killing of the King, 1776," *Journal of American History* 60(September 1973): 294–308; Gregory Claeys, *Thomas Paine: Social and Political Thought* (Boston: Unwin Hyman, 1989); Eric Foner, *Tom Paine and Revolutionary America* (London: Oxford University Press, 1976) and Pauline Maier, *From Resistance to Revolution: Colonial Radicals and the Development of American Opposition to Britain, 1765–1776* (New York: W.W. Norton and Company, 1972). See Appendix for an historiographical overview of the scholarship surrounding *Common Sense*.
123. unsigned [attributed to Paine], "The Magazine in America," *Complete Writings*, 1110. Paine echoed this belief about the press throughout his career. In a private letter to Nathanael Greene on Sept. 9, 1780, Paine informed Greene that he considered the press "the tongue of the world, and that which governs the sentiments of mankind more than anything else that ever did or can exist." (*Complete Writings*, 1110.) Two years later, in his *Letter to the Abbé Raynal* Paine publicly admitted that "Letters, the tongue of the world, have in some measure brought all mankind acquainted, and by an extension of their uses are every day promoting some new friendships." (*Letter to the Abbé Raynal, August 21, 1782*, in *Complete Writings*, 241.)
124. Thomas Paine, *The Rights of Man, Part II*, in *The Life and Major Writings of Thomas Paine*, ed. Philip S. Foner (New York: The Citadel Press, 1948), 406n.
125. Ibid.
126. Ibid.
127. Ibid.
128. Thomas Paine, *Letter to the Abbé Raynal*, 338. This work was one of Paine's favorites; it was the closest he ever came to writing an actual history of the Revolution, a project he one day looked forward to pursuing.
129. Ibid.
130. Bruce Woodcock, "Writing the Revolution: Aspects of Thomas Paine's Prose," *Prose Studies* 15(2)[1992]: 171.
131. Paine, *Age II, Collected Writings*, 830.

132. Robert A. Ferguson, "The Commonalities of *Common Sense*," *William and Mary Quarterly* 57(3) (July 2000): 502.
133. Ibid.
134. According to N. Arnold Smithline, "it is essentially [Paine] the hard-hitting advocate of republicanism and freedom who is speaking out against what he feels the clergy has used and is continuing to use as a means to control the minds and souls of men." N. Arnold Smithline, *Natural Religion in American Literature* (New Haven, Connecticut: College and University Press, 1988), 47.
135. ' "As to religion, I hold it to be the indispensable duty of government to protect all conscientious professors thereof, and I know of no other business which government has to do therewith." Thomas Paine, *Common Sense, Life and Major Writings*, 37.
136. Virginia (June 1776), Delaware and Pennsylvania (September 1776), Maryland (November 1776), and North Carolina (December 1776). See Gordon Wood, *The Creation of the American Republic, 1776–1787* (New York: W.W. Norton and Company, 1969), 133.
137. Paine, *Age I*, 465. The other two epiphanies of Paine's life were of course his rejection of Christianity as a child and his conversion to deism as a young man.
138. Edward H. Davidson and William J. Scheik, *Paine, Scripture, and Authority* (Bethlehem, Pennsylvania: Lehigh University Press, 1994), 18.
139. Thomas Paine, "Letter to John Inskeep, Mayor of the City of Philadelphia, February 1806," in *Complete Writings*, 1480.
140. Robert Francis Smith, Jr., "Thomas Paine and the American Political Tradition" (Ph.D. diss., University of Notre Dame, 1977), 270.
141. Thomas Paine, The American *Crisis* Number II, *Life and Major Writings*, 72.

NOTES TO CHAPTER FIVE

1. Edward Larkin, "Inventing an American Public: Thomas Paine, the *Pennsylvania Magazine*, and American Revolutionary Discourse," *Early American Literature* 33(i3)(Fall 1998): 177–178.
2. Cecilia M. Kenyon, "Where Paine Went Wrong," *The American Political Science Review* 45(1951): 1096.
3. Eric Foner, *Tom Paine and Revolutionary America*, (London: Oxford University Press, 1976), 87.
4. Thomas Paine, *The Rights of Man, Part I*, in *The Life and Major Writings of Thomas Paine*, ed. Philip S. Foner (New York: The Citadel Press, 1948), 318.
5. Thomas Paine, *The Age of Reason, Part I, Life and Major Writings*, 498.
6. Paine, *Age I*, 465.
7. Ibid., 484.
8. Ibid.
9. Paine, *Age I*, 463.
10. Paine, *Rights of Man II*, 406n. (author's note)

Notes to Chapter Five

11. Thomas Paine, The American *Crisis* Number I, December 1776" *Life and Major Writings*, 56.
12. Thomas Paine, "The Forester, Number Four, April 1776" *The Complete Writings of Thomas Paine*, ed. Philip S. Foner (New York: The Citadel Press, 1945), 85.
13. Paine, *Crisis I*, 56.
14. Paine, *Rights of Man I*, 266.
15. Paine, "Epistle to the Quakers," *Complete Writings*, 56.
16. Paine, *Rights of Man I*, 248.
17. Ibid., 485.
18. Paine, "The Forester, Number Four," 83.
19. Ibid., 446.
20. Thomas Paine, *The Rights of Man, Part II*, *Life and Major Writings*, 450.
21. Paine, *Common Sense*, 18.
22. Ibid., 7 and 17.
23. Ibid., 3.
24. Paine, *Rights of Man II*, 415.
25. Ibid., 421.
26. Thomas Paine, *Letter to the Abbé Raynal*, 1782, *Complete Writings*, 243.
27. Ibid.
28. Ibid.
29. Ibid., 244.
30. Ibid., 243 and 244.
31. Paine, *Rights of Man I*, 353.
32. Paine, *Rights of Man II*, 421.
33. Thomas Paine, "Serious Address to the People of Pennsylvania, December 5, 1778," *Complete Writings*, 290.
34. Ibid., 297.
35. Ibid.
36. Ibid., 449.
37. Ibid.
38. Paine, *Rights of Man II*, 447.
39. Paine, *Rights of Man I*, 248.
40. Ibid., 487.
41. Thomas Paine, *The Age of Reason, Part II*, in *Thomas Paine: Collected Writings*, ed. Eric Foner (New York: Literary Classics of the United States, 1995), 827.
42. Thomas Paine, *Case of the Officers of Excise*, *Complete Writings*, 15.
43. Paine, *Common Sense*, 43.
44. Paine, *Rights of Man I*, 279.
45. Paine, *Common Sense*, 5.
46. Paine, *Rights of Man II*, 357.
47. Paine, *Age II*, 500.
48. Eric Foner, *Revolutionary America*, 92–93.
49. Paine, *Common Sense*, 6.
50. Ibid., 43.

51. Ibid., 6.
52. Paine, "The Forester, Number Four," 85.
53. Thomas Paine, The American *Crisis* Number X, March 5, 1782 *Collected Writings*, 205.
54. Ibid.
55. Thomas Paine, "The Necessity of Taxation, April 4, 1782," *Collected Writings*, 310–311.
56. Thomas Paine, "Prospects on the Rubicon, August 20, 1787," *Complete Writings*, 623.
57. Ibid., 631.
58. Paine, *Rights of Man II*, 444.
59. Paine, *Crisis I*, 54. Unlike many deists, Paine did not believe in a "clockmaker" God who created the world and left it to run according to the physical laws God established.

    Rather, Paine believed in an active God. In this first *Crisis* paper Paine declared, "I have as little superstition in me as any man living, but my secret opinion has ever been, and is still is, that God Almighty will not give up a people to military destruction, or leave them unsupportedly to perish, who have so earnestly and so repeatedly sought to avoid the calamities of war. . . . Neither have I so much of the infidel in me, as to suppose that He has relinquished the government of the world, and given us up to the care of devils" (50–51). He continued, "throw not the burden of the day upon Providence, but '*show your faith by your works*,' that God may bless you" (55).
60. Paine, *Rights of Man I*, 267.
61. Ibid., 373.
62. Ibid., 374.
63. Ibid., 342.
64. Paine, *Age I*, 464.
65. Paine, *Rights of Man I*, 274.
66. Paine, *Common Sense*, 9.
67. Ibid.
68. Paine, *Rights of Man I*, 274–275.
69. Paine, "Serious Address," 286.
70. Ibid., 287.
71. Paine, *Rights of Man I*, 273.
72. Ibid., 274.
73. James Anthony Betka, "The Ideology and Rhetoric of Thomas Paine: Political Justification Through Metaphor" (Ph.D. diss., Rutgers University, 1975), 275.
74. There is considerable debate among historians about whether or not Paine included women and slaves in his fight for equal rights, or his definition of "equality." Paine never refers specifically to either group when mentioning the rights of man (or mankind for that matter) thus there is no concrete way to discern his true meaning. Paine expresses, in a few scattered sentences, his contempt for slavery, but says nothing about women. I speculate that Paine truly

Notes to Chapter Five

believed that every individual was a child of God and therefore equal, but whether or not Paine believed in full political rights for women and Africans or African-Americans I cannot hazard a guess—not even an educated one.

75. Paine, *Age I*, 482.
76. Ibid.
77. Ibid., 483.
78. Ibid.
79. Paine, *Letter to the Abbé Raynal*, 241.
80. Paine, *Common Sense*, 3.
81. Thomas Paine, The American *Crisis* Number VII, *Life and Major Writings*, 146.
82. Thomas Paine, The American *Crisis* Number II, *Life and Major Writings*, 58.
83. Thomas Paine, The American *Crisis* Number IX, *Life and Major Writings*, 166, and "Serious Address," 287.
84. Paine, *Rights of Man II*, 342.
85. Paine, *Letter to the Abbé Raynal*, 255.
86. Ibid.
87. Ibid., 256.
88. Ibid., 292.
89. Paine, *Age I*, 506.
90. Ibid., 464.
91. Ibid., 490.
92. Thomas Paine, The American *Crisis* Number VIII, *Life and Major Writings*, 164.
93. Harry Hayden Clark, "Toward a Reinterpretation of Thomas Paine," *American Literature* 5 (March 1933-January 1934): 141.
94. Paine, *Rights of Man I*, 266.
95. Paine, *Case of the Officers of Excise, Complete Writings*, 14.
96. Paine, *Crisis II*, 72.
97. Thomas Paine, A Supernumerary *Crisis* [To Sir Guy Carleton], May 31, 1782, *Life and Major Writings*, 217, and *Rights of Man II*, 405. The quotation is exactly the same in both works.
98. Paine, *Rights of Man I*, 258.
99. Darrel Abel, "The Significance of the Letter to the Abbé Raynal in the Progress of Thomas Paine's Thought," *Pennsylvania Magazine of History and Biography* 66 (1942): 178.
100. Thomas Paine, "Public Good, December 30, 1780," *Complete Writings*, 304.
101. Ibid.
102. Paine later expressed his concern about the Confederation government. He accurately predicted that the lack of centralized power the autonomy of the states would put America's economy and safety in jeopardy.
103. Thomas Paine, "Six Letters to Rhode Island, January 31, 1783," *Complete Writings*, 362.
104. Thomas Paine, "Dissertations on Government; the Affairs of the Bank; and Paper Money, February 18, 1786," in *The Complete Writings of Thomas Paine,* ed. Philip S. Foner (New York: The Citadel Press, 1945), 372.

105. Ibid.
106. Ibid.
107. Paine, *Rights of Man I*, 275.
108. Foner, *Revolutionary America*, 218–219.
109. Ibid.
110. Norman Sykes, "Thomas Paine," in *The Social and Political Ideas of Some Representative Thinkers of the Revolutionary Era*, ed. F.J.C. Hearnshaw (London: George G. Harrap and Co., Ltd., 1931), 137.
111. Ibid., 361.
112. Ibid., 449.
113. Ibid.
114. Paine, *Rights of Man II*, 400.
115. Ibid., 356.
116. Ibid., 406n. [author's note]
117. Ibid., 413–414.
118. Ibid., 353.
119. Ibid., 370.
120. Ibid., 398.
121. Ibid., 392.
122. Ibid.
123. Ibid., 405 and 355.
124. Ibid., 398.
125. Ibid., 432.
126. Ibid., 434.
127. Ibid., 436.
128. Ibid.
129. Ibid., 424.
130. Ibid., 425.
131. Ibid., 429.
132. Ibid.
133. Ibid.
134. Ibid.
135. Ibid., 428.
136. Ibid., 426.
137. Ibid., 427.
138. Ibid., 426. Perhaps this is the most remarkable aspect of Paine's pension program; even the Social Security Act of the United States, when it was adopted, excluded large segments of the labor force and discriminated against various ethnic and racial groups. Paine was clearly ahead of his time.
139. Ibid., 426.
140. Ibid., 427.
141. Ibid., 430.
142. Ibid.
143. Ibid., 429.
144. Ibid., 431.

145. Ibid., 452.
146. Peter J. Stanlis, review of *Thomas Paine's American Ideology*, by A. Owen Aldridge, In *Modern Age* (31–32) 1987: 157.
147. Linda Kirk, "Thomas Paine: a Child of the Enlightenment?" *Bulletin of the Society for the Study of Labour History* 52(3)[1987]: 11.
148. Paine, *Common Sense*, 5.
149. Paine, *Rights of Man II*, 397.
150. Kirk, "Child of the Enlightenment?" 11.
151. Walter Woll, *Thomas Paine: Motives for Rebellion*, Anglo-Saxon Language and Literature Series (Frankfurt am Main: European University Studies, 1992), 9.
152. Paine, *Common Sense*, 29.
153. Paine, *Rights of Man I*, 291.
154. Paine, *Common Sense*, 37.
155. Ibid.
156. Paine, *Rights of Man I*, 291.
157. Paine, *Age I*, 504.
158. Harry Hayden Clark, "An Historical Interpretation of Thomas Paine's Religion," *University of California Chronicle* 35(1933): 60.

NOTES TO THE CONCLUSION

1. Thomas Paine, "To a Committee of the Continental Congress, October 1783," in *The Complete Writings of Thomas Paine*, ed. Philip S. Foner (New York: The Citadel Press, 1945), 1239.
2. Ibid.
3. Ibid.
4. Thomas Paine, "To Henry Laurens, September 14, 1779," *Complete Writings*, 1179.
5. Paine, "To the Continental Congress," 1239.
6. Ibid., 1241.
7. Ibid., 1240.
8. Ibid.
9. Ibid., 1242.
10. Thomas Paine, *Letter to the Abbe Raynal*, August 21, 1782, *Complete Writings*, 215.
11. Ibid.
12. Ibid.
13. Paine, "To the Continental Congress," 1239.
14. Sean Wilentz, review of *Thomas Paine: Collected Writings*, edited by Eric Foner, *Thomas Paine: Apostle of Freedom*, by Jack Fruchtman, and *Tom Paine: A Political Life*, by John Keane, In *The New Republic* 212(17)(April 24, 1995): 39.
15. Henry Leffman, "The Real Thomas Paine, Patriot and Publicist: A Philosopher Misunderstood," *Pennsylvania Magazine of History and Biography* 46(1922): 98.

16. Paine, "To the Continental Congress," 1240.
17. Ibid.
18. Thomas Paine, The American *Crisis*, Number XIII, April 19, 1783, in *The Life and Major Writings of Thomas Paine*, ed. Philip S. Foner (New York: The Citadel Press, 1948), 235, and Paine, *The Rights of Man, Part II, Life and Major Writings*, 406.
19. Paine, *Letter to the Abbé Raynal*, 214.
20. Ibid.
21. Paine, *Rights of Man II*, 406.

NOTES TO THE APPENDIX

1. Elaine Kaner Ginsberg, "The Rhetoric of Revolution: an Analysis of Thomas Paine's *Common Sense*" (Ph.D. diss., University of Oklahoma, 1971) and Bruce Woodcock, "Writing the Revolution: Aspects of Thomas Paine's Prose," *Prose Studies* 15(2) [1992]: 171–186.
2. Edward Larkin, "Inventing an American Public: Thomas Paine, the *Pennsylvania Magazine*, and American Revolutionary Discourse," *Early American Literature* 33(i3)(Fall 1998):252.
3. Robert A. Ferguson, "The Commonalities of *Common Sense*," *William and Mary Quarterly* 57(3)(July 2000): 492–493.
4. Eric Foner, *Tom Paine and Revolutionary America* (London: Oxford University Press, 1976), 84.
5. Bernard Bailyn, "The Most Uncommon Pamphlet of the Revolution," *American Heritage* 25(1973): 93.
6. See A. Owen Aldridge, *Thomas Paine's American Ideology* (Newark: University of Delaware Press, 1984), and Sean Wilentz, review of *Thomas Paine: Collected Writings*, edited by Eric Foner, *Thomas Paine: Apostle of Freedom*, by Jack Fruchtman, and *Tom Paine: A Political Life*, by John Keane, In *The New Republic* 212 (17)(April 24, 1995): 34–41.
7. Ferguson, "Commonalities of *Common Sense*," 465–504.
8. Thomas Paine, *Common Sense*, in *The Life and Major Writings of Thomas Paine*, ed. Philip S. Foner (New York: The Citadel Press, 1948), 17.
9. Ferguson, "Commonalities of *Common Sense*," 486.
10. Thomas Paine, *Common Sense*, 29 and 14.
11. Winthrop Jordan, "Familial Politics and the Killing of the King, 1776," *Journal of American History* 60(September 1973): 297.
12. Stuart Andrews, "Paine's American Pamphlets," *History Today* 31(July 1981): 7. For discussions of the influence of Paine's rhetoric, see any of the literary studies previously noted or, likewise, Bailyn and Jordan's brilliant essays.
13. James J. McCormack, "The Evolution of Thomas Paine's *Common Sense*" (M.A. thesis, St. John's University, 1947), 39.
14. Albert Matthews, "Thomas Paine and the Declaration of Independence," *Proceedings of the Massachusetts Historical Society* 43(1910): 243.
15. Ibid.

16. Ibid.
17. See Joseph Lewis, *Thomas Paine: Author of the Declaration of Independence* (New York: Freethought Press Assn., 1947) and Albert Matthews, "Thomas Paine and the Declaration of Independence." There is no evidence that Paine had any part in the actual drafting of the Declaration, and a great deal of evidence that proves that Jefferson acted alone.
18. Ibid.
19. Ibid., 85.
20. Ibid.
21. Jordan, "Familial Politics," 295.
22. Pauline Maier, *From Resistance to Revolution: Colonial Radicals and the Development of American Opposition to Britain, 1765–1776* (New York: W.W. Norton and Company, 1972), 269.
23. The recent consensus is that because there is no way to quantify or prove scientifically a link between *Common Sense* and the Declaration, it should not be discussed further in any conclusive way. It would also be fair to mention that there are a number of studies which give very little credence to the influence of ideas in the creation of American Independence. Among them is a very fine study by Robert Gross entitled *The Minutemen and Their World* (New York: Hill and Wang, 1976).
24. John Adams, *The Autobiography of John Adams,* in *The Adams Papers: The Diary and Autobiography of John Adams,* vol. 2, ed. L.H. Butterfield (Cambridge, Massachusetts: The Belknap Press of Harvard University Press, 1961), 330.
25. Foner, *Revolutionary America,* 123.
26. Ibid.
27. Ibid., xi.
28. Bernard Bailyn, *The Ideological Origins of the American Revolution* (Cambridge, Massachusetts: The Belknap Press of Harvard University Press, 1967), 286.
29. Ibid., 285.
30. Robert Francis Smith, Jr., "Thomas Paine and the American Political Tradition" (Ph.D. diss., University of Notre Dame, 1977), 5.
31. Sean Wilentz, review of *Thomas Paine: Collected Writings,* edited by Eric Foner, *Thomas Paine: Apostle of Freedom,* by Jack Fruchtman, Jr. and *Tom Paine: A Political Life,* by John Keane, In *The New Republic* April 24, 1995: 36.
32. Cecilia M. Kenyon, "Where Paine Went Wrong," *The American Political Science Review* 45(1951): 1086–1099.
33. Ibid.,1099.
34. Ibid.
35. Robert Ferguson and other literary scholars, for example, easily reach the conclusion that Paine's pamphlet was original because of his rhetoric, giving little attention to his political arguments.
36. Wilentz, "Review," 36.
37. Ibid., 40.

38. Ibid.
39. For a complete discussion of universalism as a theme in Paine's writing see Chapter Five.
40. Gregory Claeys, *Thomas Paine: Social and Political Thought* (Boston: Unwin Hyman, 1989), 216.
41. Smith, "American Political Tradition," 5.
42. According to Ferguson, "Orthodox colonial readers could still reach their Calvinist God through Paine's construct, but just as available were a Quaker God (an image in the human heart), a deistic God (at work in nature's design), and a Scottish moral-sense God (instilling inextinguishable feelings for good and wise purposes). The Supreme Being remains scrupulously abstract in the pages of *Common Sense*." Ferguson, "Commonalities of *Common Sense*," (487). See also Paine, *Common Sense, Life and Major Writings*, 30.
43. I am referring of course to Paine's argument that the book of Samuel denounces monarchy.
44. Aldridge, *American Ideology*, 95.
45. Ibid., 102, 105.
46. The first is on page 8, when Paine refers to Parliament as "a house divided against itself." (King James Version Mark 3:25) The second is on page 10 when Paine argues, "*Render unto Cesar the things which are Cesar's* is the scripture doctrine of courts, yet it is no support of monarchical government, for the Jews at that time were without a king, and in a state of vassalage to the Romans." (KJV Matthew 22:21 and Luke 20:25) In fact Paine uses a Christian citation to demonstrate the anachronism inherent in arguments surrounding the origin of kings.
47. Paine, *Common Sense*, 10.
48. Jack Fruchtman, Jr., "The Revolutionary Millennialism of Thomas Paine," in *Studies in Eighteenth-Century Culture*, vol. 13, ed. O.M. Brack (Madison, Wisconsin: University of Wisconsin Press, 1984), 68.
49. Ibid.
50. Ibid., 65–66.
51. Ruth Bloch, *Visionary Republic: Millennial Themes in American Thought, 1756–1800* (Cambridge, England: Cambridge University Press, 1985), xvi.
52. Ibid., 194.
53. Claeys, *Social and Political Thought*, 104.
54. Bloch, *Visionary Republic*, 75.
55. Ibid., 86.
56. Ibid., 93.
57. Catharine Albanese, *Sons of the Fathers: The Civil Religion of the American Revolution* (Philadelphia: Temple University Press, 1976), 114.
58. Ibid., 115.

Bibliography

Abel, Darrel. "The Significance of the Letter to the Abbé Raynal in the Progress of Thomas Paine's Thought." *Pennsylvania Magazine of History and Biography* 66(1942): 176–190.
Adams, John. *The Autobiography of John Adams.* In *The Adams Papers: The Diary and Autobiography of John Adams,* vol. 2, ed. L.H. Butterfield. Cambridge, Massachusetts: The Belknap Press of Harvard University Press, 1961.
Aitken, Robert. "Proposal For Printing by *Subscription,* THE PENNSYLVANIA MAGAZINE of the AMERICAN REPOSITORY of useful knowledge." *The Pennsylvania Packet,* November 21, 1774.
Albanese, Catharine. *Sons of the Fathers: The Civil Religion of the American Revolution.* Philadelphia: Temple University Press, 1976.
Aldridge, A. Owen. *Thomas Paine's American Ideology.* Newark: University of Delaware Press, 1984.
Andrews, Stuart. "Paine's American Pamphlets." *History Today* 31(July 1981): 7–11.
"Atlanticus." "Useful and Entertaining Hints." In *The Complete Writings of Thomas Paine.* Edited by Philip S. Foner. New York: The Citadel Press, 1945.
———. "Reflections on the Life and Death of Lord Clive." In *The Complete Writings of Thomas Paine.* Edited by Philip S. Foner. New York: The Citadel Press, 1945.
Bailyn, Bernard. *The Ideological Origins of the American Revolution.* Cambridge, Massachusetts: The Belknap Press of Harvard University Press, 1967.
———. "The Most Uncommon Pamphlet of the Revolution." *American Heritage* 25(1973): 36–41, 91–93.
———. *Voyagers to the West: A Passage in the Peopling of America on the Eve of the Revolution.* New York: Vintage Books, 1986.
Barclay, Robert. *An Apology for the True Christian Divinity: Being an Explanation and Vindication of the Principles and Doctrines of the People Called Quakers.* London: Thomas Tegg, 1825.
Barlow, Joel. "To James Cheetham, August 11, 1809." In *Life and Letters of Joel Barlow, Poet, Statesman, Philosopher.* Edited by Charles Burr Todd. New York: The Knickerbocker Press, 1886; reprint, New York: Burt Franklin, 1972.

Berthold, S.M. *Thomas Paine: America's First Liberal*. Boston: Meador Publishing Co., 1938.
Betka, James Anthony. "The Ideology and Rhetoric of Thomas Paine: Political Justification Through Metaphor." Ph.D. diss., Rutgers University, 1975.
Bloch, Ruth H. *Visionary Republic: Millennial Themes in American Thought, 1756–1800*. Cambridge, England: Cambridge University Press, 1985.
"Bucks County." "The Dream Interpreted." In *The Complete Writings of Thomas Paine*. Edited by Philip S. Foner. New York: The Citadel Press, 1945.
Calverton, V.F. "Thomas Paine: God-Intoxicated Revolutionary." *Scribner's* 95(January 1934): 15–22.
Campbell, R. *The London Tradesman*. London: [publ.?]: 1747. Reprint, New York: A.M. Kelley, 1969.
Chadwick, John W. *Thomas Paine: The Method and Value of His Religious Teachings*. New York: Chas. M. Green, 1877.
Chapin, Chester. "Oliver Goldsmith and Thomas Paine." *ANQ—A Quarterly Journal of Short Articles Notes and Reviews* 11(2)[1998]:22–23.
Claeys, Gregory. *Thomas Paine: Social and Political Thought*. Boston: Unwin Hyman, 1989.
Clark, Harry Hayden. "An Historical Interpretation of Thomas Paine's Religion." *University of California Chronicle* 35(1933):56–87.
———."Toward a Reinterpretation of Thomas Paine." *American Literature* 5(March 1933–January 1934): 133–145.
Colley, Linda. *Britons: Forging the Nation, 1707–1837*. New Haven, Connecticut: Yale University Press, 1992.
Conner, Jett Burnett. "Thomas Paine and the First Principles of Democratic Republics." Ph.D. diss., University of Colorado at Boulder, 1980.
"Contents." *The Pennsylvania Magazine,* January 1775.
———. *The Pennsylvania Magazine,* February 1775.
———. *The Pennsylvania Magazine,* May 1775.
———. *The Pennsylvania Magazine,* July 1775.
———. *The Pennsylvania Magazine,* August 1775.
Conway, Moncure D. *The Life of Thomas Paine*. In 2 volumes. New York: G.P. Putnam's Sons, 1908.
Crosby, Alan. *A History of Thetford*. Sussex, England: Phillmore & Co., Ltd., 1986.
Davidson, Edward H. and William J. Scheik. *Paine, Scripture, and Authority*. Bethlehem, Pennsylvania: Lehigh University Press, 1994.
Dennis, Donald Dean. "The Deistic Trio: A Study in the Central Religious Beliefs of Ethan Allen, Thomas Paine, and Elihu Palmer." Ph.D. diss., University of Utah, 1979.
A Description of the Diocese of Norwich: or, The present state of Norfolk and Suffolk. giving an account of the situation, extent, trade, and customs, of the city of Norwich in particular. And of the several market-towns in those counties . . . By a gentleman of the Inner Temple, and native of the diocese of Norwich. London: for T. Cooper, 1735.

Dickinson, H.T. Review of *Tom Paine: A Political Life* by John Keane and *Thomas Paine: Apostle of Freedom* by Jack Fruchtman. In *History* 81 (262 [1996]): 228–237.
Dyck, Ian. "Local Attachments, National Identities and World Citizenship in the Thought of Thomas Paine." *History Workshop Journal* 35(1993): 117–135.
Eliot, T.S. "The Lovesong of J. Alfred Prufrock." *T.S. Eliot: The Complete Poems and Plays (1909–1950)*. New York: Harcourt Brace & Company, 1980.
Emerson, Ralph Waldo. "Self-Reliance." In *The Norton Anthology of American Literature*, ed. by Nina Baym, et al., 3rd Edition, vol. 1, 956–972. New York: W.W. Norton and Company, 1989.
"Esop." "Cupid and Hymen." In *The Complete Writings of Thomas Paine*. Edited by Philip S. Foner. New York: The Citadel Press, 1945.
Falk, Robert. "Thomas Paine: Deist or Quaker?" *Pennsylvania Magazine of History and Biography* 63(1938): 52–63.
Ferguson, Robert A. "The Commonalities of *Common Sense*." *William and Mary Quarterly* 57(2)(July 2000): 465–504.
Foner, Eric. *Tom Paine and Revolutionary America*. London: Oxford University Press, 1976.
Fruchtman, Jack Jr. "The Revolutionary Millennialism of Thomas Paine." In *Studies in Eighteenth-Century Culture*, vol. 13, ed.O.M. Brack, Jr., 65–77. Madison: University of Wisconsin Press, 1984.
———. "Nature and Revolution in Paine's Common Sense." *History of Political Thought* 10(3)[1985]: 421–438.
———. *Thomas Paine and the Religion of Nature*. Baltimore: The Johns Hopkins University Press, 1993.
———. *Thomas Paine: Apostle of Freedom*. New York: Four Walls Eight Windows, 1994.
Gimbel, Richard. *Thomas Paine: A Bibliographical Check List of Common Sense with an Account of Its Publication*. Port Washington, New York: Kennikat Press, 1956.
Ginsberg, Elaine Kaner. "The Rhetoric of Revolution: an Analysis of Thomas Paine's Common Sense." Ph.D. diss., University of Oklahoma, 1971.
Godfrey, Walter H. *At the Sign of the Bull, Lewes*. With an account by J.M. Connell. London: Eyre and Spottiswoode, Ltd., 1924.
Gross, Robert A. *The Minutemen and Their World*. New York: Hill and Wang, 1976.
Gwyn, Douglas. *Apocalypse of the Word: The Life and Message of George Fox (1624–1691)*. Richmond, Indiana: Friends United Press,1984.
Hail, Francina Kercheville. "Thomas Paine: An Interpretive Study of the Treatment of Paine by Biographers, Historians and Critics." Ph.D. diss., University of New Mexico, 1977.
Halévy, Elie. *The Birth of Methodism in England*. Trans. and ed. Bernard Semmel. Chicago: The University of Chicago Press, 1971.
Harris, Ian. "Paine and Burke: God, nature and politics." In *Public and Private Doctrine: Essays in British History presented to Maurice Cowling*, ed. Michael Bentley, 34–62. Cambridge: Cambridge University Press, 1993.

Hindmarch, George. "Thomas Paine: The Methodist Influence." *Thomas Paine Society Bulletin* (March 1979): 59–78.
Jones, Rufus. M. *The Later Periods of Quakerism*. In 2 volumes. London: Macmillan and Co., Ltd., 1921.
Jordan, Winthrop D. "Familial Politics: Thomas Paine and the Killing of the King, 1776." *Journal of American History* 60(September 1973): 294–308.
Kashatus, William C. III. "Thomas Paine: A Quaker Revolutionary." *Quaker History* 73(1984): 38–61.
Keane, John. *Tom Paine: A Political Life*. Boston: Little, Brown and Company, 1995.
Kenyon, Cecilia M. "Where Paine Went Wrong." *The American Political Science Review* 45 (1951): 1086–1099.
Kiley, Michael Mills. "The Republic of Reason: The Political Ideas of Thomas Paine." Ph.D. diss., University of California at Santa Barbara, 1979.
———. "Thomas Paine: An American Founder and Political Scientist." *Biography* 8(1) [1985]: 51–67.
King, Arnold K. "Thomas Paine in America, 1774–1787." Ph. D. diss., University of Chicago, 1952.
Kirk, Linda. "Thomas Paine: a Child of the Enlightenment?" *Bulletin of the Society for the Study of Labour History* 52(3)[1987]: 3–13.
Larkin, Edward. "Thomas Paine and the New Literature of Revolutionary Politics." Ph.D. diss., Stanford University, 1998.
———. "Inventing an American Public: Thomas Paine, the Pennsylvania Magazine, and American Revolutionary Discourse."*Early American Literature* 33 (i3) (Fall 1998): 250–275.
Leffman, Henry. "The Real Thomas Paine, Patriot and Publicist: A Philosopher Misunderstood." *Pennsylvania Magazine of History and Biography* 46(1922): 81–99.
Locke, John. *The Second Treatise of Government*. Cambridge Texts in the History of Political Thought, ed. Peter Laslett. Cambridge, England: Cambridge University Press, 1988.
"A Lover of Peace." "Thoughts on Defensive War." In *The Complete Writings of Thomas Paine*. Edited by Philip S. Foner. New York: The Citadel Press, 1945.
Lyttle, Charles H. "Thomas Paine's Religion of Humanity." *Unity* 118(1937): 192–193.
McConnell, Bishop Francis John. *Evangelicals, Revolutionists, and Idealists: Six English Contributors to American Thought and Action*. New York: Abingdon-Cokesbury Press, 1942.
McCormack, James J. "The Evolution of Thomas Paine's *Common Sense*." M.A. thesis, St. John's University, 1947.
McGovern, John. "Ben Franklin and Tom Paine." *National Magazine* 23(1906): 426–452.
Maier, Pauline. *From Resistance to Revolution: Colonial Radicals and the Development of American Opposition to Britain, 1765–1776*. New York: W.W. Norton and Company, 1972.

Bibliography

Matthews, Albert. "Thomas Paine and the Declaration of Independence." *Proceedings of the Massachusetts Historical Society* 43(1910): 241–253.

Mayhew, Jonathan. *A Discourse Concerning Unlimited Submission and Non-Resistance to the Higher Powers.* American Classics Facsimile Series III, ed. Norman E. Tanis. Northridge, California: Santa Susana Press, 1976.

Metzgar, Joseph Valentine. "Thomas Paine: A Study in Social and Intellectual History." Ph.D. diss., University of New Mexico, 1965.

Middlekauf, Robert. *The Glorious Cause: The American Revolution,1763–1789.* New York: Oxford University Press, 1982.

Milton, John. *Paradise Lost.* In *The Norton Anthology of English Literature.* Vol. 1. Fifth Edition. Ed. M.H. Abrams, et al. New York: W.W. Norton & Company, 1986.

———. *A Defence of the People of England* [London 1658]. In *John Milton: Political Writings.* Ed. Martin Dzelzainis. Transl. Claire Gruzelier. Cambridge, England: Cambridge University Press, 1991.

Nash, Gary. *The Urban Crucible: The Northern Seaports and the Origins of the American Revolution.* Cambridge, Massachusetts: Harvard University Press, 1979.

Norman, Charles J. "'The American Crisis' By Thomas Paine: A Rhetorical Analysis." Ph.D. diss., Lehigh University, 1988.

"P." "*Trifles, light as air, Are to the jealous confirmations strong.*" Supplement to *The Pennsylvania Packet and General Advertiser. The Pennsylvania Packet,* August 30, 1773.

———. "Of Love of Country, from the St. James Chronicle." *The Pennsylvania Packet,* January 23, 1775.

"Pacificus." Untitled. *The Pennsylvania Packet,* November 20, 1773.

Paine, Thomas. Letter to the Board of Excise, July 3, 1766. In *The Complete Writings of Thomas Paine.* Edited by Philip S. Foner. New York: The Citadel Press, 1945.

———. *Case of the Officers of Excise,* 1772. In *The Complete Writings of Thomas Paine.* Edited by Philip S. Foner. New York: The Citadel Press, 1945.

———. Letter to Oliver Goldsmith, December 21, 1772. In *The Complete Writings of Thomas Paine.* Edited by Philip S. Foner. New York: The Citadel Press, 1945.

———. Letter to Benjamin Franklin, March 5, 1775. In *The Complete Writings of Thomas Paine.* Edited by Philip S. Foner. New York: The Citadel Press, 1945.

———. *Common Sense.* In *The Life and Major Writings of Thomas Paine.* Edited by Philip S. Foner. New York: The Citadel Press, 1948.

———. "Epistle to the Quakers, 1776." In *The Complete Writings of Thomas Paine.* Edited by Philip S. Foner. New York: The Citadel Press, 1945.

———. "The Forester's Letters, Number IV, April 1776." In *The Complete Writings of Thomas Paine.* Edited by Philip S. Foner. New York: The Citadel Press, 1945.

———. The American *Crisis,* Number I, December 1776." In *The Life and Major Writings of Thomas Paine.* Edited by Philip S. Foner. New York: The Citadel Press, 1948.

———. The American *Crisis,* Number II, January 1777." In *The Life and Major Writings of Thomas Paine.* Edited by Philip S. Foner. New York: The Citadel Press, 1948.

———. "Candid and Critical Remarks on a Letter Signed Ludlow, June 4, 1777." In *The Complete Writings of Thomas Paine.* Edited by Philip S. Foner. New York: The Citadel Press, 1945.

———. The American *Crisis,* Number V, March 21, 1778. In *The Life and Major Writings of Thomas Paine.* Edited by Philip S. Foner. New York: The Citadel Press, 1948.

———. "Serious Address to the People of Pennsylvania, December 5, 1778." In *The Complete Writings of Thomas Paine.* Edited by Philip S. Foner. New York: The Citadel Press, 1945.

———. Letter to Henry Laurens, January 14, 1779. In *The Complete Writings of Thomas Paine.* Edited by Philip S. Foner. New York: The Citadel Press, 1945.

———. Letter to Henry Laurens, September 14, 1779. In *The Complete Writings of Thomas Paine.* Edited by Philip S. Foner. New York: The Citadel Press, 1945.

———. The American *Crisis,* Number VIII, May 1780. In *The Life and Major Writings of Thomas Paine.* Edited by Philip S. Foner. New York: The Citadel Press, 1948.

———. The American *Crisis,* Number IX, June 9, 1780. In *The Life and Major Writings of Thomas Paine.* Edited by Philip S. Foner. New York: The Citadel Press, 1948.

———. Letter to Nathanael Greene, September 9, 1780. In *The Complete Writings of Thomas Paine.* Edited by Philip S. Foner. New York: The Citadel Press, 1945.

———. "Public Good, December 30, 1780." In *The Complete Writings of Thomas Paine.* Edited by Philip S. Foner. New York: The Citadel Press, 1945.

———. "The Necessity of Taxation, April 4, 1782." In *Thomas Paine: Collected Writings.* Edited by Eric Foner. New York: Literary Classics of the United States, 1995.

———. The American *Crisis,* Number X, March 5, 1782. In *The Life and Major Writings of Thomas Paine.* Edited by Philip S. Foner. New York: The Citadel Press, 1948.

———. Supernumerary *Crisis,* May 31, 1782. In *The Life and Major Writings of Thomas Paine.* Edited by Philip S. Foner. New York: The Citadel Press, 1948.

———. *Letter to the Abbé Raynal, August 21, 1782.* In *The Complete Writings of Thomas Paine.* Edited by Philip S. Foner. New York: The Citadel Press, 1945.

———. Letter to George Washington, September 7, 1782. In *The Complete Writings of Thomas Paine.* Edited by Philip S. Foner. New York: The Citadel Press, 1945.

———. "Six Letters to Rhode Island, January 31, 1783." In *The Complete Writings of Thomas Paine.* Edited by Philip S. Foner. New York: The Citadel Press, 1945.

———. The American *Crisis,* Number XIII, May 19, 1783. In *The Life and Major Writings of Thomas Paine.* Edited by Philip S. Foner. New York: The Citadel Press, 1948.

———. To A Committee of the Continental Congress, October 1783. In *The Complete Writings of Thomas Paine*. Edited by Philip S. Foner. New York: The Citadel Press, 1945.

———. "Dissertations on Government; the Affairs of the Bank; and Paper Money, February 18, 1786." In *The Complete Writings of Thomas Paine*. Edited by Philip S. Foner. New York: The Citadel Press, 1945.

———. "Prospects on the Rubicon, August 20, 1787." In *The Complete Writings of Thomas Paine*. Edited by Philip S. Foner. New York: The Citadel Press, 1945.

———. To the Marquis of Landsdowne, September 21, 1787. In *The Complete Writings of Thomas Paine*. Edited by Philip S. Foner. New York: The Citadel Press, 1945.

———. *The Rights of Man, Part I, 1791*. In *The Life and Major Writings of Thomas Paine*. Edited by Philip S. Foner. New York: The Citadel Press, 1948.

———. *The Rights of Man, Part II, 1792*. In *The Life and Major Writings of Thomas Paine*. Edited by Philip S. Foner. New York: The Citadel Press, 1948.

———. *The Age of Reason, Part I, 1794* . In *The Life and Major Writings of Thomas Paine*. Edited by Philip S. Foner. New York: The Citadel Press, 1948.

———. *The Age of Reason, Part II, 1795*. In *The Life and Major Writings of Thomas Paine*. Edited by Philip S. Foner. New York: The Citadel Press, 1948.

———. *The Age of Reason, Part II, 1795*. In *Thomas Paine: Collected Writings*. Edited by Eric Foner. New York: Literary Classics of the United States, 1995.

———. "Worship and Church Bells: A Letter to Camille Jordan, 1797." In *The Complete Writings of Thomas Paine*. Edited by Philip S. Foner. New York: The Citadel Press, 1945.

———. To Anonymous. In *The Complete Writings of Thomas Paine*. Edited by Philip S. Foner. New York: The Citadel Press, 1945.

———. "To the Citizens of the United States, November 19, 1802." In *The Complete Writings of Thomas Paine*. Edited by Philip S. Foner. New York: The Citadel Press, 1945.

———. Letter to Samuel Adams, January 1, 1803. In *The Complete Writings of Thomas Paine*. Edited by Philip S. Foner. New York: The Citadel Press, 1945.

———. "The Prospect Papers, 1804." In *The Complete Writings of Thomas Paine*. Edited by Philip S. Foner. New York: The Citadel Press, 1945.

———. Letter to John Innskeep, February 1806. In *The Complete Writings of Thomas Paine*. Edited by Philip S. Foner. New York: The Citadel Press, 1945.

———. To Andrew Dean, August 15, 1806. In *The Complete Writings of Thomas Paine*. Edited by Philip S. Foner. New York: The Citadel Press, 1945.

———. "My Private Thoughts on a Future State, 1807." In *The Complete Writings of Thomas Paine*. Edited by Philip S. Foner. New York: The Citadel Press, 1945.

———. The Will of Thomas Paine. In *The Complete Writings of Thomas Paine*. Edited by Philip S. Foner. New York: The Citadel Press, 1945.

Pearson, Hesketh. *Tom Paine: Friend of Mankind*. New York: Harper Brothers, 1937.

Punshon, John. *Portrait in Grey: A Short History of the Quakers*. London: Quaker Home Service, 1984.

Remsburg, J.E. *Thomas Paine: The Apostle of Religious and Political Liberty*. Boston: J.P. Mendum, 1889.

Rickman, Thomas Clio. *The Life of Thomas Paine*. London: Thomas Clio Rickman, 1919.
Roper, Ralph. "Thomas Paine: Scientist-Religionist." *Scientific Monthly* 58(1944): 101–111.
Roosevelt, Theodore. *The Life of Gouverneur Morris*. New York: Houghton-Mifflin Co., 1888.
Rorbaugh, W.J. *The Alcoholic Republic: An American Tradition*. New York: Oxford University Press, 1979.
Rush, Benjamin. "Travels Through Life." In *The Autobiography of Benjamin Rush: His "Travels Through Life" together with His Commonplace Book for 1789–1813*. Edited by George W. Corner. New Jersey: Princeton University Press, 1948.
———. "To James Cheetham, July 17, 1809." In *The Letters of Benjamin Rush*, vol. 2, ed. L.H. Butterfield. Princeton: Princeton University Press for the American Philosophical Society, 1951.
Skemp, Sheila L. *Benjamin and William Franklin: Father and Son, Patriot and Loyalist*. Boston: Bedford Books of St. Martin's Press, 1994.
Smith, Frank. "New Light on Thomas Paine's First Year in America, 1775." *American Literature* 1(1929–1930): 348–356.
———. "The Authorship of 'An Occasional Letter on the Female Sex.'" *American Literature* 2[November 1930]: 277–280.
Smith, Robert Francis Jr. "Thomas Paine and the American Political Tradition." Ph.D. diss., University of Notre Dame, 1977.
Smithline, Arnold. *Natural Religion in American Literature*. New Haven, Connecticut: College and University Press, 1966.
Spater, George. "Introduction." In *Citizen of the World: Essays on Thomas Paine*, ed. Ian Dyck. New York: St. Martin's Press, 1988.
Stanlis, Peter J. Review of *Thomas Paine's American Ideology*, by A.Owen Aldridge. In *Modern Age* (31–32) 1987: 152–158.
Stone, Lawrence. *Broken Lives: Separation and Divorce in England, 1660–1857*. London: Oxford University Press, 1993.
Strickler, Gerald Brenner. "An Analysis of the Writings of Thomas Paine with Respect to His Philosophy of Religion." Ph.D. diss., Temple University, 1955.
Sykes, Norman. "Thomas Paine." In *The Social and Political Ideas of Some Representative Thinkers of the Revolutionary Era*, ed. F.J.C. Hearnshaw. London: George G. Harrap and Co., Ltd., 1931.
Thompson, Ira M. *The Religious Beliefs of Thomas Paine*. New York: Vintage Press, 1965.
Tolles, Frederick B. *Quakers and the Atlantic Culture*. New York: The Macmillan Co., 1960.
The Town Book of Lewes, 1702–1837. Sussex Record Society. ed. Verena Smith, no. 69. Lewes, England: The Society of Barbican House, 1972.

Trueblood, D. Elton. *Robert Barclay.* New York: Harper and Row, 1968.
Turner, James. *Without God, Without Creed: The Origins of Unbelief in America.* Baltimore: The Johns Hopkins Press, 1985. *The Universal Magazine of Knowledge and Pleasure,* July 1770, frontispiece.
Unsigned. "Publisher's Preface." *The Pennsylvania Magazine,* January 1775.
———. "Utility of this work evinced." *The Pennsylvania Magazine,* January 1775.
———. "Useful Hints—Curious Deception—Query on Salt-Petre." *The Pennsylvania Magazine,* June 1775.
———. "Account on the Manufactory of Salt-Petre." *The Pennsylvania Magazine,* June 1775.
———. "Elegy on the Memory of American Volunteers, who fell on April 19." *The Pennsylvania Magazine,* June 1775.
———. "from London, May 26." *The Pennsylvania Magazine,* July 1775.
———. "Arabella's *Complaint of the* CONGRESS." *The Pennsylvania Magazine,* September 1775.
Vickers, Vikki J. "The Origins of the Religious Beliefs of Thomas Paine." M.A. Thesis, University of Missouri-Columbia, 1996.
"The Visitor." "The White Cliffs of Dover: Methodism in a Great Fortress." *Methodist Recorder and General Christian Chronicle* August 16, 1906: 9.
Walters, Kerry S. *The American Deists: Voices of Reason and Dissent in the Early Republic.* Lawrence, Kansas: University Press of Kansas, 1992.
Wesley, John. *The Journal of the Reverend John Wesley.* vol. 8, ed. Nehemiah Curnock. London: The Epworth Press (Edgar C. Barton), 1938.
Wilentz, Sean. Review of *Thomas Paine: Collected Writings,* edited by Eric Foner, *Thomas Paine: Apostle of Freedom,* by Jack Fruchtman, and *Tom Paine: A Political Life,* by John Keane. In *The New Republic* 212(17)(April 24, 1995): 34–42.
Williams, L. Glen. "Thomas Paine and the Birth of American Patriotism." Ph.D. diss., Indiana University, 1993.
Wilson, Jerome D. and William F. Ricketson. *Thomas Paine: Updated Edition.* Boston: Twayne Publishers, 1989.
Woll, Walter. *Thomas Paine: Motives for Rebellion.* Anglo-Saxon Language and Literature Series. Frankfurt am Main: European University Studies, 1992.
Wood, Gordon. *The Creation of the American Republic, 1776–1787.* New York: W.W. Norton and Company, 1969.
Woodcock, Bruce. "Writing the Revolution: Aspects of Thomas Paine's Prose." *Prose Studies* 15(2)[1992]: 171–186.
Young, Alfred. "George Robert Twelves Hewes: Shoemaker and Patriot." In *The Private Side of American History: Readings in Everyday Life,* vol. 1, eds. Gary B. Nash and Cynthia J. Shelton. Fort Worth: Harcourt Brace Jovanovich College Publishers, 1987.

Index

A
Abel, Darrell, 116
Adams, John, 2, 4, 8, 37, 48, 98–99, 137
Adams, Samuel, 14, 25, 33, 37, 94
Addison, Joseph, 82
Aitken, Robert, 19–24, 29, 31, 35–36; see also *The Pennsylvania Magazine*
Albanese, Catharine, 41
Aldridge, A. Owen, 48, 83, 98, 134, 139
American Independence, *see* American Revolution
American Philosophical Society, 12, 16
American Revolution
    Articles of Confederation, 116
    Boston Massacre, 25, 70
    Boston Tea Party, 15, 17
    the Coercive Acts, 17, 22, 43
    committees of correspondence, 18, 27
    Continental Association, 17, 18
    Continental Congress, 2, 7, 17–18, 28, 38, 41–42, 45–46, 57, 100, 116, 127, 128, 135–137
        Committee for Foreign Affairs, 2
    Declaration of Independence, 60, 128, 135–136
    Declaration of Rights, 17
    Lexington and Concord, 2, 25, 27, 35–36, 38, 100
    nonconsumption, 17
    Sons of Liberty, 31
    Stamp Act, 39, 70, 74
    Townshend duties, 70, 74
    Treaty of Paris, 117, 130
    War of Independence, 25, 37
Anglicanism, *see* Church of England

Antoinette, Marie, 3
Apology for the True Christian Divinity, 81, 83, 84; *see also* Barclay, Robert

B
Bache, Richard, 18
Bailyn, Bernard, 11, 59–60, 133, 136–137
Barclay, Robert, 64, 81, 82, 83, 84
Barlow, Joel, 3, 5, 95
Betka, James, 113
Bevis, Doctor, 66, 87
Bloch, Ruth, 140–141
Burgess, Hazel, 68
Burke, Edmund, 2, 110, 113, 116–117; *see also Reflections on the Revolution in France*

C
Carey, James, 20
Case of the Officers of Excise, 14, 53–57, 72, 110, 116
Chalmers, George, 4–6, 62, 92
Cheetham, James, 5, 62
Church of England, 62–64, 78, 80, 86–87, 101–102
Claeys, Gregory, 9, 139, 140–141
Clark, Harry Hayden, 10, 78, 115, 124
Colley, Linda, 69
Common Sense, 2, 8–9 20–21, 30, 33, 35–57, 59–61, 63, 75, 77, 83, 98–103, 105–107, 109–112, 114, 116, 122–123, 128–130, 133–142
Conway, Moncure, 78–80, 136
Curnock, Nehemiah, 91–93

183

Index

D
Death, William (Captain), 66
de Bonneville, Madame, 5
de Bonneville, Nicholas, 5
Defence of the People of England; 48, *see also* Milton, John
Deism, *see* Thomas Paine
Dickinson, John, 14

E
Excise, 1, 13–14, 53–57, 68, 71–73

F
Falk, Robert, 81
Federalist Party, 3
Ferguson, James, 66, 87–88
Ferguson, Robert, 134, 139
Foner, Eric, 10, 17–18, 21, 61, 97, 106, 111, 117, 133, 136–137
Foner, Philip, 11
Fox, George, 79
Franklin, Benjamin, 1, 4, 14–16, 18–19, 22, 29, 73–74
French Revolution, 2–3, 6, 94, 97, 99, 106, 108–110, 112, 118
Fruchtman, Jack Jr., 5, 140–141

G
George III, 28, 38, 50–52, 62, 69, 73, 75, 134, 141
Gimbel, Richard (Colonel), 12
Goldsmith, Oliver, 72
Greene, Nathanael, 2
Gwyn, Douglas, 81

H
Halévy, Elie, 91
Hamilton, Alexander, 7, 138
Hancock, John, 25, 37
Hindmarch, George, 92; *see also* Methodism
Hutchinson, Thomas, 15

I
Independence, *see* American Revolution

J
Jacobite Uprising, 62, 65
Jefferson, Thomas 3–4, 7–8, 60, 122, 135–136
Jones, Rufus, 83
Jordan, Winthrop, 47–48, 51, 59, 134, 136, 138

K
Keane, John, 5, 78, 92
Kearsley, John, 18
Kent, England, 1, 67–68, 91–93
Kenyon, Cecilia, 7, 105, 138
Kiley, Michael, 71
King, Arnold, 7
Kirk, Linda, 122
Knowles, Reverend William, 66

L
Larkin, Edward, 23, 29–31, 137
Laurens, Henry, 28
Lee, William, 72
Lewes, England, 1, 13, 17, 68–74, 92
Lewes Journal, 92
Lewis, Joseph, 136
Locke, John, 7, 22, 39, 60; *see also Two Treatises of Government*
London, England, 1, 2, 13, 15, 17, 53–57, 66–68, 72–74, 87–88, 120
London Packet, 18
Louis XVI, 3
Luxembourg Prison, 3, 95; *see also* French Revolution

M
McCormack, James, 135
Madison, James, 7–8, 138
Maier, Pauline, 136
Martin, Benjamin, 66, 87
Mathews, Albert, 135–136
Matlack, Timothy, 33
Methodism, 91–94
Milton, John, 40–41, 49, 129; *see also Paradise Lost* and *Defence of the People of England*
Monroe, James, 3, 95

N
New Rochelle, New York, 3
Newton, Isaac, 78, 88, 90, 93
Newtonian science 9, 66, 78, 87–91, 111–112

O
Oldys, Francis, *see* Chalmers, George
Oliver, Andrew, 15
Ollive, Elizabeth, 1, 13, 69, 72
Ollive, Esther, 68–69
Ollive, Samuel, 1, 68–69

Index

P

Pain, Elizabeth, 63, 80
Pain, Frances Cocke, 11, 63–64, 80
Pain, Joseph, 1, 63–65, 79–80
Paine, Mary Lambert, 1, 67–68
Paine, Sarah, 68
Paine, Thomas
  biographical information
    arrival in America, 18
    birth of, 1, 62–63, 91
    children, 68
    conviction for libel, 2
    death, 3
    delegate in National Convention (France), 2
    education, 1, 64–67
    family, 1, 63–64, 79–80
    imprisonment, 3
    marriages, 1, 13, 67–69, 72–73
    religion (deism), 4, 9, 77–103
    scientific pursuits, 2, 16, 65, 73
  biographies, 4–5, 11, 62, 78–79
  as Founding Father, 4, 7–8, 74, 130–131
  "mission," 105–125
  occupations
    Continental Army, 2
    editor, 2, 13–33, 35–36
    excise officer, 1, 13, 16, 31, 53–57, 68, 71–73
    privateer, 1, 14, 66
    secretary to the Committee for Foreign Affairs, 2
    stay-maker, 13–14, 16, 63, 65–68
    teacher, 17, 19, 31–32
    vestryman, 13, 71
  scholarly interpretations, 4, 7–10, 20–21, 29–31, 59–60, 78, 94, 99, 111, 115–117, 121–122, 124, 128–130, 133–142
  works
    The Age of Reason, 3–4, 9, 11, 61, 63, 77–103, 105–107, 115, 117, 123, 128
    Agrarian Justice, 93
    The American Crisis, 2, 99, 103, 107, 111, 114–116
    Case of the Officers of Excise, 14, 53–57, 72, 110, 116
    Common Sense, 2, 8–9, 20–21, 30, 33, 35–57, 59–61, 63, 75, 77, 83, 98–103, 105–107, 109–112, 114, 116, 122–123, 128–130, 133–142
    "Dissertations on Government," 117
    "Epistle to the Quakers," 83
    Letter to the Abbé Raynal, 109, 114, 128
    "Public Good," 116
    The Rights of Man, 2, 4, 11, 73, 88, 93, 99, 106, 109, 112–113, 116–120, 122–123, 125, 128
    "Serious Address to the People of Pennsylvania," 113
    "Useful and Entertaining Hints," 24, 36
    "Utility of this work evinced," 23
Paradise Lost, 40, 48
Paris, France, 2–3, 94–95
Pennsylvania Journal, 99
Philadelphia, Pennsylvania, 13–33, 35–38
Pitt, William, 15
Price, Richard, 141
Priestley, Joseph, 140–141
Pseudonyms, 20–21, 24–28, see also *The Pennsylvania Magazine*

Q

Quakers, 9, 63–64, 66, 78–86

R

Raynal, Abbé, 109–115, 128
Reflections on the Revolution in France, 2, 113; see also Burke, Edmund
Republican Party, 3
Reviews and Parliamentary Debates, 67
Revolution, see American Revolution, French Revolution
Rickman, Clio, 5–7
Rittenhouse, David, 33, 66
Robespierre, 3; see also French Revolution
Roosevelt, Theodore, 4, 8
Rorbaugh, W. J., 6
Rush, Benjamin, 5, 17, 33, 36–38, 137

S

Scott, George Lewis, 14, 73
Second Great Awakening, 4
Seven Years' War, 1, 56, 62, 65
Smith, Robert Francis, 10, 20–21, 103, 137, 139
Society of Friends, see Quakers
Spater, George, 92

Stanlis, Peter, 121,
Sykes, Norman, 117

T

The Age of Reason, 3–4, 9, 11, 61, 63, 77–103, 105–107, 115, 117, 123, 128
The American Crisis, 2, 99, 103, 107, 111, 114–116
The Autobiography of John Adams, 98, 99
The Gentleman's Magazine, 67
"The Headstrong Book," 70
The Methodist Recorder, 91
The Pennsylvania Magazine, 2, 13–33, 35–36, 53, 100, 129
    essays and poems
        "Account on the Manufactory of Salt-Petre," 36
        "Arabella's *Complaint of the* CONGRESS," 29
        "On the Continental Fast," 28
        "Cupid and Hymen," 25
        "The Dream Interpreted," 27
        "On the Fall of Empires," 27
        "The Farmer's Dog Porter," 20
        "Internal Riches of the Colonies," 24
        "Introduction to the Pennsylvania Magazine," 20
        "Liberty Tree," 28
        "Life and Death of Lord Clive," 24
        "Method of Making Mortar Impenetrable to Moisture," 29
        "The Monk and the Jew," 24
        "New Anecdotes of Alexander the Great," 20, 24
        "An Occasional Letter on the Female Sex," 21
        "To the Publisher on the Utility of Magazines," 20
        "Publisher's Preface," 22
        "References to the Plan of Gen. Gage's Lines," 29
        "Substitutes for Tea," 24
        "Thoughts on a Defensive War," 28
The Pennsylvania Packet, 20–22
    essays
        "Of Love of Country," 20
        "A Mathematical Question Proposed," 20
        "*Trifles, light as air, Are to the jealous confirmations strong,*" 20
The Rights of Man, 2, 4, 11, 73, 88, 93, 99, 106, 109, 112–113, 116–120, 122–123, 125, 128
Thetford, England, 1, 12, 62–65, 68, 79, 86
The Town Book of Lewes, 71
The Universal Magazine of Knowledge and Pleasure, 67
Trueblood, D. Elton, 83, 85
Two Treatises of Government, 39, 60; see also Locke, John

V

Voltaire, 83, 84

W

Walters, Kerry S., 94
War of Jenkins' Ear, 65
Warren, Joseph, 17
Washington, George, 2, 4, 61
Wesley, John, 69, 91–92; see also Methodism
White Hart Club, 69–70
Wilentz, Sean, 7, 9, 130, 134, 138
Wilkes, John, 69–70
Wilkes Movement, 69
Woll, Walter, 9, 122
Woodcock, Bruce, 133

Y

Young, Alfred, 11

For Product Safety Concerns and Information please contact our EU
representative GPSR@taylorandfrancis.com
Taylor & Francis Verlag GmbH, Kaufingerstraße 24, 80331 München, Germany

www.ingramcontent.com/pod-product-compliance
Lightning Source LLC
Chambersburg PA
CBHW030344240426
43661CB00052B/1737